For Kendrich
Summer Institute of
Theology & Disability
Atlanta 2015

Disability, Providence, and Ethics

SRTD
STUDIES IN RELIGION, THEOLOGY, AND DISABILITY

SERIES EDITORS

Sarah J. Melcher
Xavier University (Cincinnati, Ohio)

and

Amos Yong
Fuller Theological Seminary (Pasadena, California)

Disability, Providence, and Ethics
Bridging Gaps, Transforming Lives

Hans S. Reinders

BAYLOR UNIVERSITY PRESS

Scripture quotations, where not an author's own translation, are from the New Revised Standard Version Bible, copyright 1989, Division of Christian Education of the National Council of the Churches of Christ in the United States of America. Used by permission. All rights reserved.

Cover Design by Alyssa Stepien
Cover image: The Blind Dancing at Night; Les Aveugles dansent la Nuit, 1956 (oil on canvas), Ernst, Max (1891–1976) / Private Collection / Photo © Christie's Images / The Bridgeman Art Library. © 2014 Artists Rights Society (ARS), New York / ADAGP, Paris

Library of Congress Cataloging-in-Publication Data

Reinders, Hans S.
  Disability, providence, and ethics : bridging gaps, transforming lives / Hans S. Reinders.
  248 pages cm. — (Studies in religion, theology, and disability)
  Includes bibliographical references and index.
  ISBN 978-1-4813-0065-0 (hardback : alk. paper)
  1. Providence and government of God—Christianity. 2. People with disabilities—Religious aspects—Christianity. I. Title.
  BT135.R45 2014
  231'.5--dc23
                        2013049569

Printed in the United States of America on acid-free paper with a minimum of 30% post-consumer waste recycled content.

Nobody knows what suffering or sacrifice means—except, perhaps, the victims.

—Joseph Conrad

God tempers the wind for the shorn lamb.

—Anthony Trollope

SERIES INTRODUCTION

STUDIES IN RELIGION, THEOLOGY, AND DISABILITY brings established and newly emerging scholars together to explore issues at the intersection of religion, theology, and disability. The series editors encourage theoretical engagement with secular disability studies, while also supporting the reexamination of established religious doctrine and practice. The series fosters research that takes account of the voices of people with disabilities and the voices of their family and friends.

The volumes in the series address issues and concerns of the global religious studies/theological studies academy. Authors come from a variety of religious traditions with diverse perspectives to reflect on the intersection of the study of religion/theology and the human experience of disability. This series is intentional about seeking out and publishing books that engage with disability in dialogue with Jewish, Christian, Buddhist, or other religious and philosophical perspectives.

Themes explored include religious life, ethics, doctrine, proclamation, liturgical practices, physical space, spirituality, or the interpretation of sacred texts through the lens of disability. Authors in the series are aware of conversation in the field of disability studies and bring that discussion to bear methodologically and theoretically in their analyses at the intersection of religion and disability.

Studies in Religion, Theology, and Disability reflects the following developments in the field: First, the emergence of disability studies as an interdisciplinary endeavor that has impacted theological studies, broadly defined. More and more scholars are deploying disability perspectives in their work, and this applies also to those working in the theological academy. Second, there is a growing need for critical reflection on disability in world religions. While books from a Christian standpoint have dominated the discussion at the interface of religion and disability so far, Jewish, Muslim, Buddhist, and Hindu scholars, among those from other religious traditions, have begun to resource their own religious traditions to rethink disability in the twenty-first century. Third, passage of the Americans with Disabilities Act in the U.S.A. has raised the consciousness of the general public about the importance of critical reflection on disability in religious communities. General and intelligent lay readers are looking for scholarly discussions of religion and disability as these bring together and address two of the most important existential aspects of human lives. Fourth, the work of activists in the disability rights movement has mandated fresh critical reflection by religious practitioners and theologians. Persons with disabilities remain the most disaffected group from religious organizations. Fifth, government representatives in several countries have prioritized the greater social inclusion of persons with disabilities. Disability policy often proceeds based on core cultural and worldview assumptions that are religiously informed. Work at the interface of religion and disability thus could have much broader purchase—that is, in social, economic, political, and legal domains.

Under the general topic of thoughtful reflection on the religious understanding of disability, Studies in Religion, Theology, and Disability includes shorter, crisply argued volumes that articulate a bold vision within a field; longer scholarly monographs, more fully developed and meticulously documented, with the same goal of engaging wider conversations; textbooks that provide a state of the discussion at this intersection and chart constructive ways forward; and select edited volumes that achieve one or more of the preceding goals.

CONTENTS

Foreword   xi
Stanley Hauerwas

1   Disability and Divine Providence   1

2   Cosmic Fairness?   31

3   Providence: Intervention and Transformation   53

4   Does the Cosmos Contain Keys?   73

5   A Man Named Job   97

6   *Fons Omnium Bonorum*   125

7   Providence in Christ   145

8   Stories We Live by   167

Notes   191

Bibliography   221

Index   229

FOREWORD

"The Christian belief in providence is also faith in the strict sense to the extent that, with reference to its object, it is simply and directly faith in God Himself, in God as the Lord of His Creation watching, willing and working above and in world-occurrence." I take this statement by Karl Barth in *Church Dogmatics*[1] to be the heart of Hans Reinders' extraordinary account of how the Christian understanding of providence helps us be people better able to be with the disabled. How providence so understood should work to have that effect is not easily displayed, which is why this is such an important book. Reinders' clear and compelling account of the relation of providence and disability does not need to be "explained" by me, but I want to try to explain why that is the case.

Of course, as Reinders helps us see, one of the words that often creates problems—when appeals to providence are made to "explain" why bad things happen to good people—is the word "explain." It is, of course, an indication of our humanity to ask "why," in an attempt to explain why X or Y happened, but just to the extent we think an explanation is possible, we run the risk of giving false comfort for ourselves and others; and that often makes matters worse. That we want to explain why a child is born with Down syndrome is perfectly understandable. But "explanation" can tempt us to believe that what we have experienced is "really good for us or others in the long run," which traps us in a mechanistic universe in which God can make no difference.

That is why Reinders' refusal to associate providence with theodicy is so important. For interestingly enough, theodicy—that is, the attempt to show how terrible events can be reconciled with the presumption that God exists primarily to ensure we are all right—is not really about God; rather, theodicy is all about us. Thus Reinders' refusal to read Job as an exercise is theodicy. When Job is read as the attempt to justify the ways of God to our satisfaction, we miss how Job is able to help us better understand the God who refuses to let us be alone in our suffering. In short, theodicy is an attempt to overcome the contingent character of our creaturely status.

Contingency, moreover, is the heart of providence when providence is appropriately understood as the expression of God's care of God's creation. It is not accidental that within the *Church Dogmatics*, Barth's account of providence develops within the doctrine of creation. We, and all that is, did not have to be, but we are. The only way to comprehend that which did not have to be but is, is through showing the connections between that which did not have to be through a narrative. Providence is the name Christians use to express God's care of the contingent in a manner that the contingent remains contingent. Thus contingency is viewed as gift—not burden.

These are heady theological waters that are not easily navigated. The false alternative is to think that God is the direct "cause" of every happening or God is not present at all. The latter alternative cannot help but result in deism, and the former turns God into a manipulative tyrant. Reinders reminds us that the problem with these alternatives is the presumption we know what we say when we say "cause." The very language of cause, particularly when cause is understood as efficient causation, presumes that if God is to be present in creation, then episodic intervention by God will be required. But the very presumption that God must intervene presumes that God has a problem in being present to that which would not exist except by God's grace. In short, "intervention" language is the language of deism.

What must be remembered is "creation" is a concentrated way to tell the story of God's love of all that which is not God. Providence is but a further elaboration of that story that witnesses to God's ongoing care of that whose very existence depends on God's delight in what God has created.

What providence makes possible is that our lives can be and are in fact storied. Indeed the very demand "to explain" "Why This? Why Me?" can be understood as a testimony to the presumption that our existence is not the result of blind chance. The problem is not that the questions "Why This? Why Me?" are asked, but the problems come when we try to answer them using the grammar of "explanation."

That is why this book centers around the stories Reinders marshals to help us see that the birth of a mentally handicapped child, as well as those who have suffered a traumatic brain injury, cannot be explained, but they can be storied. Through stories we are able to make connections between contingencies that cannot be connected by cause and effect but nonetheless can be shown to be parts of an ongoing pattern of life. Stories may not "explain" what happened, but they can help us know how to go on. Of course, as Reinders makes clear, it is not just any story that shapes the stories Christians tell to make sense of our lives. For Christians, it is the story of Jesus that tests any stories we would tell of our lives.

Reinders' account of the christological character of the doctrine of providence echoes Barth's understanding that in its substance the Christian belief in providence is faith in Christ. The word of God that makes faith possible and that illumines all existence by making it possible to see the lordship of God in the history of creaturely being, Barth maintains, "is the one Word of God besides which there is no other—the Word which became flesh and is called Jesus Christ."[2] Accordingly the Christian belief in providence is given content and form, and is therefore in distinction from other similar forms, by the fact that the lordship of God is not just any Lordship, but the fatherly lordship manifest in the Son of God, Jesus Christ.

Barth is unrelenting in his critique of Protestant accounts of providence that divorce an account of providence from its proper christological home. When providence is divorced from Christology, it cannot help but become an expression of absolute will of an absolute power in an absolutely subjected sphere of power. Though such a view of providence was promulgated by orthodox Protestant theologians, Barth identifies them as "liberals" because their account of providence was "liberated" from the constraint of faith in Christ as the one word of God. Barth notes, for example, that such a view of providence not only proved inadequate in the face of the Lisbon earthquake, but when a general conception of providence is divorced from Christian substance, it becomes, for example, a favorite word on the lips of Adolf Hitler.

Reinders knows most of us are captured by the general account of providence identified and critiqued by Barth. He does not blame us for that, but rather gently and patiently leads us through exercises designed to help us recover the Christological character of our faith in God's care of us through providence. If he had begun with his chapters on Calvin's account of providence, many of us would have found Calvin far too "dogmatic." But by taking us through witnesses who have learned not to lie to themselves about their child's disability, we are prepared to begin to appreciate why providence is the name given to the transformation of our lives that is required if we are to be able truthfully to go on.

Such a transformation is made possible by having our lives engrafted into the story that is Jesus. That story—that is, the story of Jesus—means we are not determined by the past. Indeed the past is not even the past until it has been redeemed: thus Reinders' suggestion that the Joseph story indicates that the "past" is not fated to be the past because we do not even know what the past is until we see the past in the light of the future that is Christ. Reinders' use of stories like Martha Beck's story is not therefore an illustration of a point that can be isolated from the story of Martha Beck, but the story is constitutive of the argument of the book.

Stories like the story of Martha Beck help us see that providence is best understood as an exercise in retrospective judgment. The great temptation is to think some account of providence will give us a handle on history by underwriting the presumption that where we are and where we are going is inevitable. But providence is best understood as a retrospective exercise that helps us see that what we thought "happened" is open to being described in a manner that is redemptive.

One of the extraordinary features of this book is the way Reinders has been able to engage difficult and complex questions dealing with God's way of being and what can only be characterized as pastoral concerns. Though he acknowledges his indebtedness to John Swinton's *Raging with Compassion*, a book with extraordinary pastoral insight, Reinders' way of storytelling in itself is a response to the isolation suffering entails. Providence becomes the way our aloneness is overwhelmed through our mutual recognition made possible by the stories we must tell to one another. Such stories have the ring of truth because they are told by those who have nothing to lose.

Reinders rightly concentrates on stories of disability because so often disability occurs in contexts in which we have our highest expectations. We rightly want our children born "all right." We have high expectations for those we bring into existence. Unsure about why we have this desire that our children have a "normal" and "happy" life, we are led to compensate for our uncertainty by ensuring that for them "everything will be all right." But sooner or later, in everyone's life, something will become "not all right." We seek to blame or explain, but neither "works." Reinders' book is an extended meditation on why Christians have an alternative to that unhappy choice.

Some may think this book is primarily directed at those who have disabled children or family members. Hopefully those so situated will be led to read this book, but it would be a tragedy if the book only had such readers. This is a book that addresses theologically fundamental human questions in a manner that has implications for all lives. Hopefully it will be read widely as a model for the difference being Christian makes for the way we live.

—*Stanley Hauerwas*
Duke Divinity School

1

DISABILITY AND DIVINE PROVIDENCE

There are but three alternatives for the sum of existence:
chance, fate, or Deity.

—*James Douglas*

Introduction

What, if anything, has divine providence to do with disability? The question is by no means an obvious one to ask, except for the fact that a remarkable number of people hold strong opinions on the matter, both with regard to the question itself as well as to what seem to be plausible answers. To start with the former, for some the question as such betrays a suspicious desire to overcome disability by spiritual means. It inevitably pitches the realm of the fallen, rejected body against the realm of the soul, where healing, and ultimately redemption, can be found. For others the question as such is not suspect, and the answer is important, at least to them, even when none of the plausible answers goes uncontested. For some there is great consolation in the belief that disability is part of divine purpose, which for others again is totally unacceptable.[1]

Surfing on that endless sea of popular opinion called the Internet, I came across the site of "BBC Disability Ministry" and was quite surprised in finding the following expression of faith on the matter:

> We exist to spread a passion for the supremacy of God in all things
> for the joy of all peoples through Jesus Christ. We joyfully live with
> a hard and glorious truth: God purposes disability in his creation for
> his glory and for our good.[2]

The surprise was because my European mind led me to assume that behind
these lines was the respected public institution of the British Broadcast-
ing Corporation. Of course this was a mistake. "BBC Disability Ministry"
turned out to be a volunteering group of people with disabilities attached
to Bethlehem Baptist Church, which was unspecified on this site. Its statement is a particularly strong example of the claim that God uses disability
for his own glory, as well as for the good of the people involved. Without
further qualification not very many people would be prepared to accept
this.

Moving on in cyberspace, I stumbled upon one of the most succinct dis-
missals of this view that I have ever come across. I found it in a poem called
"Ars Poetica" written by the American poet Gregory Fraser. In this poem
Fraser sets out to define the nature of his poetry in light of the existence of
his brother Jonathan who lives with spina bifida: "All poetry begins, from
now on, with my brother's legs." Fraser has no patience for endearing talk
about God's friendship, let alone love, for his disabled brother. For those
who are tempted to make sense of disability in religious language, he has a
very clear message: "Call God 'cause' and be done with it."[3]

This comment not only squarely opposes the triumphant tone of
exalted views on what faith can do for you; Fraser also puts his finger on
the spot where religious "explanations" hurt the most. People with disabilities have been harassed by comments about their sin, lack of faith, or inadequate prayer. Get rid of all this religious stuff, Fraser suggests; replace
divine will by "cause" and there remains nothing to explain.

Particularly offending are religious explanations when they are felt as
exonerating God, while blaming the victims. In his book *Vulnerable Communion*, Tom Reynolds makes this point:

> Making the victim responsible is a typical path toward resolving the
> issue. . . . We look for a reason, someone or something to blame. And if
> God is not culpable . . . then the individual is presumed at fault, either
> bringing on divine punishment as a response to sin, or pre-empting the
> healing process because a lack of faith.[4]

When religious explanations of disability come up, people sooner or later find themselves discussing the will of God. If God's will has anything to do with it, then what does he want? So, the question arises of what religious traditions mean when they say that what happens in our lives is an expression of God's will. "Traditions" can be written plural, in this connection, because this question is not only found in Christian discourses on disability, but in Jewish and Islamic discourses as well.[5]

It is with regard to this question that Gregory Fraser's blunt advice is particularly poignant. Forget about the "why" question, I take him to say, because there is no divine intention here, just natural cause. Not everybody agrees, though. "I know my daughter's disability has nothing to do with sin or lack of faith, but yet the question must be asked."[6] Since the "why" question is on virtually everybody's lips, it is apparently hard to avoid.

But I should not get ahead of my argument; I should say a bit more about what this book is supposed to do. Looking at the two opposite statements above, the question that interests me primarily is not what divides them, but rather what they have in common—and not only these two, but a whole range of similar statements. What they have in common is that in discussing the issue of "making sense" of disability, each of them is dependent on some conception of the universe, a particular way of looking at the world and our temporal existence in it. The controlling picture in the background seems to be something like this: in the ordinary flow of things, the world appears a pretty reliable place, a stable habitat for humanity, if you will. Occasionally things seem out of joint, however. People's lives are turned upside down, shaking their belief in reliability. Tragic events and horrific accidents occur in their lives. This is when the question arises: Why this? Why me? The world throws all kinds of events upon people, some of which raise this question in that they disrupt what they would ordinarily expect from their lives. Apparently, being confronted by disability is one of such events.

Yet people's responses differ, and they differ widely. According to some the universe is a well-ordered space, *kosmos* rather than *chaos*, to use ancient Greek terminology. According to others, however, there is no rule in the universe but chance and fortune, which makes the notion of a stable and reliable world anything but certain. The issue of making sense of disability, then, is ultimately about what kind of space one believes the universe to be. This is a question that warrants investigation.

The perspective from which I will pursue this investigation is that of religion. Religious traditions have characteristically adhered to the notion of a well-ordered universe (at least the traditions of the Abrahamic religions of Judaism, Islam, and Christianity have). The reason is their belief in a Creator God who "rules heaven and earth," as the Hebrew Bible puts it. This is why "God" in these traditions is spoken of as a providential God. The notion of a well-ordered universe goes hand in hand with the notion of divine providence, and this notion is the central concern of this study.

However, in investigating divine providence, I will not start with investigating sacred texts and classical treatises based upon them, the kind of sources that theologians usually start with—not because I think other sources of wisdom are preferable, but because I think that theological explanation is at its strongest when it addresses questions that spring from our own experience. When, for example, Gregory Fraser—or anyone else for that matter—in view of his brother's disability suggests that we "call God 'cause' and be done with it," then the question is what experience makes such a statement intelligible. What are its presuppositions, and what are its implications? The same goes *mutatis mutandis* for any competing statement on the same subject. It seems to me there is no better way to understand what people believe, and why, than by following the logic of how they try to make sense of their experience, as they report it, and then turning to the wisdom and insights of ancient sources to see whether—and, if so, how—these sources shed their light upon that experience.

Given the strong sentiments when it comes to "disability experience" and the many different ways of representing it, however, it is clear that I am entering a minefield here. The danger of offending people's most intimate feelings lies on every corner of the road ahead. This cannot always be avoided, and in the present case there is a particular reason to be very cautious indeed: I am not a disabled person myself, at least not for the time being.

In starting with the question of how disability experience is accounted for and what this tells us about the underlying beliefs, I can only speak from what I have heard and read from people with disabilities and their families. Representing their views, however, is a sensitive issue indeed. In recent times, the experience of being misrepresented has been abundantly testified. Representation of disability is a tricky business, apparently, particularly because there are issues of stigmatization and marginalization at stake, especially when those who are not stigmatized and marginalized are the ones that are producing statements about how people feel about their disability. Regarding such statements people have learned to ask who is behind personal pronouns like "we," "they," "us," "them," "our," or "theirs." In the present case this is as well a relevant question to ask.

Even though I do not speak from firsthand experience, I do think it is possible to listen to what people say, and listen carefully, in order to try and understand what they are saying. One of the ways this can be done is what I intend to do in this book, which is to find out what convictions and beliefs make their experience intelligible. Therefore, listening carefully to what people say about the meaning of the question "Why this? Why me?" in their lives is the appropriate way to start.

Finally, in taking the "why?" question as my point of departure, it appears this inquiry is buying into the premise of disability as a tragedy, comparing it to horrific accidents and other catastrophes, against which many people with disabilities and their families would level strong objections. As a matter of fact, I do not believe that disability is first of all a tragedy, because what makes it a tragedy, if at all, are mostly other people's responses.[7] But even if disability per se is not necessarily a tragedy or a disaster, the experience of being confronted by it certainly is, at least initially. This experience turns people's lives upside down, as the literature of their first-person accounts abundantly testifies. Of course it can be argued that disability will only appear as a tragedy because the people involved have been socialized within the "cult of normalcy," to borrow Tom Reynolds' phrase.[8] But precisely because they are so socialized, the experience of tragedy cannot but be very real to them. The fact that underlying the notion of tragedy are often mistaken beliefs about disability is something they do not know at the time of their experience. At that time, people have yet to find out ways to regain confidence and trust that there is life "beyond tragedy." As I have put it elsewhere, for most people the experience of disability as tragedy is real because it is prior to discovering the grounds on which that experience can be contested.[9]

Making Sense of Disability

Before we proceed, however, I need to clarify the language of "making sense" of disability. It is not unusual for theologians to think about the kinds of questions they raise as questions about *meaning*. This holds for questions about disability as well. The late Nancy Eiesland, for example, expressed in her work a wholehearted commitment to the struggle of the disability rights movement of which she considered herself to be a part. But at the same time, she confessed that this commitment failed to respond to some of her spiritual and theological questions, such as the question, "What does my disability mean?"[10] Similarly Arne Fritzon, a Swedish theologian with cerebral palsy and a member of the Ecumenical Disability Advocates Network (EDAN), writes about "Disability and Meaning."[11] Together with Samuel Kabue from Kenya, Fritzson was one of the authors of the document "A Church of All and for All," issued by the World Council of Churches in 2003, in which they argue that "those disabled people who share a Christian faith ... have relied upon certain theological tools to address their existential need to explain the mystery and paradox of love and suffering, coexisting and giving meaning to their lives."[12] Referring to Jacob's struggle that left him disabled (Gen 32:24-26), the document further states:

> In our wrestling with God, as disabled people we all ask the same basic questions, but the theological enquiry involved may be complex. Why me, or my loved one? Is there a purpose to my disability? The answers to those questions can be influenced by the expected time-span of a disability, and by the time and circumstances of its onset.[13]

What we find, then, is testimony by people with disabilities and their families of the spiritual need to come to terms with their disability. However, as the above quote indicates, what people go through will vary, because their disabilities vary, as well as their living conditions.

This is a fact that often goes unrecognized by those who are talking about "disability" in general, as if the rule *one size fits all* were applicable. It is not, because the lives of people with disabilities differ from each other just as widely as the lives of people in any other segment of the general population. Disability experience is a fragmented reality because it is identity related. It is not just that people go through different things in their lives; they do so as people with different convictions and beliefs, the mix of which shapes different identities.

In order to address at least some of these differences, I propose to look at two "kinds" of disabilities in particular. The first usually occurs at birth, as the manifestation of a genetic condition, and results in a cognitive or developmental disability. The terminology continues to be shifting, but what I have in mind here used to be named "mental retardation," and is now internationally addressed as "intellectual disability." The second occurs as the result of an accident that results in acquired brain damage, now generally known as "traumatic brain injury" (TBI). These widely different conditions provide an example of how various "kinds" of disabilities can get lumped together as if they were similar, apparently because both result in cognitive problems. Ignorance of the difference is demonstrated by the fact that people with TBI are frequently approached as if they had an intellectual disability.

In listening to their stories, it turns out that the main point in which they differ is that people with an intellectual disability have never known themselves otherwise than in their present condition, whereas for people with TBI, their lives are divided into two episodes: the life before and the life after their accident. This difference entails very different issues when it comes to learning to live with a disability. Characteristically, what an intellectual disability means and how you learn to live with it is a question faced by families into which a child with such a condition is born. Most first-person accounts of what families go through in that situation begin with the experience of "devastation," as we will have ample opportunity to see. "Making sense" is very different in that case from the question of how to adjust to a new kind of life in which you have lost much of what was very dear, as in the case of people who suffer from TBI after an accident.

The act of sense making can be depicted as a spiritual struggle of people in view of their disabling condition, but it need not be. Many people would argue that they do not suffer so much from their disabling condition as they do from other people's responses to it. In terms of a classical distinction, if there is evil in disability—*and this is a big "if"*—then it is a "moral" rather than a "natural" evil. It is "deeds" rather than "facts" that hurt the most. In respect of this distinction, we may read what people say about their disability as an act of resisting what they regard as wrong responses. Many would say that they feel neither wronged nor harmed by their disability, but by how other people treat them.

There is, in other words, a way of making sense of disability that proceeds from the perspective of a social ethic. People with disabilities have a right to a place under the sun, just like other people, which demands opposing any view that makes their disability a problem to be fixed or, worse, depicts it as a natural evil. Here the role of religion can be particularly damaging, as is testified in a passage taken from Nancy Eiesland's testimony of her own spiritual journey:

> As a person with a disability, I could not accept the traditional answers given to my own query of "What is disability?" Since I have a congenital disability, I have had opportunities to hear and experience many of these so-called answers through the years. They included "You are special in God's eyes, that's why you were given this painful disability." Imagine it didn't seem logical. Or "Don't worry about your pain and suffering now, in heaven you will be made whole." Again, having been disabled from birth, I came to believe that in heaven I would be absolutely unknown to myself and perhaps to God. My disability has taught me who I am and who God is. What would it mean to be without this knowledge? I was told that God gave me a disability to develop my character. But by age six or seven, I was convinced that I had enough character to last a lifetime. My family frequented faith healers with me in tow. I was never healed. People asked about my hidden sins, but they must have been so well hidden that even I misplaced them. The theology that I heard was inadequate to all of my experience.[14]

The quest for meaning as it is stated in Eiesland's question "What is disability?" suggests a spiritual problem, something that is for theologians to deal with. Not everybody would accept that there is such a problem, however, as it appears from the development of social and cultural "models" of disability. These are ways of representing disability that basically answer the question of what disability is in ways I just indicated. Rather than the result of biological or physiological conditions, disability is seen as the effect from social and cultural conditions. Eiesland deserves to be credited for bringing home this message to the field of Christian theology. "Disability" is the result of social and cultural processes of naming and shaming "unproductive" and "dysfunctional" bodies.[15] Behind these processes lies a mostly unarticulated "ableist" ideal of human perfection, such that being confronted by bodies distorting this ideal causes fear and rejection, hence the demand of the disability rights movement—namely, to restore people with disabilities in the power of "naming." A truthful representation of disability will only occur when they tell their own stories, or at least these stories need to be told from their point of view.[16]

Now if all of this is true, what then is left unanswered in the question of what disability *is*? If understanding disability as resulting from social and cultural patterns in responding to dysfunctional bodies is all we need to know, then what more could there be that is wanting of an explanation?

One way to read this question is to say that the quest for meaning is in fact the remainder of a continuing misrepresentation of disability as a "natural defect." It is only when people wonder whether it is caused by some cosmic agent—"fate," "chance," "the gods," "God"—that the "why" question begins to make sense in the first place. But as disability studies scholars are quick to point out, nature only produces variations in human bodies; it does not produce meanings. The meanings attached to some of these bodies as being "defective," "deformed," or "dysfunctional," these scholars would argue, have very little to do with "nature." A critical understanding of disability will show it primarily to be a social and cultural phenomenon. What follows is that this critical understanding of disability dethrones the theological quest for meaning as a remainder of ableist assumptions.

Of course Nancy Eiesland knew all this, as the disability rights movement taught her "to see the problem not within [her] body or the bodies of other people with disabilities, but with the societies that have made [people with disabilities] outcasts and viewed and treated [them] in demeaning and exclusionary ways."[17] But she did not want to give up her theological query—"I am a theologian by necessity"[18]—if only because she believed, perhaps, that there had to be more intelligible answers from religion than the ones she was confronted with in her childhood. Thus she contended:

> It may be possible to find within Christian sources and history glimpses of more adequate answers to the query: what are the theological responses to people with disabilities in our midst? Thus, the challenge for people of faith is first to acknowledge our complicity with the inhumane views and treatment of people with disabilities, and second, to uncover the hidden, affirming resources in the tradition and make them available for contemporary reflection, finding new models of the church in which full participation is a sign of God's presence.[19]

From the perspective of the disability rights movement, then, one might expect the argument that religious explanations are to be rejected because historically they have contributed to the marginalization of people with disabilities and their families. For Nancy Eiesland this could not be the whole story, however. Reflecting upon her formative years in the disability rights movement, she says something of her own spiritual needs that in this connection deserves to be quoted at length:

> While the disability rights movement and activism addressed my experience, it didn't always respond to my more spiritual and theological questions such as, "What is the meaning of my disability?" For a long time, I experienced a significant rift between my participation in the disability rights movement and my Christian faith. The movement offered me opportunities to work for change that were unavailable in Christianity, but my faith gave a spiritual fulfillment that I found elusive in the rights movement. Yet, I also had to name the ways in which Christian communities participated in our silencing. Within the church, often other people with disabilities were uninterested in political and activist matters. In the rights movement, fellow participants saw religion as damaging or at least irrelevant to their work. Although I began to answer my own question of the meaning of my disability by articulating God's call for justice for the marginalized, thus including people with disabilities, yet I nonetheless felt spiritually estranged from God.[20]

Following Eiesland's line of reasoning, one might say that the theological task of reflecting critically on disability begins with listening to people's stories, and then rereading the sources of the tradition in the light of these stories. In this way theological investigation may help to counteract stigmatization and marginalization of people with disabilities in their religious communities and organizations. One could also say that theology's responsibility in this connection is to clean up its own mess, so to speak—a task that, by the way, holds true for a few other academic disciplines as well.[21]

But there is more to her view than a need for such sanitizing operations in Christian theology, important as they are.[22] Nancy Eiesland was yearning for "intimacy with God"—as she did put it—to overcome her feeling of estrangement toward the God of her youth that alienated her from her own self. The faulty answers she received in her youth did not only separate her from other people, and from the community of her church, they also instructed her about her relationship with God in a way that she could not, and would not, accept. So it appears that when all that is said and done is said and done in terms of social and political action, there still appears to be a *spiritual* remainder. Such was at least the case for Nancy Eiesland. "What does my disability mean in light of my relationship with God?" The question, perhaps, may be rephrased in this way: "What does my disability mean in view of God's relationship with me?"

I take it that something similar holds for many people who find themselves perplexed by the same query. Yearning for an intimacy with God is a truly spiritual need that is properly addressed by theological reflection. It cannot be dismissed in the manner of some quarters of critical social studies—namely, as nothing but a remainder of the false ideology of ableism. After all, "nothing but" arguments to unmask religion, spirituality, or morality as ideology are the hallmark of scientific reductionism, and have been so at least since the nineteenth century.

Christian Responses to Disability

Looking at the literature on people's responses to disability in the last decades, it is hard to avoid the conclusion that, generally speaking, religious traditions have a bad reputation in this regard. In considering some of the most familiar themes in this literature, I will look exclusively at responses from the Christian tradition because that is the focus of this study.

With regard to these, we find most authors emphatically denying that people with disabilities are defective human beings in the eyes of God. The prominent attention for this theme in their work suggests, however, that what they deny is widely accepted within their religious communities. One has only reason to deny what other people affirm. As a matter of fact, many religious people *do* believe that disabled people *are* defective human beings and that their disability is a sign of their defectiveness. Even the Gospel implies the belief that connects disability with divine judgment: "Rabbi, who sinned, this man or his parents, that he was born blind?"[23]

This view, which I will call the view of popular religion, holds that there must be something wrong with disabled persons, because if there were nothing wrong, why then are they disabled? One way to respond to this view is to dismiss it outright as religious bigotry, but I think that would be a mistake. It warrants critical reflection because it may tell us something important about the way people have come to understand their Christian beliefs.

As the earlier quote from Nancy Eiesland already indicated,[24] there are both negative and positive meanings assigned to disability. On the negative side, it has been named a curse; a punishment for sins committed, either by the disabled persons themselves or by others; a lack of faith; a sign of imperfection indicating God's judgment; or a blemish that renders this person unfit to approach God in worship. These are the responses one finds time and again mentioned in the literature, and they are universally rejected by the authors in the field, many of whom have been writing about disability from personal experience. More specifically, they have been writing from personal experience of what it means to be wounded by religious people.[25] Some of them testify that they have considered withdrawing from the church altogether. As wounded people they come to a community looking for consolation only to find judgment, which is about the opposite of what they hoped for.[26]

At the other end of the spectrum, we find what are intended to be positive responses. Among these we find naming disability as a blessing, a token of God's love, a special task to fulfill, or an opportunity for spiritual growth. Disabled children have been called "holy innocents" and God's "little ones"; they have also been named as "the poor"—as in the beatitudes.[27] While such positively intended comments seem to forestall religious accounts of disability as an affront, they are nonetheless also strongly rejected. Whether a curse or a blessing, it is argued, the underlying assumption in both negative and positive responses is that disability is a *special* condition of human being. The language of "special" is considered suspect, however. One finds it in standard phrases such as "special needs" and "special education," or "Special Olympics," all of which share the same implication: "special" refers to people excluded from mainstream society. The language of "special" predicates a culturally mediated dichotomy: there is "special" as distinct from "general," and there is "abnormal" as distinct from "normal," each of which reflects the basic opposition: there is "disabled" as distinct from "non-disabled."[28] One way or another, any view of disability as a special condition is to be criticized for being dependent on patterns of exclusion. Whether God has blessed you or punished you, in both cases you are set aside from his other creatures about whom such verdicts usually are not communicated. That is what is wrong with such views.

Attending to people with disabilities in religious communities as individuals with special needs is usually part of well-intended pastoral ministry programs. Particularly resented about such programs, however, is that they frequently trade on the question "What can we do for them?" It is a question that robs people with disabilities from the possibility of participation.[29] What people with disabilities suffer from, if anything, is the lack of people who are thinking critically about their own position as occupying the center stage of ableism.[30] God has too often been perceived as being on the side of "normal" people, represented by "us," leaving anybody perceived as "abnormal" out, meaning "them." Whatever religious responses have contributed to the experience of people with disabilities, therefore, empowering them in living their daily lives has very rarely been part of it. So the question before us is this: what does theological explanation have to say to people with disabilities that does not set them apart from the rest of humanity?

Rethinking Providence

As indicated above I will suggest that the answer starts with reflecting critically upon the controlling framework underlying religious beliefs. Whether it is named a "curse" or a "blessing," in both cases the occurrence of disability is attributed to a divine will operating in a universe under its control. The underlying assumption is that disability receives its religious or spiritual meaning from being "caused" somehow by God. This assumption introduces the theological subject of this study, which is the question of providence. The belief of disability being caused by the divine will invokes the language of providence which expresses the view that God is in control of a moral universe, and that whatever happens must be attributed to his judgment in governing our lives.

In the theological literature, this view is usually known as a theology of retribution.[31] Many theologians have argued that this theology is in fact highly implausible, which, if true, suggests there is reason for rethinking providence as the view that God controls the universe according to a scheme of moral geometry. To indicate what this reason is, let me present a few preliminary observations. Some of them can be made in terms of human experience of what is happening in people's lives. Others regard the understanding of who God is and what he does.

An example of the first is a point about deserts and culpability. The view of a moral universe controlled by a divine will implies that nothing happens in the world that people do not somehow deserve. This view reflects the logic of providence as it is found in many popular religious systems. It is the logic underlying the disciples' question in the Gospel of John already referred to: "Rabbi, tell us, who sinned so that this man was born blind?" The question presupposes a moral geometry that regards the occurrence of disability in terms of what people deserve.

From what human experience tells us, however, the idea of a moral geometry ruling our lives does not appear very plausible. For example, to believe that God sends a disabling condition upon people to punish them for their wrongdoings is implausible because in most cases it is hard to see that their wrongdoings exceed those of the people holding this belief. Since the latter have not been punished similarly, the conclusion should follow that divine justice is a mockery. The only way to escape this conclusion is to assume that only God sees through the human heart and that people therefore may be at fault in ways that only God knows of. This escape might work except for the fact that it cannot credibly explain the suffering of newborn children, which in connection with disability experience is a very serious consideration indeed. To argue that disability in newborn children results from their "original" sin does not help, of course, because original sin does not differentiate between individual human beings.

But perhaps there will be those who would affirm that the notion of divine justice is *indeed* a mockery, given the innocent suffering in the world. It is hard to see, however, how religious people can say the same. If it were true that God sends disabling conditions upon some but not on others without there being a clear moral difference between them, this would mean that in distributing good and evil, the divine will works about as randomly as chance and fortune. This would render the very notion of a *divine* will meaningless. A will that in its operation is indistinguishable from chance or fortune cannot be "divine" in any meaningful sense of the term. Without a direct link with divine justice, this is to say, the very notion of "God" does not make much sense. Looking at it from the perspective of human experience, therefore, the idea of a moral universe controlled by an all-powerful divine will leaves us with an understanding of God in which the distinction between God and chance or fortune is hard to make.[32]

There is a second observation about human experience that I want to present in this connection, however. It also will show why attributing disability to culpability and merit is highly implausible. This attribution necessarily implies that there is no contingency in human lives. If whatever happens to people happens because of a divinely controlled moral geometry, there is no logical space left for the idea that some things just happen for no reason at all. Without contingency, however, religious believers could *never* be uncertain about God's will because nothing of whatever happened in their lives could *not* be his will. Consequently, they could never be in the dark about the question of why God commands bad things. As a matter of fact, it would be hard to explain how bad things can be bad if God wills them. In view of the fact that bad things occasionally happen to good people, it is not easy to explain how good people can be good if God judges them to deserve such things.

A theology of providence that eliminates contingency is implausible, then, because all people of all times have experienced that its moral equations do not add up. Too often people who deserve to be punished walk away freely; and too often undeserving people have been hit hard by life's contingencies. The cry for a providential God is most intensely felt precisely at those moments when life itself turns against us. So it is rather *because of* the overwhelming force of life's contingencies that questions about divine justice arise in religious minds.

If it were not for this experience—the experience that a morally geometrical universe does not add up—the Hebrew Bible probably would not know of the book of Psalms. Likewise we would not have known about the story of a man named Job. Crying out in agony for God's help at one moment, the psalmist exalts in God's praise in the next, reassuring himself that he will not be forsaken.[33] Providence is what you need in the face of being swept from your feet by life's contingencies. Put differently, it is the benumbing experience of moral *perplexity*—trying to find God *in his absence*, rather than the supposition of a moral *geometry*—that invokes the question "Why this? Why me?" As we will see later on, this is exactly at issue in the book of Job.

The arguments from human experience against a theology of retribution, then, all point in the same direction. Understanding the adversities that people face in their lives in terms of culpability and merit is plausible *only* as long as one leaves oneself out of the picture. In pondering what is happening in our lives, or in the lives of our children, it can hardly be understood consistently in terms of punishments and rewards.[34] In first-person accounts of disability experience, one frequently reads phrases like "I must have done something wrong" without the person involved having a clue what it could be. The fact that religious people nevertheless hold on to such a scheme of direct retribution when *other* people are concerned is thoughtless at best, and hypocritical at worst.

But there are other arguments as well. The above conjectures about popular religious belief regarding disability point to a conception of how God rules the world, which introduces a theological point of view. The notion of a universe controlled by the divine will seems to have as a necessary corollary the notion of God's incomprehensibility.[35] At the very least, it must be admitted that some of the things that God presumably wills cannot but escape human understanding. It is hardly credible to maintain that the calamities and disasters in people's lives are willed by the same God that the Christian faith tells us is the Father who "so loved the world that he gave his only son" (John 3:16).

In view of the biblical testimony of God's love for the world, many theologians have proclaimed that the divine will escapes human understanding, John Calvin being one of the more prominent among them. This is hardly an innocent maneuver, however. It leaves much more to explain, as we will see, than a convincing theology of providence can bear. Just how incomprehensible can God's providential will be, before the belief that it is the will of the loving Father collapses altogether?

The above considerations are meant to introduce the concern that governs this inquiry into the theology of providence. What must a theology of providence be like if it is to sustain people existentially and spiritually in their experience of living with a disability, or sharing their lives with someone who lives with a disability? What does it take for a theology of providence to be capable of doing so? These are by no means easy questions, particularly given the classical view of providence, at least in the Protestant tradition. Its negative reputation, at any rate, suggests that divine providence is about the last thing to empower people in facing life's contingencies. But is the notion of providence that presupposes a belief in God's omnicausality in fact true? Is it sound Christian theology?

Reflecting upon these questions is the main theological objective of this study. Sustaining people existentially and spiritually is a practical concern, however, which is to say that the point of this study is not to offer a "theological solution" to "the problem of suffering." Books do not solve practical issues; people do. The practical concern therefore is to show how a different theology of providence may inspire other responses to disability than the ones I have listed above. The theology of providence rejected in this study leans toward explaining providence in terms of judgment, which on a practical level translates into people being judged when they find themselves confronted by the experience of disability. A theology that pulls in a different direction may hope to enable different responses.

No Theodicy

In investigating the doctrine of providence, I want to keep at arm's length a question that is often treated as closely related—namely, the question of theodicy.[36] This is the question of how a supposedly benign God can rule the world without being responsible for all the evil that occurs in it. It is typically dealt with in treatises on the philosophy of religion. However, the theodicy question will not be discussed in this study.

To explain why, I will take my lead from John Swinton's powerful book *Raging with Compassion*, which has many interesting things to say on the matter.[37] Swinton starts with pondering the question of what to say on the accidental death of the child of his friend George. He realizes that his studies of classical treatises on theodicy leave him speechless because the logic they explained "was smashed on the rock of George's lament: 'Why, Lord?'"[38] This remark indicates an important distinction between the question of theodicy as an intellectual problem and the "why" question as a pastoral problem. The question addressed in this study, as in Swinton's book, is about *lament*. It is not about the intellectual conundrum of saving God's face in view of all the evil in the world.

The distinction is important because the philosophical approach to theodicy does nothing for the pastoral question of how to respond to the lament of grief about loss. To see why, I invite the reader to try the following thought experiment. Suppose you have lived happily through a pregnancy—either yours or your spouse's—that is now carried to term. You have made preparations in your home and are full of expectations about a happy family life. But it turns out, unfortunately and unexpectedly, that your child is born with a disability. So your plans for the immediate future are gone, or at least this future will be very different from what you expected it to be. Consequently, you stumble into a crisis in which your belief in God is deeply challenged. Why would God allow this to happen to you? *Why an innocent baby?*

Now suppose your best friend John Swinton, who happens to be a very bright theologian, comes to visit you. After the first exchange of tears and comforting words, you cannot hold back the question *"Why John?"* upon which your friend takes a deep breath and then responds with explaining his view on the matter.[39] Suppose further—for the sake of argument—that he does so in an intellectually satisfying manner. Do you think that when you wake up the next morning your struggle about why God allowed this to happen to you and your baby is gone?[40]

I expect the answer to be that this thought experiment is actually quite ludicrous. Even when we would take the hypothetical question seriously, we would respond that our friend might be a smart theologian, but he is certainly a very bad minister.[41] Raising the "why" question is an act of lament, in which people do not address an intellectual problem. They are deeply wounded and seek to be comforted. Their trust in life is fundamentally shattered. Therefore the "why" question is not truly a question at all, at least not in an intellectual sense, but much more a cry in despair. This is why many would say that at such a time, they expect something else from a theologian other than an explanation.

Leaving aside hypothetical questions, there is another reason why philosophical accounts of theodicy are missing something from a practical point of view. What do such accounts look like from the perspective of the lament of loss? Swinton answers:

> It was the moment when I suddenly and quite powerfully was forced to recognize that the theological framework that I had built around me to protect me from the reality of pain, suffering, and evil was in fact the emperor's new clothes.[42]

From a practical pastoral point of view, philosophical explanation seems to serve as a shield against the agony and pain. To be sure, this comment does not eradicate the question of how God can be just in view of all the evil in the world. It does suggest a kind of practical rule, however: philosophical reasoning on theodicy is the least helpful when the pastoral problem is most acutely felt. As said before, suffering is not primarily an intellectual problem, as it appears in philosophical treatises, but a human experience to be lived with.[43]

No doubt, many philosophers of religion would agree, and argue, that this is why thinking about the question of theodicy is something to be pursued only "in a cool hour." This is fair enough, but this still leaves the question of why the treatises produced by philosophical theology are cast in such complicated arguments that it takes an extensive training in philosophical reasoning to be able to read, let alone understand, them. So it is not only that there are right and wrong moments to engage in that kind of activity,[44] but it is also the fact that as an academic genre, philosophical treatises are less than helpful for the practice of lament. "Practicing theodicy," to use Swinton's phrase, is a very different thing from practicing (analytic) philosophy.[45] The difference is one between the practice of lament as a first-order experience and thinking philosophically about theodicy as a second-order activity.

Apart from formal differences, however, there are problems of a more substantial nature too. Basically what philosophical treatises do is to seek the theoretical reconciliation of two apparently irreconcilable premises: the premise that God is good and all-powerful, and the premise that evil in the world exists. A powerful formulation of the problem comes from David Hume:

> Is God willing to prevent evil, but not able? Then God is impotent. Is God able to prevent evil, but not willing? Then God is malevolent. Is God both willing and able to prevent evil? Then why is there any evil in the world?[46]

This is the question that is at the heart of the theodicy problem. It is supposedly a powerful question for the Christian religion in the sense that unless it can be answered convincingly, it provides the critics of the Christian religion with a very strong reason to reject it. Before we buy into this supposition, however, we need to look at how the question is posed. It is stated from an omnipersonal point of view. As Gerrit Berkouwer wrote, "One tries, in theodicy, to open conversation within neutralized territory, in which, for the sake of the contact, one does not intrude the content of one's own Christian faith into the discussion."[47] Theodicy discourse is decontextualized thought.[48] The issue is supposedly the same for everyone. This supposition is clearly inaccurate.[49] Left out of the equation is the first-person question of whether one actually trusts and loves God. The discipline of theodicy, according to Surin,

> finds an authoritative manifestation in common-sense rationalism and empiricism [that] would cease to be what it essentially is if it were required to posit a subject whose self-definition requires her or him to *live* and *think* as a servant of God.[50]

If one *does* posit such a religious subject, I would argue, it is rather strange to suppose that whether the theodicy question can be answered convincingly is in any way decisive for one's belief in God, not to mention the fact that what may convince the believer may not necessarily convince the unbeliever. Of course there is a point in trying to understand what one actually believes, but there is also a point in keeping "faith" and "understanding" in their relative order of priority. That is to say, there is a point in arguing that faith comes first, and understanding comes second. As far as I know, people do not become believers because they are persuaded by the compelling logic of an argument proving the existence of God. Rather they have been persuaded by a particular experience, or a testimony, or a story, that has touched them deeply. Consequently, it is the way religious belief illuminates their experience and not reason that grounds their faith.

To put this point in terms of a well-known ancient phrase from the Christian tradition, *fides quaerens intellectum* ("faith seeking understanding"), this phrase was never meant to imply that if understanding cannot be achieved then faith would be groundless.[51] The reason is that understanding was never the ground of faith to begin with. When Abraham, the father of all believers, left the land where he was born to answer the call he received from God, it was not because he *understood* it, but because he trusted there was something to the promise he received.

Finally, if loving God would be dependent on understanding him, faith would most likely be an empty concept. When understanding is the condition of love's duration, not many love relationships would actually survive.

In moments of crisis, such as discussed here, it is trust that is tested, not understanding. Understanding could not take the pain away. Again, the cry for a providential God is most intensely felt precisely at those moments when life itself seems to turn against us, so that it is because of the experience of God's absence, rather than his presence, that the question "*Why, Lord?*" arises. It is a cry in the dark absence of divine light.[52]

For all these reasons, I agree with Swinton that if thinking theologically about providence is to make a difference, the question has to be an eminently practical one. How can it empower people to face the contingencies of living with adversity, not knowing where the journey will take them? Again, theology is not a solution, but it may inspire people to be witness to the promise that God will not forsake the work he began.

Providence in the Age of Reason

There is something important about the cultural context within which the question about divine providence arises, in the present case by and large the cultural context of western society as it has been shaped by modernity. It appears that in modern times "providence" has changed. Particularly since the rise of science in the seventeenth and eighteenth centuries, a major issue in theology has been how to adjust religious doctrine with scientific knowledge.

In his magnificent book *A Secular Age*, Charles Taylor speaks about a turning point in this connection, in which he refers to "deism" to explain what happened to providence.[53] According to Taylor, deism shifted the understanding of the Christian religion from its emphasis on human salvation to its potential contribution to prosperity and progress. Christianity came to be understood as a culture-shaping force. In Taylor's account of this historical development, the turn to human prosperity is named as the "anthropocentric shift":

> The order God designed was there for reason to see. By reason and discipline, humans could rise to the challenge and realize it.[54]

"Deists" were people who turned away from religious strife over "orthodox" doctrine that had caused a serious threat to the leading European nations in the era of religious civil wars. Turning away from orthodox conceptions of salvation, deists were intent on viewing Christianity as a practical religion. Particularly in its ecclesial shape, "orthodoxy" became synonymous with the "dark" forces of religious conservatism.

The anthropocentric shift had important consequences for the deistic conception of providence. Deists did not deny that God rules the universe, but they asserted that once his creative work was set in motion, God had no reason to interfere. In fact, deism reiterated the conception of divine providence in antiquity as the explanation for a well-ordered universe, which had always been part of "natural religion."[55] In the optimism of the age of reason, the deists developed their natural religion in a different direction. They defended the notion of a remotely present God, for which they coined the metaphor of the "clockmaker God," who designed the world in order to let it run according to its own laws. God was not directly involved and never interfered with the "natural" course of events.[56] There was no need for human beings to be saved. Consequently, there was no need for redemption either. The central doctrines of Christianity lost their force. Deism preached providence without Christ.[57]

With this shift, the overriding concern of Christian orthodoxy—human salvation from the corruption by sin—was dethroned. At the beginning of the eighteenth century, many still maintained that virtue could not survive without the belief in God's rewards and punishments—Taylor mentions Locke as an important voice in this respect—which still retained a sense of the classical doctrine of providence: God governed the world by ordering what happened to those who were faithful and those who were wicked. But as the age of reason progressed, this claim lost more and more of its ground, according to Taylor, such that the eighteenth century witnessed "the decline of hell."[58] The belief that God was in control of human destiny was no longer on people's minds in the same way as it had been in previous times. But there were other consequences as well. Divine providence came largely to be identical to "nature":

> If God's purposes for us encompass only our own good, and this can be read from the design of our nature, then no further mystery can hide there. If we set aside one of the central mysteries of the Christian faith, that of evil, of our estrangement from God, and our inability to turn to him unaided, and we see all the motivation we need already there, . . . then there is no further mystery in the human heart.[59]

This loss of mystery meant that divine providence had in fact been emptied. If reason "reads" God's plan from nature, then the notion of divine intervention in particular instances no longer makes sense. But what is more, in relying on reason as the source of human progress, deism had given up on the necessity of human transformation. Deist providence, as indicated before, had no need for mystery, neither for grace, nor for the work of Christ. Consequently, as Taylor puts it, "religion is narrowed to moralism."[60]

To the extent that this anthropocentric shift has entered into our cultural history, people do not seem to have much reason to believe what orthodoxy used to preach about how God governs the world. If divine providence is about explaining how the world works without recourse to direct divine intervention, then a much more reliable source is available for understanding the human condition than what Christian orthodoxy had on offer. It is called "science."

Leaving aside whether or not the rise of science is sufficient to explain the decline of providence as direct intervention—Taylor maintains that it is not[61]—it has surely been one of its main beneficiaries. Science is generally believed to replace providence, wherefore it is not by accident that "providence" continues to be at the heart of modern debates on the relation between science and religion.[62] Here is what the *Encyclopaedia of Science and Religion* has to say about the "natural" conception of providence:

> In establishing the fundamental structures of the created world, God sets the parameters of its history, building in various possibilities and ruling out others. In the modern era, this has often been interpreted in terms of God's role as the creator of the structures of natural law that the sciences seek to disclose. By establishing these causal laws and setting the conditions under which they operate, God directs the developing history of the universe.[63]

It is needless to add that from a "scientific" perspective there is little room left for any other notion of providence than the one described. When providence directs the universe through laws of nature, there is no use for direct intervention. Indeed, inasmuch as God's intervention would go *against* the laws of nature, science could only question the reliability of God's governance.

"Who Is in Control?"

Where does this leave the doctrine of providence in our present day and age? Developments in the history of ideas are usually much too complex for linear connections, but this is not to deny signs of the deist heritage in our times. To give just one example, let us look at a theological discussion of the Human Genome Project and see how the ultimate theological question in that discussion turns out to be "Who is in control?"

Research into the genetic basis of a number of disabling conditions has produced knowledge about genetic dispositions, mutations, and chromosomal anomalies. This means that henceforth, there is no reason to attribute the occurrence of these conditions to the imperious forces of fate, chance, or fortune. The promise of genetics, we have been told, is that it enables people to gain control over their own lives regarding human reproduction. We now are in a position to intervene at the basic level of our individual human nature, and are—in that sense—in control of our own destiny. But now another question arises: does this mean that humanity has taken over creation? Are we playing God?

In a book with the same title, the American theologian Ted Peters raises this very question.[64] When the genetic code in our cells is the product of divine creation, are we allowed to change it and engineer our own genetic code? Would it mean that in our capacity as creatures we are taking the place of our Creator? In other words, would we be playing God?[65]

What interests me about the language of "playing God" is its implicit conception of divine providence. The language of "playing God" captures the mind, Peters argues, because in pursuing genetic research, human beings seem to be taking control over their own destinies. Read in this way, the language of "playing God" brings out a similarity with deism's providence. Deism believed that providence is about *control*. God is in control of the universe by means of the natural order that he created. In changing this order—for example, by intervening in the distribution of genetic "defects"—human beings apparently intervene in creation. Only on this assumption does the language of "playing God" begin to make sense. In the Human Genome Project, mankind is taking control over its own destiny insofar as its genetic imprint is concerned. In doing so, it appears to be trading places with God.

Deism's doctrine of providence as divine control over nature is therefore not so remote from our present culture as one might be inclined to think. If science starts "tinkering" with the fundamental structures of human life—"intending implicitly or explicitly to alter human traits," as Francis Collins, the director of the Human Genome Project, has it[66]—then, yes, this presumably means it is playing God. The underlying assumption must be that when human genetics puts us in control of the order of nature, it is taking away control over nature from deity.

The heritage of deism, then, is reflected in understanding providence as a doctrine about control over nature for the good of mankind. In view of this doctrine, I want to suggest that it may well account for the intellectual demise of the belief in providence. Since the age of reason, science has assumed control over nature as its main objective. It will be the main contention of this study, however, that God's providence is not about controlling the universe by the laws of nature. Theologically speaking, there is no doubt that God governs the world, but it proceeds in a way that worldly wisdom does not recognize as such, to put it in Pauline language (1 Cor 1:18). God's ways of governing our lives is folly in the eyes of the world because he rules by way of his spirit, the spirit that unites him with his Son, which is the spirit of love, not force. To the extent that our culture understands "government" as being in control by the use of legitimate force, the folly of this view from the perspective of worldly wisdom is evident from its implication: without the use of force, God cannot be in control. Consequently, but mistakenly, the conclusion is often drawn that he does not govern at all.

There is yet another observation to be made on the cultural context of this inquiry. In our culture the notion of God being in control of the universe has as its opposite the notion of human freedom. This explains why the relation between God and human beings is frequently misunderstood as a relation of competition. The relation between freedom and control is thus conceived as a zero-sum game: the one wins what the other loses. Where God controls, human beings cannot be free. Where humans take over, God can be no longer God.[67]

This book will argue against understanding the notion of providence in terms of divine control because it rejects, among other things, the relation between God's government and human freedom as a zero-sum game. The reason is theological, or, better, christological. To say that God the Father governs our lives is to say that he is present in the Spirit that he has sent upon us in the name of his Son. Providence, in other words, requires

Trinitarian display. In the light of the Spirit, people will learn to see how God is present to bridge the gap between past and future in the midst of their afflictions and tribulations. The question of what it means that God is in control of our lives cannot be understood, this is to say, without addressing the need for transformation, the transformation that enables people to see that God's love, not control, governs their lives.

The Plan

If it is true that many contemporary Christians have a hard time understanding the notion of providence, this should not be surprising. Given what our culture teaches us about being "the authors" of our own lives, which makes the "meaning of life" very much appear as a matter of control, it will be obvious that a theological inquiry about providence must find a way to capture the readers' attention. There is a rhetorical effort to be made, which in this inquiry will take the form of beginning with listening to people's stories of their experience with disability.

We will start therefore by looking at what people report about the "why" question. In this connection it is important to see that their accounts are diverse, as should be expected. Just as the theodicy issue is not very helpful when it is posed as a philosophical problem that is the same for everyone, everywhere, the same is true of the "why" question. That is to say, being hit by whatever adversity turns people's lives upside down is never a general problem, but is an experience of particular people in particular situations. "Adversity" is highly contextual, shaped by people's identities, their beliefs, and their social ties, among other things. "Adversity," in other words, forces itself upon people as contingency. Contingency, however, requires narrative for its explanation. That is why listening to people's stories is a proper way to start our reflections.

After some introductory stage setting, in which we explore the "why" question in view of disability experience (chapters 1 and 2), I will proceed therefore with a close reading of a few contemporary stories before saying anything about how Christian theology has understood divine providence. The first of these stories is Martha Beck's book *Expecting Adam*, in which she tells us about what happened to her and her husband, John, in the nine months before their son, Adam, was born with Down syndrome. Although it probably has not been on the author's mind at all—Beck does not claim any religious conviction, at least not very explicitly—the way she tells her story makes it very much a story about providence. As a matter of fact, there are two clearly identifiable conceptions of providence at work in her story that I will bring to the surface (chapter 3). They illuminate the issue that is central to this inquiry, which is whether providence is rightly regarded as God's supernatural control over natural forces.

The experience with devastating accidents is clearly different from that of giving birth to a child with a disability, which is why in chapter 4 we will turn to stories by people confronted by acquired brain damage. First we will read Jean-Dominique Bauby's book *The Diving Bell and the Butterfly*, in which he tells about how he awakes from a major CVA (*cerebrovascular accident*) with a condition called locked-in syndrome. This is a condition in which one's mind is left intact without virtually any possibility to communicate with the outside world. Then we will read Cathy Crimmins' *Where Is the Mango Princess?* This is an account of what happened after her husband Alan Forman had a serious accident from which he recovered as a "TBI survivor." Crimmins' powerful story teaches us that traumatic brain injury is about the opposite condition of a locked-in syndrome. Her husband appears to everyone as the same guy he has always been. But this is only appearance, because in is his case, everything is left intact except his brain. Despite appearances the "old Al" is not there anymore, because his personality has changed, while the new Al is largely a stranger to his wife. The point of reading these two stories together is to explore the problem that the notion of providence seeks to address. It is the problem of how to negotiate the connection between "the great Before and After," as Cathy Crimmins calls it, at the time when people are stuck right in the middle of it. Looking into the abyss of a frightening and dreadfully uncertain future, people attempt to understand what is happening to them by seeking to find the story that connects the two time frames they find themselves caught in between: the familiar past they know to be discontinued and the unfamiliar future they fear. Between the two they are caught in a bewildering present they do not yet know how to make sense of or respond to.

The various themes that have been explored in this way come together in what is without a doubt one of the greatest classics in religious imagination, the story of a man named Job, as it appears in the Hebrew Bible (chapter 5). I have read this story also from the perspective of its main character. Many of the commentaries that I consulted proceed from the premise of Job's righteousness, as God attests it in negotiating his wager with Satan. But of course Job and his friends do not have a clue of what has been arranged between them in the heavenly courtroom. What comes out of this reading is a story of a man who fights for his right not to be trampled upon by the one to whom he is most beholden. The questions and comments by Job's friends make him understand, however painfully, that there is also this other side of God, the side where he appears in his *inscrutable* majesty. Recognizing that there is this other side, Job faces a distinction between two accounts of divine justice: the justice according to the law that God has given to his people, as distinct from the justice that follows from the unfathomable distance between the Creator of the universe and his creatures. In this reading, the climax of the story is Job praying to the God he knows, asking him to be his intercessor now that he is facing the God he does not know.

Having staged the scene for a theological inquiry in this way, I propose to take the bull by the horns and discuss John Calvin's doctrine, which is generally regarded as the most unpalatable theology of providence (chapters 6 and 7). Calvin's theology in this respect has been characterized as "an iron cage for iron believers." Incidentally, Calvin has given much thought to the story of Job, and particularly to what he coins "a double justice." The ontological difference between the Creator and the Creator's creatures appears to Calvin such that—regardless of original sin—no human being could ever appear righteous before his or her Maker. So even when there is no evident transgression of God's law to be blamed for, as seems to be the case in the story of Job, the creature is still wanting in righteousness simply because it is a creature, and therefore infinitely distanced from the infinite goodness of its Maker. Consequently, we find Calvin struggling with keeping both of these sides of God connected with each other. A particularly aggravating problem resides in Calvin's reliance on the conceptual distinction between primary and secondary causation. Describing God's intervention in a way that turns his action into an alternative of natural causality, this distinction fails to be helpful in discerning the specific Christian understanding of providence.

Providence is not about God being causally in control of the universe, or so I will argue in the final chapter (chapter 8). Instead it is about his Triune presence to sustain the promise that he will not abandon his creation. This presence is mediated by the Spirit. It is through the Spirit that we will learn to see with different eyes. Finally, to demonstrate what this entails, we will look once more at a first-person account of disability experience. It is found in Amy Julia Becker's book *A Good and Perfect Gift*, in which the task of bridging the gap between the "before" and "after" is interpreted explicitly in terms of transformation. Only to the extent that they manage to discover a new self will people succeed in moving beyond the initial experience of disability as a tragedy. To so succeed, one needs to learn to see differently. Providence is the active presence of God, mediated by the Spirit, to guide us in learning to see what there is to be seen.

2

COSMIC FAIRNESS?

There must be some misunderstanding; there must be
some kind of mistake.

—*Phil Collins, Genesis (band)*

Introduction

In a book full of stories about the spiritual lives of disabled children, the American theologian Brett Webb-Mitchell tells the tale of his friendship with Joshua. Joshua is a little boy whose disabling condition is assessed as "autism." Autism is a condition that is characterized—the DSM (*Diagnostic and Statistical Manual of Mental Disorders*) tells us—by, among other things, strongly repetitive and self-centered behavior. Like many other autistic individuals, Joshua is difficult to communicate with in direct conversation. To circumvent the difficulty, Webb-Mitchell organizes "music sessions." In these sessions he discovers that the boy has a remarkable talent for piano playing. Among the songs that Joshua has learned to play, there is one song in particular that keeps coming back. It has these opening lines: "There must be some misunderstanding; there must be some kind of mistake." Unsurprisingly, these lines capture Webb-Mitchell's attention, and they induce him to ponder about the meaning of this song. Here is what he says:

I began thinking that these words state the problem I have in understanding the problem of autism. God, who created us, probably agonizes over the plight of anyone who is autistic, a condition that cripples and limits a child's relationship with self and the world. But since there is autism in the lives of children "there must be some misunderstanding; there must be some kind of mistake." Is Joshua's disabling condition a cosmic mistake?[1]

The question of whether the lives of disabled human beings like Joshua betokens a "cosmic mistake" is a question of meaning. When confronted by disability, people often raise questions like the one Webb-Mitchell asks. Parents of a child with a disability, for example, will tell you that their world fell apart when they were confronted by the prospect of parenting a disabled child. That is apparently what "disability" means, at least initially. Their lives knew some sort of order, presumably, that now has ceased to exist. The life they thought they were living no longer adds up. Normal patterns break down. That is when the "why" question arises.

Does It Matter to Ask "Why?"

Giving birth to a disabled child does not affect just a part of you, but your entire life: your plan for the future is gone. Something similar is true when people become disabled later in their lives, say, due to brain injury caused by an accident or a progressive disease. They have to redefine their story, find ways to live a new life with old selves that must change. To be able to do this, people need answers. Over and over again, one finds the same question: Why is this happening to me? What did I do? What does it mean?

Lives are usually turned upside down in the months following a brain injury, and the first two years are usually busy with rehabilitation and recovering as much as possible. But with time the big questions start emerging: "I've led a good life, so why was I left with a brain injury but the drunk driver who smashed into me was unscathed?" or "Why am I now the lifelong carer for my five-year-old son after encephalitis, what did he do to deserve this?" How we answer these philosophical questions can have a direct bearing on how well things turn out in the long run, as how we make sense of adverse situations is a key factor in our resilience, our ability to "bounce back."[2]

Answering the "why" question is a "key factor in our resilience" and will help us to find out how to go on living. But not everybody agrees. Some folks argue that the "why" question does not really matter. What matters is getting over it. A young university student from New Zealand reports that asking herself "why" she has traumatic brain injury (TBI) is a sign of a bad day:

> If I'm having a good day, I feel great and I can achieve anything even though I still need to make sure I am super organized. On a bad day, particularly if I'm tired, I'll feel stink, I won't be able to concentrate, I'll probably cry several times throughout the day, someone might say something that annoys me. If I don't have too busy a day, I might buy a big block of chocolate and get into bed and watch a DVD. It's very frustrating on those days. Recently I had a bad day at uni. On those days I think, "Why me, why can't I do this, why am I so tired, why do I have to get these headaches?"[3]

Apparently the "why" question is the type of question that shows you are off track. A disability is just that: a disability. Period. Tedious questions about what it all means get you caught up in inaccessible philosophical discussions that are not helpful at all:

> I thought questions of "why?" and particularly "why me?" were a waste of time and a reflection of skewed self-centeredness that inflates the questioners' importance, implying there must be some grant reason that they, in all their fabulousness, should have to suffer so.[4]

A "motivational speaker" from the United States tells his audience how he struggled with his TBI, which he acquired through falling down a flight of stairs:

> Many folks ask "why me?" and the answer is likely "why not me?" Nobody "deserves" to fall and sustain a serious head injury . . . but those things happen. You can either respond—which is positive, or react— which is negative. When you respond, the results are better by far. Being hotheaded and self-centered, or seeking to place blame never leads to a positive outcome.[5]

The message is clear: asking the "why" question is not helpful at all. Those things just happen. It brings you off track from seeking positive goals. A similar message comes from the brochure of a UK-based organization called Brain Injury Rehabilitation Trust (BIRT), which is written by a neurologist, Professor Oddy:

> We have a natural tendency to want to blame someone or at least something. It is part of our desire to be able to explain the world, to make things out there predictable and understandable. Human beings do not like being in the dark about things, unable to explain what is going on. It makes us feel insecure. However, the simple fact is that all brain injuries occur through accidents and illnesses. It is often just a case of being in the wrong place at the wrong time. Even when there is someone else who is clearly to blame, they may not have acted deliberately. Brain injury can happen to anyone, from any section of the community at any time.[6]

There is no cause other than the fact that things just happen. To suppose that there is a cause reflects the "natural tendency" to blame someone or something, but this is a mistake. There is no one to blame, and even when there is, "they may not have acted deliberately." The simple fact about all brain injuries is that they occur through accidents and illnesses. They may hit anyone at random. Before looking more closely at this message, however, let us see what Miranda Schwartz has to say about the effects of her mother's brain injury:

> I truly believed that I would learn, Mom would learn, we all would learn from Mommy's head injury. As a family, we would become closer, more understanding, more empathetic, and loving. Twenty-one years later: I have trust issues. My father retreats into his intellect and can solve intricate 19th century math problems in his head. My mom is as open and frank with me about her TBI as she is emotional.
> "Mom, do you think your head injury was positive at all?"
> "No. It ruined my life."
> My mother was a piano prodigy. Music was the heartbeat of my childhood home. She woke me daily with intricate Schubert, Chopin, Mozart, gorgeous lilting, soulful piano music.

Last summer, my boyfriend asked her to play piano. Mom refused, coy, not wanting to show off.

"The truth is I can't play anymore. It's gone," she later told me.[7]

In view of this experience, I am not sure whether people who lament a life that is gone are really comforted by the notion that it is just their "desire to explain the world" that is playing out, pace Professor Oddy. In Catherine's case it is not just the loss of part of her life that she must overcome, but the loss of its very essence, music, which to her is like "the loss of breathing."

Professor Oddy respectfully disagrees, however. The problem with asking the "why" question is precisely that it does not help. It is self-destructive and does nothing to improve our situation. People with TBI have better things to do:

> Perhaps it helps make the world slightly less uncertain if we can understand why something has happened to us, but does it help in the long run? The answer is probably not. Rather than dwell on what has happened, the important thing to do is to rebuild our lives and look for the positives. Pondering the negatives is itself a negative pastime and will lead us nowhere. Spending time trying to apportion blame and looking for someone or something to be made responsible takes us away from thinking about those we care about and those who care about us. We may become bitter and twisted. This is self-destructive, and does nothing to improve our situation or help us deal with it. If we can acknowledge there is no answer to "why me?" then we can leave it behind and move on.[8]

One way to respond to the "why" question, then, is to turn to psychology and explain why people raise that question. They long for certainty, including the certainty that they themselves are not to blame. The result is not helpful in the long run, it is argued, because people need to get their shattered lives together, and spending time in lamenting "why?" does not help.

No doubt, there is practical wisdom in this advice, but something is missing too. As a response to the "why" question, it does not appear as a way of taking people seriously in their grief, does it? Of course it is always possible to explain their lament in terms of a psychological need ("human beings do not like to be in the dark about things, it makes them feel insecure"), but the fact of the matter is that in asking the "why?" question, people do not merely report a *feeling*. They report a sense of crisis in their worldview also. Part of their agony is that they find the world they knew shattered. It is falling apart, and they themselves seem to be falling apart also. The remaining question, therefore, is whether or not there is anything to say about this crisis that makes sense, other than explaining it away.

Apart from this, however, it is awkward to see the *performative contradiction* in the above statement. Professor Oddy does precisely what he discourages TBI survivors to do, which is to explain why the brain injury happened to them ("the simple fact is that all brain injuries occur through accidents and illnesses. It's often just a case of being in the wrong place at the wrong time"). Only he prefers an explanation that does not leave room for the "why" question to make sense. Furthermore, the neurologist's comment presupposes that people raise this question for *therapeutic* reasons, which is odd. People do not lament a traumatic experience because it will help them in any way, or make them feel better, but because they are *grieving*. That is why the "why" question does matter.

Looking for Answers

The prospect of living with a disability varies between people, of course, but it always tends to have the same effect, as we have seen. It is disruptive, overwhelming:

> I had been reading about the tsunami that had devastated the island of Indonesia a year earlier. I read that before the wave hit, all the water had rushed out to the sea, leaving a dry floor littered with fish. It must have been an eerie calm, watching, waiting, wondering if the water would return. After the doctors left the room, I felt like a woman standing on that beach. I didn't believe what was happening, and so I watched, as if it were someone else's life. As if the water never would come back. As if there weren't a tidal wave on its way.[9]

The literature that comes out of these confrontations is full of stories that testify nothing less than despair, at least in the initial stage. It is unjust, unfair, it should not have happened. "What did my five-year-old son do to

deserve a lifelong disability?" a mother once said to me. People find themselves thrown off their feet. "I didn't say anything. I felt as though I were
falling through space," recalls Martha Beck when she received a phone
call from a woman from the fertility clinic, Judy, to inform her that the
baby she expected was diagnosed with Down syndrome.[10] Judy tells her
that her fetus is "a typical trisomy-twenty-one." Martha asks her what this
means. Judy tells her what went wrong during conception with the process
of cell division, but she gets interrupted: *"I know that!"* Martha barks into
the phone. "I've taken biology, for God's sake! I said what does it *mean?"*[11]

Evidently, under the circumstances, people turn to specialists—medical or otherwise—for answers. But most of the time the answers given by
specialists fail to offer much comfort. They can explain the factors that are
causally responsible for the disabling condition and that can predict, to
the extent that they know, the outcomes that these factors may produce.
Specialists, this is to say, explain causes and effects.

What people want to understand, however, is not "how?" but "why?"
They are not asking for a scientific explanation of the cause but for an
answer about meaning or a purpose. Their world is falling apart, so what is
the point of carrying on? A mother of a severely disabled daughter recalls:

> The why question was inescapable. Why and what for? And why our
> daughter? What is the meaning of this life brutally violated? Could it be
> God's will that life be damaged even before it gets a chance of becom-
> ing? Why me?[12]

Shortly after the birth of her first child, Amy Julia Becker tells her readers,
the message that her daughter is born with Down syndrome makes her
begin to question her view of how the world works:

> Before Penny was born, I would have assumed that an extra chromo-
> some was just that, a crack in the cosmos, evidence of the fractured
> natured of all creation. But how could I imagine such a thing about my
> daughter? I couldn't figure it out.[13]

What happened is not just incomprehensible. Something or someone
ought to be accountable. There must be someone who is responsible.
Unsurprisingly, this craving for accountability often comes with a strong
sense of guilt:

A little monster, that was how it was described. How could that be? What had I done wrong? And then the feeling that I never should have gotten pregnant to begin with. This blaming of oneself. I did that very strongly. That was very fundamental. We had decided to have a baby together. And then there was this feeling of guilt. "If only I had not allowed myself—" That feeling was very strong.[14]

In many instances people speak of experiencing a strong sense of injustice in what has happened to them, like the above quote from Martha Beck's book *Expecting Adam*. This sense of injustice, however, suggests a particular conception of the universe, as was already indicated in the previous chapter. It presupposes a conception of the universe that is ruled by some kind of moral geometry. Presumably this moral geometry is violated by the occurrence of disability:

I had come into the hospital with a grid that ordered my sense of how the world worked. I believed that all people were created in the image of God, that every human being bore the mark of God's goodness and light. But I also believed that everything that went wrong in the world was a consequence of sin. I didn't think that God was doling out tornados or cancer or malaria as punishment for us doing bad things or something like that. I just believed that ultimately all the pain in the world could be traced back, somehow, to the human refusal to love God.[15]

Then a newborn with Down syndrome comes along, and the thought of attributing her life to a refusal to love God withers away. It simply does not seem right. This is a view that people quite frequently seem to express. What happened is not just sad, but wrong, which indicates the sense that someone is victimized. Consequently, "justice" is an issue that must be addressed.

The second issue is silence. Despite the fact that people may have grieved about what has happened to them, and even when they continue to do so, the "why" question may be stifled nonetheless. What is there to say, anyway? Of course, the question may also just go away because people manage to get on with their lives.

Dropping the question out of resignation, however, is another matter. It suggests a conception of the universe in which adverse things happen at random. There is no rule other than chance or fortune, which means there is simply nothing to say. Silence is all that is left.

We will look at how both issues emerge from what people say about their experience with disability. Before we start, we will pay (at least to some extent) attention to the wide variety in their experiences, and we will look at two different types of circumstances. One is the situation in which people find themselves confronted by the birth of a disabled child. The other is the situation in which they find themselves confronted by traumatic brain injury.

Traumatic Brain Injury

Through all the stories we have been considering so far runs the theme of a shattered life. Whether it is being confronted by the birth of a disabled child parents did not know was coming, or with a terrible road accident resulting in brain injury, in all cases there is a "before" and an "after." But it matters to sort out differences and similarities in this respect. The experience of people suffering the consequences of brain injury is different from the experience of people who are born with a disability. The same is not necessarily true of the experience of their families.

The causes of brain injury can be manifold, and include strokes, CVAs, neurological disease, respiratory failure, assaults, or traffic accidents. Usually the resulting brain damage is not the first concern, however. The first concern is that the medical condition of the patient is stabilized. In severe cases this may take a few months. The resulting condition is called TBI. Then the next stage comes up, which is to assess the extent of permanent brain damage. The question arising is to what extent the patient and the family will be able to go on with their lives, which introduces the task of rehabilitation.

Here the main difference between the two conditions begins to show itself. The notion of "rehabilitation" entails assisting people to "fit" into their lives again. For the person involved, there is a sense of "the life before," which is not the case for the person who is born with a disability. Persons with TBI have known a different life. So there is loss, sometimes a huge loss, in a way that persons with a congenital disability have no experience with. As a matter of fact, the latter often complain that they are approached with pity, which they abhor because to them their lives are perfectly normal; they have never known themselves otherwise than with the condition they were born. This is the very point of the debate on "disability identity"—namely, that a congenital disability at least in part defines who you are.[16] But this is not true for the condition of TBI. That condition, at least in its initial stages, is *alien* to who you are. So part of what is gone is not only your life, but also *you* as you knew yourself before:

> Outsiders cannot grasp how much a brain injury changes who a person is; how it changes one's sense of self to the very core. After an injury the brain just works different. Or, in reality, it doesn't work well in certain ways so a brain-injured person has to learn *work-arounds*. And *work-arounds* do not always *work* well. They take far more energy and are still faulty because the tasks that a brain should just take care of automatically now have to be done manually. A brain injury survivor can no longer count on herself in the way she used to.[17]

As indicated above, after vital health conditions are stabilized, the first concern is to determine the extent to which one's cognitive capabilities may be affected by the injury. This requires assessing a degree of consciousness, which is measured by the Glasgow Coma Scale (GCS), an internationally accepted standard in the field.[18] Consciousness varies from "the person does not respond at all" to "the person is fully aware of its circumstances and has the capacity for mobility and speech." It varies in length as well, from a few seconds to many months. The longer unconsciousness lasts, the more likely the result will be a severe brain injury.

When people emerge from a state of unconsciousness, a rehabilitation program is put in place to find out the extent to which the remaining brain injury affects one's ability to continue one's life where it broke off. People will find out that their TBI may have consequences on various levels. They are often confused and unable to say where they are or what happened. Particularly aggravating is the fact that *short-term memory* loss is a common impairment following TBI, while frequently, *long-term memory*—such as recall of historical information, childhood, and other events prior to injury—is often preserved.[19] This means that memories of the life "before" can be stronger than those attached to the life "after," which of course only adds to the sense of loss. Short-term memory is defined as the brain's ability to remember information over the course of a few hours, or across a day or week after a TBI. Some examples of short-term memory loss include things like forgetting where you put things away or what tasks you have taken care of and therefore do not need to do again. But particularly damaging is losing a train of thought during a conversation, or forgetting the question, or repeating the same question again and again.[20] It undermines a person's sense of self-esteem. This situation can be most alarming for both the person as well as for the family. For instance, a mother of a son with TBI wants to know whether there is medication for this problem. She says:

> I am at my wit's end and it hurts because he now thinks he is stupid. He is 35 and has a CAD degree. He is very smart and because he can't remember simple things, he is at the point that he does not want to be around people much.[21]

Dan Windheim is a brain stem injury survivor who was in a car accident when he was sixteen. He was in a coma for two and a half months. Over the years he has been through extensive rehabilitation to help improve his still-slurred speech, injured leg, and weakened left arm. But the problems with which he struggles most are the cognitive deficits caused by his head injury. In his book *Out of My Mind*, he talks about how his brain injury affects him. The loss of short-term memory is one of the things he has to deal with. "I sometimes fabricate the way I think things were. I don't do this purposely. It's really the way I think things went even if they didn't . . . . It's frustrating and annoying. It makes me feel guilty, that I am being dishonest."[22]

The question of recovery is very difficult to answer. Recovery is not impossible, but it is hard to say when and how much, which means that rehabilitation prepares people for the longer-term effects of their TBI. These effects will vary and are distinguished as physical effects (e.g., motor skills, sensory abilities), cognitive effects (e.g., memory, concentration), and behavioral effects (e.g., self-control, temper). They complicate the possibilities of taking up work or school again. Dan Windheim explains:

> I have trouble remembering the order in which things have to be done. For example, everyone knows that to operate a washing machine you first have to put in your laundry, and then the soap, and you have to remember to bring quarters. But I often find that I have trouble sequencing or thinking through the entire process.[23]

When someone will not be able to continue the daily activities that they used to perform, or continue them at a less demanding level, the question of alternative activities arises. This is frequently when the sense of loss hits hard. The school where one was studying, the job one enjoyed, the career that was valued: they may be gone for good. In this connection the issue of self-esteem is particularly poignant because it is frequently reported that families often misinterpret the inability of the person with TBI to go to work as before. An anonymous blogger explains that the family atmosphere can be a great challenge for the brain injury survivor, particularly when there is a lack of emotional support:

> My family shows no interest in trying to understand my injury or help me with it. My mother is always telling me I must get a job although I am unable to work due to my dizziness, which can be severe at times and other injuries I am still challenged by, due to being crushed. Getting your family to understand that you cannot work, you have a brain injury and just why can't they understand, this is nearly impossible. It wells up in frustration and anger. You just want them to understand. You want them to give you a hug, tell you that it will be better and that you will get better with time. You just want *support*. I can't get that with my family.[24]

However, even when there is strong emotional support, the fact remains that the effects of brain injury on the person, as described above, quite often lead to a confusing experience for the family. A different person seems to have recovered from the state of unconsciousness.

These accounts of the experiences of people living with TBI indicate how this condition may affect one's life and the life of one's family. People have to let go of their lives as they knew them. Something similar is true when children with a disability are born into their family, but in a different way. Families in which a child with a disability is born suffer the loss of unfilled, and unfulfillable, expectations. They have to let go of expectations they may have had for their child, as well as for themselves as parents.[25]

For families of TBI survivors, their loss is different. Not only do they have to adjust to a different kind of life, often filled with a heavy load of responsibilities for care and support, but they also mourn the loss of the person they once knew and loved. There are no photographs of people with a congenital disability showing them in a condition different from their disabled one. There are such photographs of people with acquired brain injury. Actually they may be of two kinds: the one kind is showing the people in their younger years, healthy and flourishing; the other kind is showing the people as survivors. The difference between the two indicates the many respects in which that person's life has radically changed.[26] It is therefore not inappropriate to think about the event that caused the brain injury as the moment that divides life into two episodes: the time before, and the time after. Given the grief over the experienced loss of a previous life, as distinct from the bleak necessities of the life that remains, it is not uncommon to think about both of these lives as before and after *the fall*. To some the life they used to live appears from a far distance as "paradise lost": "Sometimes I would like to go back to my old life . . . when I was 16 . . . when life was great, when I was told that I had the world by its tail."[27]

Justice

The "why" question often does not come alone. It is accompanied by another equally painful question: "why me?" So, there is not only the experience of "normal" expectations denied; there is also the fact that seeing them fulfilled has been denied to "me." Dan Windheim reports that many people with TBI share the sense of being cheated out of life, which is why he speaks of the "why me?" *syndrome*:

> A lot of the people with whom I correspond feel that they have been robbed of their lives. They feel cheated. In reality, head injury survivors have been cheated. You can't focus on that. You have to go on. And that's what I try to get across in my book.[28]

Being "cheated" implies being wronged, which introduces the issue of justice. The "why" question as such can be raised from a disinterested point of view—as we have seen in the way philosophers frequently talk about it—but this changes as soon as the question "why me?" is asked. It makes it personal. Martha Beck recalls her feeling of injustice when she found out about the Down syndrome of her future child. The baby she expected was "killed" but she was still pregnant: "The whole thing seemed wildly unfair to me."[29]

The experience of unfairness and injustice is strongly present in the stories that people tell about the news that they are expecting, or gave birth to, a child with a disability. There are different ways of expressing this experience, however, bringing to light different aspects of justice that are worthwhile to consider.

Justice and injustice—in this context as well as in any other—are about equations. The underlying principle of justice is always *suum cuique*, "to each his due." To explore the issue of justice, we may start with thinking about the book of Job, particularly the scene where Job calls upon the heavens that God may be his witness against God so that justice be done:

> O earth, do not cover my blood; let my outcry find no resting place. Even now, in fact, my witness is in heaven, and He that vouches for me is on high. My friends scorn me; my eyes pour out tears to God, that he would maintain the right of a mortal with God.[30] (Job 16:18-21)

The powerful image of a heavenly court arising from Job's prayer indicates the "why" question as a matter of justice. Is there no address in heaven to plead innocence? Job argues he has a witness in heaven, which means there is a higher court of appeal for justice. Job feels he is punished undeservingly. So he cries out to God so that he may plead for man against God.

This ancient story expresses the experience of injustice in a way that is also reflected in present day stories. There are striking examples of this to be found in the literature. First of all, there is a strong need for accountability. There must be a culprit!

> I believed in the idea of external cause. If there was a problem, it must necessarily have a source, a reason, an explanation. If Adam's cognitive ability was permanent, as every evaluator seemed to agree, I wanted a culprit to accuse, a disease to blame, a named pathology. I had the kind of anger that could be ameliorated only through understanding that could be accepted only after every stone had been upturned.[31]

In order for an accusation to make sense, there must be an "external cause," so that I am justified in my complaint that I have been defrauded of a normal family life I am entitled to. This perceived externality of the cause generates the experience of being assaulted, for which "bad luck" is far too indifferent a term. The term "bad luck" refers to the awareness of the fact that the good and the bad are distributed at random among human beings. But at the same time it suggests equanimity: there is no point in raging against bad luck. The logic of random distribution of bad things implies that victims are hit anonymously. The outcry of the experience of injustice does not fit into that logic.

A strong motive in responses raising the issue of justice resides in a sense of fairness, as we already saw. People ought to get what they deserve; at any rate they ought to be spared from what they do not deserve. Also, the experience of brain injury appears to be viewed in that light:

> This is an almost inevitable question to ask when something as significant as a brain injury happens to us. Why did this happen to me? Why do I have to cope with all this? I've done nothing to deserve this, why am I being punished? Why me, why not someone else?[32]

There is, then, a frequently expressed element of unjust retribution. This is particularly strong when it relates to children. Apart from the "why" question, there is the additional question: "Why this child?"

> What I did ask myself that day, however, what I continue to ask myself as I watch Adam go out into a frightening world in all his gentleness, sweetness, and hope, is, "Why him? Why him? Why him?"[33]

People are frequently ready to consider the possibility that *they* are to blame, but what could their baby possibly have to do with it? This line of reasoning reinforces the notion of innocence of a newborn child that has been wronged even before its life got under way! The notion is just too horrifying to contemplate:

> I never doubted, at least I never acknowledged doubt that Adam would be found in some way "gifted" and looked forward to hearing what off-the-scale talents he might possess. I believed, at that point in my life, in a kind of cosmic fairness, in the idea that for every disability there was an equal or greater ability. Adam was an innocent if ever there was one, and innocence could not be penalized.[34]

In this quote, a father faces the violation of innocence of his son born with a disability. He maintains that this violence is just too much *not* to be repaired somehow. There must be a kind of "cosmic fairness," he believes, because innocence cannot just be "penalized."

This basic trust in cosmic fairness, it seems, is a mirror of the cosmic mistake with which we started. "There must be some misunderstanding, there must be some kind of mistake," was the line in Joshua's song that triggered this notion. It seems to be another way of saying that the reality of autism cannot be final; there must be another truth about it, which presupposes that cosmic justice exists.

The "why?" question, it appears from these quotations, is frequently followed by "why me?" and "why this child?" But there is also the question "why *not* me?" There is good and bad in the universe, and each of us will get a share of both. If justice is about an equation, then the question is if I had my share of the good, why should I not get a fair share of the bad as well? Why should this only fall upon other people? The American novelist Nancy Mairs, who lives with multiple sclerosis, recalls she had a conversation with a disabled friend about the "why" question:

> A friend who also has MS startled me once by asking, "Do you ever say to yourself, 'Why me, Lord?'" "No, Michael, I don't," I told him, "because whenever I try, the only response I can think of is 'Why not?'" If I could make a cosmic deal, whom would I put in my place?[35]

To Mairs the question "why not me?" makes more sense. Would you rather see someone else burdened instead of yourself? This alternative question suggests that there is a fixed "quantity" of adversity to be distributed in the universe so that if you do not get your share of it, somebody else will.

As the accounts gathered so far indicate, "justice" provides us with an important focal point when it comes to understanding what people are asking in raising the "why?" question, which they apparently do in various ways. A cosmic mistake, cosmic fairness, a cosmic deal: none of these notions could be coined intelligibly on the assumption that the universe is governed by chance or fortune. The goddess Fortuna is commonly conceived to be blind in her distribution of the good and the bad, which means she visits people anonymously. "To each his due" is entirely absent in her deliberation.

This observation explains why her "blindness" is an appropriate metaphor. In fortune's measurement there is no equation; there is no proportionality either. Consequently, there is no point in questioning her distribution. The "why" question, in any of its variations, is met by indifference: a stroke of bad luck, or a lucky escape, the wrong straw. There is no ground for complaint; there is nothing to be angry about. Lament before the goddess Fortuna is pointless; there is no outcry of injustice. There is only silence.

Silence

Parents of disabled children often confess to have given up on the "why" question. The question does not make sense. Nobody is going to answer it for you anyway. So, why not leave it and just get on with your life? Eventually despair may just go away. It may change into reconciliation. A father of a boy with Down syndrome recalls how that happened:

> Why has our son one chromosome too many? It is a fact about which also medical specialists have no satisfactory story. They can explain it medically, all right, but why does it happen to our child? These revolting questions regarding his life resounded for a long time. But after six months the days brightened up. There was something growing and developing. We became reconciled with his being there.[36]

Despair may develop into reconciliation, but it may develop into resignation too. Why despair what one cannot change? A father of a profoundly disabled girl once told me he had given up on the question of meaning. Not only is there no answer, but there are plenty of practical everyday worries that need attention. So, why waste energy on an unanswerable question that is better used for other things? I asked him if he meant to say that the "why" question never bothered him. He looked at me, smiled, and said, "I didn't say that."

The pragmatic posture that characterizes many families who have a person with a disability in their midst does not necessarily eliminate the question. Not many people that I have spoken to would say that it does; it is just that they have given up on asking. You have to get on with your life, so that continuing to question the inevitable does not seem to be of much help. What would there be to say anyway?

Silence in this connection can mean any number of things, of course. In his book *Raging with Compassion*, John Swinton discusses how intellectual responses—theodicies—to the "why?" question may actually contribute to silencing people, rather than empower them to speak out about their anger and despair: "Theodicies often end up silencing the lamenting voice of the sufferer."[37] A distinct way in which this may occur, according to Swinton, is produced by Augustine's platonic conception of evil as *privatio boni*. Since God is good in an absolute sense, and no part of his being is unfulfilled, it follows that evil must be that which is lacking in "being," and evil is "non-being." Thus, since only God is real, the reality of evil must be illusory. Obviously, this "solution" to the problem of evil does not solve very much, unless one wants to say to people that they are mistaken about their suffering. For them evil is a tangible reality, not an illusion.[38] Silencing the lamenting voice of the sufferer by taking the sting out of evil simply will not do.

There are other ways in which lament can be silenced. In his book *Naming the Silences*, Stanley Hauerwas discusses the development of modern medicine.[39] His case is the suffering and death of children that leaves people speechless, not knowing what to say:

> I believe the most decisive challenge, which the experience of childhood illness presents, is our inability to name the silences such illness creates. Modern medicine can and too often has become a noisy way to hide those silences.[40]

The silences Hauerwas intends to name are those created by the conception of modern medicine that turns patients into passive recipients of medical expertise, and their illnesses as senseless interruptions of their lives. In his view, medicine is not interested in the stories that constitute what meaning the lives of these patients have. It is only interested in their medical history. In other words, the only story that counts is the medical story. Consequently, illness becomes an isolated series of biological events with no connections to their biography, such that there is no vocabulary available at times when medicine fails to fulfill its promises[41]—silences as muted life stories.

Here, I am interested in yet another meaning of silence, one that I will coin the "skeptical" response. The skeptical response reflects a posture of resignation in the face of what Ricoeur named "the scandal of suffering."[42] When in previous times bad things happened, religious people used to have a sense that somehow God might change it for the good. Without a doubt, bad things happen to good and bad people alike—Christians have always known that, and the same is true for Jews and Muslims—but that was never taken as a reason for speechlessness. Prayer, lament, and even protest—"raging with compassion," to use Swinton's phrase—were appropriate responses, not speechlessness.

There has been extensive scientific study of processes of bereavement and grief over the loss of loved ones from which we have learned that it is a staged affair, in which people go through despair, anger, grief, and—at some stage—acceptance. Eventually the "why" question fades away and life takes its "normal" course. One may well wonder, however, how this return to "normality" takes place when it comes to the confrontation with disability, as, for example, in the case of surviving TBI, or of giving birth to a child with a disability:

> I remembered the final stage was acceptance. But then again, that was when the tragedy was death. What if it wasn't? What if the tragedy was born alive?[43]

Even so, things may change, and people may find a way to accept life as it goes on. There is a distinct possibility, however, that the "why" question will be lingering on, because "normality" is never going to be what it once was. There is, in other words, silence as resentment or resignation:

> Where was the fine line between acceptance of a condition I could never change and despair or, worse, indifference? When did I stop wanting, demanding, feeling that Adam had been cheated? When did I let go, quell my passion to power his life, direct his interests, think his thoughts? I was not proud of my complaints; they had long since ceased to do Adam much good.[44]

Despite the lack of a satisfactory answer, the "why" question may be neither dead nor forgotten. It may be still there, buried deep down inside. Ignoring it seems to betray something like the Stoic virtue of *apatheia*: the virtue of not letting oneself being affected by what one cannot change. Why allow yourself to complain, when you need all the energy you can muster to advocate for your child and empower its life?

Apart from Stoicism, however, there is also skepticism. In this respect, many of our contemporaries seem to share the view of the French philosopher Jean-François Lyotard, who contends that the "why" question leaves us speechless because the experience of blind fate has no vocabulary.[45] In other words, there is nothing to say. Speechlessness, according to Lyotard, is not necessarily generated by the experience of being struck by disaster. Rather it results from the fact that there is no language because there is no address, no court of appeal that one can turn to, to file a complaint. The injustice is not so much that innocent people are victimized by chance, or fate, says Lyotard, but it is rather in the fact that there is no one there to be held accountable. Consequently, the "why" question is not cried out loud; it gets smothered in silence.

However, when there is no language to express people's experience with adversity in their lives, the consequence must be that the things happening to them are mere "events." The notion that there is no one to be addressed necessarily implies that there is no agent involved, and therefore no action. What remains are mere sequences of events. Consequently, a universe that consists of sequences of events has no purpose, nor has it any meaning other than that what happens, happens. The things happening to people are either prearranged by fate, or they happen as a matter of chance. Beyond these two, there seems to be only one possibility left, which is that the universe is not left to its own devices, but answers to the will of its Creator.

In this inquiry the "why?" question will be examined, therefore, from the perspective of Christian theology. Christians never believed in fate or fortune as blind and anonymous forces—neither did Jews nor Muslims, for that matter. They believed in God who governs the universe and fulfills his promises. There certainly can be silence in the experience of God's absence, but it is very different from Lyotard's speechlessness. Here is a prayer from Nicholas Wolterstorff's *Lament for a Son*:

> Here in the darkness I cannot find you. If I had never looked for you, or looked but never found, I would not feel this pain of your absence. Or is it not your absence in which I dwell but your elusive troubling presence? Will my eyes adjust to this darkness? Will I find you in the dark—not in the streaks of light which remain, but in the darkness? Has anyone ever found you there? Did they love what they saw? Did they see love? And are there songs for singing when the light has gone dim? The songs

I learned were all of praise and thanksgiving and repentance. Or in the dark, is it best to wait in silence?[46]

Silence while waiting for God is *painful*. Even then it is different from an act of resignation. In the face of resignation, "waiting" is senseless because there is no one to wait for.

The theological notion central to the belief in God's presence in the midst of people's agony is the notion of providence. "Providence" raises the question of how divine action is involved in whatever befalls human beings in their lives. "The Lord will provide" is a promise, the *locus classicus* for which is the scene where Abraham binds his only son Isaac on the altar. It is a promise that Abraham wants to be reminded of, wherefore he gave the place where God tested him the name of this promise: *The Lord will provide* (Gen 22:14). Consequently, the important question is what difference the belief in God's promises makes for how we respond to what happens in our lives. But then it must also be asked what these promises entail, and how they infuse a language of faith that does not belittle or humiliate, but that shapes people's action to empower them in facing adversity.

3

PROVIDENCE
INTERVENTION AND TRANSFORMATION

There are more things in heaven and earth, Horatio, than are dreamt of in your philosophy.

—*Hamlet in William Shakespeare,* Hamlet

Expecting Adam

In her book *Expecting Adam*, Martha Beck tells the story of how her son Adam came to be part of her family as a boy with Down syndrome. It is the kind of story that the subtitle announces: a true story of birth, rebirth, and everyday magic. As we will see, it is also in many ways a story about providence. In fact, it is a story within which two distinct conceptions of providence are at work, not necessarily in competition, but very different indeed. The first is a conception of providence as direct intervention by supernatural force; the second is a conception of providence as God's promise that what we fear most may turn out differently. To bring these different conceptions up front is my aim in retelling Martha Beck's story.

The language of providence is not at all the kind of language that Martha Beck uses to talk about what happened to her family, however. Although both she and her husband John were raised in Mormon families in Utah, they have left "religion" behind and have been converted to a presumably more respectable worldview, which is the one Beck ascribes to

53

the community of Harvard scholars. At least that is the case at the point where their story begins. Beck is not very elaborate on the years preceding their arrival at Harvard.[1] But there is little in her book that indicates hard feelings against the Mormons, except for some very critical comments on some of their religious beliefs, as we will see, including their belief in providence. The picture one gets is that of young people experiencing the intellectual and emotional distance that often comes with leaving their parents' home to enter a new world, particularly when this new world is as strange a place as Harvard University. As a matter of fact, Martha never told anyone in Harvard that they were from Utah, "a state that doesn't register as part of the known universe to anyone in the Ivy League."[2]

Harvard University turns out to be a place where you not only keep to yourself certain facts about your own history, but also where you are not supposed to think particular kinds of thoughts and have particular kinds of feelings. At least that is how the Becks experienced it in the late eighties. Martha recalls that in their undergraduate years, they had been thoroughly "Harvardized," which meant, among others things, that one develops an intense drive to succeed as a scholar. Harvard students would volunteer for the most demanding academic tasks and assignments if that was what it would take to distinguish oneself in the eyes of one's teachers.

Harvard was definitely an exciting place, according to Martha Beck, but it was far from pleasant. Signing up for classes at the beginning of a semester, for example, was a returning experience of great anxiety. Without ever admitting this to one another, both Martha and John were afraid of not being accepted by the teaching professor. It took some time for them to begin to understand that this kind of experience was not at all unusual to Harvard students. Feelings of anxiety betrayed a lack of self-confidence, a state of mind one would hardly admit to oneself, let alone to other people, because at Harvard the appearance of confidence is essential to social survival. So, they learned to fake self-confidence, largely unaware of the fact that most graduate students did the exactly same. Looking back in later years, Martha wonders if she actually ever met someone at Harvard who *did* find it pleasant.

Academic reputation was everything, which for Harvard students meant this was their top priority. The Becks, however, had stained their reputation with something as distractive as a child. Katie was born when they were both in their first year in grad school. Martha knew that pregnancies were quite unusual among graduate students at that time, and frequently considered a mistake. She recalls that several of her friends obtained abortions when accidental pregnancies threatened to interfere with their academic programs. That the Becks decided to have a baby was a clear sign that they had let "personal reasons" get in the way of their careers. Success at Harvard demanded the willingness to put personal reasons right at the bottom of one's priority list.

John, for example, made the mistake of missing a day of classes in order to support Martha while she was giving birth to Katie. For this offense his professor called him "a disgrace" for the school he attended. The professor made absolutely clear that with this attitude John would never succeed in his scholarship. The Becks tended to take this kind of criticism very seriously, something that even after years continues to amaze Martha. But at the time, she was adamant to show that one can be a scholar and a mother both at the same time, and a feminist too, of course.

The impression that something was lacking in the dedication to their academic careers reached an alarming level, obviously, when Martha got pregnant for the second time. She herself regarded it a most irresponsible deed and for most of her gestation period, she tried to hide her physical condition as long as she could. Both she and her husband pretended to go on, as if a pregnancy was just a minor inconvenience that could be ignored altogether. They decided that this pregnancy had to be kept absolutely secret. John would accept a well-paying consultancy job, while at the same time he would be working on his dissertation to be submitted to the Harvard Business School even though this job would take him to Asia two times a month! Martha would also be working on her Ph.D. in the sociology department, while teaching undergraduate classes and taking care of Katie. In good spirits they set out on this plan that demanded both of them to work like crazy, and so they did.

Unfortunately, however, the pregnancy could be anything but ignored. Martha suffered heavy attacks of nausea and could not keep food and fluid in her stomach, up to the point where she had to be hospitalized for dehydration. Meanwhile John was wearing himself out with his impossible job. He was simultaneously working on his research, as much as he could, as well as stepping in for his wife to care for the three of them as soon as he was home.

Somehow they managed to hang on with this work pace, until the decisive blow came. This was when they found out that the child she was carrying had Down syndrome. Their lives would never be the same. Harvard graduate school had to be cancelled as their number one priority. But it took a severe crisis in their lives before they arrived at that conclusion.

The Bunraku Puppeteers

Before we get to this stage, however, let me begin to explain why I have read Beck's book as a book about providence. It actually begins with the moment the couple is busy conceiving Adam. It is the first time Martha senses the influence of imaginary beings that later in her book she will explain as supernatural powers. They will not appear on a radar screen for sure, but Martha cannot deny their presence in the world of cause and effect.

The storyline begins when Martha tells about the first time she sensed the presence of the *Bunraku Puppeteers*. The name refers to a style of puppet theatre called Bunraku she had seen in Japan. The puppeteers are moving their puppets while standing on stage, in no way pretending they are not there. Their skills of moving their dolls make the audience actually believe the dolls are moving themselves.

> That night in our apartment, I kept expecting to see two teams of Bunraku masters standing behind John and me, pulling levers in our heads, sculpting every move we made. I could feel them. And without letting it anywhere near my conscious mind, I knew—I *knew*—that I was in the process of getting pregnant and that it was exactly what I wanted to do.[3]

From this moment onward, the story as Beck tells it unfolds as a skillfully constructed novel, which it is not, as her subtitle indicates. On one level, the story of her pregnancy develops in the world of ordinary experience in which they try to manage their frustratingly complicated lives. At this level, her contraceptive device fails her, and she becomes pregnant at an impossible moment. But at another level, the story reads as the discovery of spiritual powers intervening in their lives in order to get back on track again, away from the demands of Harvard's scholarly community.

Beck confesses that previous to the present version of *Expecting Adam* she had written the book twice before, both times as a novel. She worried about waving good-bye to her rational beliefs about how the real world works. Presenting it as a novel, she would not be held responsible by Harvard-type intellectuals for irrational talk about miracles in her life. It did not work that way, however, because the story would not back off; it had to be told as it happened.

Not long after the evening that they conceived their second child— which Martha did not talk about to her husband, even though she "knew"—they went for a trip through New England, and got caught in a car accident. A truck pulled off the shoulder of the freeway and blocked their path. John barely succeeded in avoiding a collision; the car got in a spin and crossed the opposite lane of the freeway. Being completely out of his wits, John kept repeating that he had lost control. Martha remained very calm, however, because it was obvious to her they had never been in danger. "The Bunraku puppeteers wouldn't have allowed it."[4]

So we understand that Martha senses their lives to be governed by supernatural forces that compel her to consider the possibility that things may be different from what they appear to be in ordinary experience.

As the story continues, the family goes through rough times more than once. Regularly, at these times, the Bunraku puppeteers show up to help out. The first time this happens is when they visit the hospital to see if the car crash did any damage to her pregnancy. They are informed that her blood test shows a lowered level of alpha-fetoprotein, which might be an indication that the baby will be born with Down syndrome. They have to take another blood sample to make sure.

To revive their spirits, John and Martha have a cup of coffee and a sandwich in a restaurant. Then they stumble into a painful argument about the possible outcome of the test. John brings up the question of aborting the fetus in case it would turn out to be "defective." Martha is infuriated, which her husband does not understand since they both have been in favor of abortion in these kinds of cases. Martha persists, "Does he not know that in China they abort a lot of fetuses just because they're female?" Is being a girl defective enough to convince him? John dismisses her attack by saying they would only be avoiding a tragedy. Martha retorts that you cannot take the tragedy out of life by killing a baby, as if it did not already exist.

Then she breaks down in tears. John is aghast because this is not how Beck women comport themselves in public. He tries once more to convince her. He does not want to hurt her feelings, but the way he sees it is that if a baby is going to be deformed, abortion will keep everyone from suffering, "especially the baby." It is like shooting a crippled horse, he says. A lame horse cannot run anymore and therefore cannot enjoy life. Running is what horses do. The analogy is clear: "If a baby is born not being able to do what other people do, I think it's better not to prolong its suffering."[5] Martha is silent. She is asking herself what it is that people do. What do human beings live to do, the way horses live to run?"[6]

Unfortunately, it turns out that the baby will indeed have Down syndrome. Martha and John are devastated, incapable of finding comfort in one another. He buries his head in work; she leaves the house to find information. As she walks to the Harvard Coop bookstore, a homeless guy sees her swollen belly and congratulates her. It embitters Martha. If the guy only knew.

Maintaining Rationalist Credibility

Martha slowly begins to realize that she no longer can ignore the fact of receiving miraculous assistance to get out of the iron cage of her Harvardized existence. Taking into account her background from rural Utah, the reader may find it remarkable that Beck rarely uses theological language to talk about Martha's experiences. Who needs the Bunraku puppeteers when she could also turn to the God she came to know as a child? But then again, when she recalls what she had been told about the God of Mormonism, the reader can understand why she wants to stay away from a God who saves some people by sending help from angels while others get trashed in freak accidents. The simple formulas that religious people have at their disposal to explain these things are less than convincing in her eyes.

Nonetheless, at the time she is expecting Adam, Martha Beck notices that her empiricist worldview is falling apart. Accepting distinctions between the natural and the supernatural, and between the normal and the paranormal, does not come easy. Among Ivy League students, any belief in the supernatural or the paranormal is a sure sign of intellectual degeneration. John and Martha both take their Harvard empiricism very seriously, so seriously that it takes a major crisis in their lives to make them rethink what they actually believe.

Apart from the car accident, there is the horrible experience of Martha being caught in a fire in their apartment building, together with Katie, while John is on one of his monthly trips to Asia. Although it is one of the most shocking episodes of her story, I will only look at its final stage where she tells how Katie and herself are rescued. Living on the tenth floor, they have to go down the staircase of the building, which is on fire on the first floor. Somewhere down that staircase, Martha is at the brink of collapsing because her body is screaming for oxygen. The sounds of other people crying for help are fading. Martha is losing it. She holds Katie tightly. Then there is a strong helper guiding her and Katie and only a few seconds later they find themselves in the lobby of the building, finally breathing fresh air.

A major fire on Massachusetts Avenue in Cambridge with people running out of a burning building does not go unnoticed, of course, so Martha and Katie appear in the evening news on TV, and on the front page of next morning's newspaper. The *Boston Herald* photographer had caught them just at the moment they were bursting into fresh air. Having somewhat recovered from how they looked on TV and in the newspaper, however, Martha notices there is something wrong with the picture. It showed her fear and exhaustion, everything, but there was something missing, Martha realized, something very important: "In the picture there was nobody behind me."[7]

The interesting thing about this episode is Martha's sense that if there were a rescuer then he should have appeared in the picture. Why is this interesting? Well, suppose you believe in divine providence of the kind that the book of Psalms talks about, and suppose you would have the experience of being miraculously saved: would you expect God to show up the next morning in a newspaper photograph? Probably not.

Martha, however, knows a rescuer has saved her, but this rescuer is missing in the picture. This staunch believer in "the facts and nothing but the facts" is not ready to give up her rationalist credibility. That has to wait until the next episode of her story, when she nearly loses her baby.

The Twilight Zone

One night, alone with Katie, after a stretch of very stressful days—grading the papers of her students and writing her own paper, while taking care of her daughter—Martha finds herself bleeding. She has no clue what is going on, but the bleeding is serious, and she decides to call a doctor for medical advice. The obstetrician is seriously worried about her story and tells her to come to the emergency room immediately. Martha promises to do so without explaining to the doctor that she has nobody around to take her there. So she stays home in her very serious condition, telling herself not to worry. But her situation deteriorates. It feels as if she is going to pass out. Slipping into a state of waning consciousness she senses that there are other beings in the room. Thus far she has always maintained her reservations about the Bunraku puppeteers. That is to say, she has not given up disbelief, and regarded her experience of their presence *as if* miraculous things were happening. Now these "as if's" are melting away, however. The presence of the Bunraku puppeteers is as real as the presence of oxygen. Finding herself and her baby in great danger she gives up all her reservations and asks for help. "You guys," she whispers to the beings in the room, "Help this baby."[8] It is the first time she addresses them directly, and it feels like she is crossing a line.

Certainly a line is crossed at this point. You may doubt the presence of God every way you want, of course, but you cannot pray *and* at the same time continue to doubt God's presence. You cannot pray *as if* you are praying, that is to say, at least not without knowingly fooling yourself. The same is true for mysterious helpers like the Bunraku puppeteers.

Martha does not believe praying is a sane thing to do, however. As a matter of fact, she believes just the opposite. She thinks that she is turning insane because the fear of losing her baby outweighs her fear of relying on irrational beliefs. Martha thus takes her apparent belief in whoever is saving her baby as a sign of her growing *insanity*.

As it turns out, however, Martha's body does not respond in a way that fits her beliefs about sanity and insanity. As soon as she asks for help, there is a flood of warmth rushing through her body: the bleeding stops. Within seconds the helpers seem to turn away. "Please, help me too," Martha whispers, which for some reason "was one of the hardest things she'd ever done."[9] Again, the response comes immediately. A set of hands are reaching out to catch her, like a father catching a falling child, and she senses how her body is supported and kept from disintegrating.

Martha Beck has willingly entered her twilight zone, that space between the world of reason and the world of supernatural assistance. Irrational beliefs are beginning to compete with things she used to believe as certainties. She has no idea what to make of her incorporeal helpers, but she clearly understands that the reason they have helped her is in the fact that she asked them to. And when she did, she *meant* it.

Giving Up on Baconian Logic

Thinking back in later years of what happened that night, Martha still does not have a clue what these beings were. The only word that comes to mind when she remembers what she experienced is "friends," and that is basically all that matters. Interestingly, she is not bothered at all by the fact that she still does not know what to make of these friends; she is not even troubled by the possibility that she made it all up. Being dehydrated and having lost a good deal of blood she could hardly be expected to think straight.

She tells us that after Adam was born she has been trying to give an accurate account of what happened during the night that she and her baby had been saved.[10] But she gave up on this attempt. Any possible explanation that people may suggest for her "paranormal" experiences is fine with her. So in hindsight Martha Beck opts for metaphysical abstinence. She does not have a clue what kind of beings helped her, and she does not care. What counts for her is what she experienced, not how to make sense of it.

This indifference was not there the next day after the event, however. She decides to write down everything she has experienced the night before, but when she reads her account it does not make sense. Nonetheless, to dismiss the whole thing as a figment of her imagination would be a lie. Acknowledging that what she believes has actually happened, on the other hand, threatens her rationality.

In view of these doubts Martha cannot help but consider the possibility that the religious folks of their childhood in Utah might be right after all, empirically speaking.[11] The very thought makes her shudder. Instead she resolves her doubts in a different direction. She decides to give up on the Baconian principle according to which things are true when proven. From here on she is willing to believe anything as long as it is not proven to be false. It is a major shift in her view of the world. "With this single decision, I expanded my reality from a string of solid facts, as narrow, strong, and cold as a razor's edge, to a wild chaos of possibility."[12]

Beck's Lingering Empiricism

Our reading of *Expecting Adam* thus far has been focusing on how Beck accounts for the strange things happening during Martha's pregnancy.[13]

As we have seen, it is a story about the help of spiritual beings in a young couple's life to guide them through unusual and often painful events. In this sense I have read it as a story about providence.

Translated in terms of classical doctrine within the Christian tradition, one would have say it is a story of direct divine intervention of the kind that usually was named "special" providence, except for the fact that "divine" in my reading of Beck's story does not refer to God, but to supernatural beings. When deism limited divine providence to the laws of nature, as we discussed in chapter 1, it ruled out the concept of special providence. God was not believed to intervene directly in the natural course of events. Orthodox theologians who wanted to retain space for this kind of divine intervention saw themselves compelled to take recourse to the sphere of the "supernatural." Thus God's providential action became restricted to the sphere of miracles and other inexplicable events, such as the resurrection of Christ.

In the next chapter we will learn about another view of providence. This is a view that has nothing to do with events transgressing the boundary of the "natural" and the "supernatural." In fact, it is not about "supernatural" intervention at all. Instead it has to do with the question of how a new future is opened up after the old one has been falling apart.

Before we continue reading Beck's story to pull out this storyline, let me finish here with a comment on how the author informs us about her own understanding of her story. As suggested before, Martha's views of what has been happening to her and John are not nearly as different from what she thinks the Mormons of Utah believe, contrary to what she assumes. When John returns from one of his Asian trips, Martha wants to tell him everything that has happened to her. John is worried about the pregnancy and wants to take her to the health clinic to make sure her condition and the condition of her baby is all right. Martha does not dare to tell him how she has been healed because she fears John will think she is crazy. But this fear of ridicule can only be justified, of course, by the fact that she actually *believes* what happened.[14]

Accounting for miraculous assistance in terms of interventions of the "supernatural" in the natural world, or of the "paranormal" in the normal world, Martha Beck assumes that the question is how we can explain unusual events. This is confirmed by the space she devotes to discussing the question, but so far she has not made up her mind as to which explanation she believes to be rationally defensible. So she decides to do what "rational" people do: she sticks to the facts about her experience.

That this is indeed the meta-text of Beck's story is sustained by what she says in the "Author's Note" with which she finishes her book. It reads as a methodology, as if, in retrospect, she has been talking all along to an academic crowd of Harvard-style skeptics. In her note she reports to have put all the details of her experience on paper, which is a way to prevent them from being distorted over time. Besides, if her book was to be published none of her academic friends and acquaintances should be able to accuse her of exaggeration or flat-out invention.[15] Her aim is to record the facts and leave the explanation as to what they mean to others.

But this is a nonstarter, of course. Nobody in her right Harvardized mind would even consider claiming the factual nature of the miraculous events that Beck reports, but immediately throw them out as delusional instead. I take it that the author knows very well that statements of fact in support of truth claims are as metaphysically loaded as the claim that God rules the universe; they only presuppose a different kind of metaphysics. "The facts," in other words, have their own way of appearing, depending on how you look at them.

Nonetheless the question of how supernatural events can be causally explained remains important for the author. How can it be that one is rescued, or healed, by invisible hands? The range of natural causes that usually enter into our explanations of mysterious facts may just be too narrowly conceived for us to really understand what is going on. But, of course, that is what the Mormon folks of Utah believe too. It is not surprising indeed that during the night she was saved, Martha begins to wonder whether this meant that these religious people might be empirically right.[16] At the time the question arises, she throws out this possibility, but the way she phrases it shows what the issue is: empirically warranted explanation.

There is a conception of providence, then, that turns on the possibility of supernatural causation. In religious language, God as a "supernatural being" breaks into the world of our ordinary experience to cause natural events in ways that we do not understand very well.[17] At the same time, following the logic of this conception, supernatural beings seem to have one thing in common with natural agents: both operate according to the principle of causality. There is a difference, but it is epistemological, not ontological. That is to say, it is not an ontological difference in the sense that both natural and supernatural causes are similar in producing effects in the empirical world. The supernatural is just as "real" as the natural; they operate on the same level of being. The difference between these types of causes is epistemological: they cannot be tested in the same way. As we will see much later in this book, however, there is reason to question whether causality is at all helpful in thinking about divine providence.

Transforming Our Stories

There is another conception of providence, as indicated. It is described in terms of God's active presence in sustaining the promises God made rather than in terms of God's supernatural interventions. Also this conception is clearly at work in Martha Beck's story, but we need to read with different eyes to see this. Looking at it from this other angle, her story is a story of transformation. A young couple is geared up to have a very successful academic career in an environment that promises everything they ever dreamed of.

Having gotten away from religion in rural Utah, which they experienced as anything but intellectually respectable, the Becks enter the world of reason Harvard style: no dodging difficult questions, no sloppy answers taken for granted, but a tough-minded naturalism when it comes to beliefs of any kind. As Martha would say, true is what can be empirically tested under controlled circumstances.

Then along comes Adam, diagnosed with Down syndrome before he is born, entering the world of Harvard scholarship as the fundamental negation of everything it stands for, at least in John and Martha's view. While turning their back on stupidity is very much part of what attracts them to Harvard University, they now have to face "the stupid little boy inside me," as Martha puts it.[18] Evidently, given their addiction to Harvard careers and all that, they refuse to face the contradiction.

More often than we realize, we tend to live the future as a way of prolonging our past. Our lives are to be what we have aspired them to be. In a sense, this is also what the Becks attempt to do. They try to shape their future so as to fit their expectations. But as it turns out, they are in for a surprise. Beck is not inclined toward a religious take on the second part of her story, but if she were, she would probably not deny the reality of God's presence, be it in very different and unanticipated ways when compared with the first part.

Phrased in terms of the doctrine of providence Martha might have said, as will be shown later, that the future of our lives is in God's hands, but this does not necessarily mean God will fulfill our expectations. Consequently, our future is what it is, because of what God brings into our lives—opportunities, calamities, friends, foes, everything. In making these contingencies part of our story, we change. In believing that whatever comes our way comes from God, we also believe that God is transforming our story, and because we are changing in the process of responding, we will discover that we no longer read previous episodes of our own story in the same light as we did when we lived them. In this sense we can say that God not only changes our future, but that God also changes our understanding of the past.

Martha Beck's book contains many episodes to illuminate this process. For example, looking back at what their life with Adam has brought them, she is astounded that being among these incredibly intimidating "Harvardized" people meant so much to them at the time when they lived there. The very act of calling them in hindsight by this name—"Harvardized" people—shows that their future with Adam turned out to be a transformative experience. By the same token, their past changed too. They had become different people, and what once appeared to them as the top of the world now had changed into a strange place. It was no longer what it seemed to be at the time when they were there.

Believing in God's providential care, in other words, entails the awareness that the coherence of our story is *not* of our own making. In this connection it is relevant to notice how time plays a role in Beck's artful construction of her narrative. First, there is the time of the strange things happening to Martha and John during her pregnancy, from the perspective of the people that they are at the time. Second, there is also the time frame of what in retrospect happened during her pregnancy, that is to say, from the perspective of Martha and John *having changed into different people*. Thus in reconstructing their past, they find a way of redeeming it. As we will see, the agent of redemption turns out to be their son Adam, which indicates the pattern of providential care that I will bring to light in the second part of my reading of Beck's book.[19]

Letting Go

John gets home from his last trip to Asia and finds Martha "trashed." She has carried her pregnancy almost to term with only a few weeks more to go. She is beginning to have contractions and wants to get it over with. She tells him she is so scared that she cannot handle a baby with Down syndrome. What if he will have all these terrible complications she has read about and may need surgery?

John tells her to calm down—the baby is not going to be premature. He reminds her of the fact that many people never have one miracle happen to them, while she had dozens, and she still wants more? Later that night Martha is alone, while John is doing the laundry. She tries to talk to God to say that she cannot take it any more. It's simply too much. Looking back Martha remembers a sense of letting go. For the first time she prayed without trying to control whatever the answer might be.[20]

This moment becomes the turning point of her life. She feels that she is taken up by some kind of personal presence in the room and filled with a radiating love. It is at this moment that she stopped grieving, a friend tells her later. She believes that is true. When she is back in the "shadow world," the world where we struggle, her body feels just as it did before, but she is no longer afraid:

> I no longer worried about going into labour. I felt utterly trustful that things were under control, though no control of mine. I was willing to bet that between them, Adam and the Being of Love probably had some kind of plan. Whatever it was, I was in it for the duration.[21]

A week after this, Martha gives birth to Adam, prematurely. The doctors do not show him right away, because there is a medical team lined up against the wall of the delivery room. The doctors take seriously both the fact of his condition and the fact that he is premature, so they first examine the baby before they will give the sign that things are okay. While waiting until they are finished, Martha feels she is no longer in the presence of the spiritual world: "I felt . . . normal."[22] John is looking intensely at the doctor's back. Martha senses what he is hoping for: the sudden announcement that there had been a mistake, that Adam was just fine. She is hoping the same. The miracle does not happen. Adam is just as medical science predicted him to be. When the baby is declared healthy, Martha holds him in her arms. That very moment she realizes that she has not been without resources at all. She loves her baby the very moment she lays her eyes upon him.

When the doctors have left the delivery room, she is alone with John and their newborn son. John confesses he believed there would be a miracle. "I really thought God would fix him."[23] Martha does not respond that their son perhaps does not need fixing. The next day, they can already take Adam home. Martha quickly recovers. Interestingly, her physical well-being seems to have another side to it, which is a "greatly diminished sensitivity to the Bunraku puppeteers."[24] During the day, there is no need for mysterious helpers because there is Adam. During the long nights, she is afraid of all the things that might happen to him, knowing that he will be someone the world rejects. During these lonely nights Martha is still expecting those helpers to assist her in overcoming her anxieties. But the miracle has disappeared. The puppeteers do not show up to assist her.

Revealing Adam

Adam turns out to be a miracle in his own right, but the true meaning of that word in connection with their son Martha and John still have to discover. Rereading their story as a story of transformation means that what came later throws a different light on what happened before. Sharing their life with Adam changes their views of many of the things they had been dreaming of, but once he is around, these things lose their attractiveness. Presumably because her book is intended to be a story about expecting Adam—as her title suggests—Beck only occasionally inserts bits and pieces about their later years with him, except for the last chapter. Before we come to this last chapter, let us look at a few of the earlier episodes.

One day, when Adam is five, Martha takes him to pick up some groceries with his two sisters (in the meantime Lizzie had arrived as number three in her family). They arrive at a supermarket, where there is a gardening display right before the entrance. While Martha is busy getting her youngest child in a shopping cart, Adam runs away. She turns around and spots him disappearing between shrubs and bushes. Calling him to come back, she is tapped on the shoulder. "Excuse me, ma'am." An elderly man with a baseball cap is standing behind her. "I was wondering if you noticed what your boy was doing just now."[25]

Martha senses trouble, because Adam has done some pretty awful things in his short lifetime. So she answers the man cautiously that she has not. "Your boy," he says, "stopped to smell every bush they have out there."[26] The man invites her to follow him.

They go outside to the gardening display, and enter a row of juniper bushes. The man leans over, his eyes closed, inhaling deeply through his nose. Then he invites her to smell, pointing to the juniper. Katie and Adam are already sniffing. Martha too starts smelling the shrub. It has a tangy, sharp scent, somewhere between citrus rind and sagebrush. The smell is amazing. With a grin on his face the farmer invites her to smell other shrubs as well. They go on smelling bushes for five or ten minutes. When they are finished, the old man straightens up and tips his hat. "Things aren't always what they seem, are they?" he gestures.[27] Martha agrees. Then the man bends over to Martha, whispering in her ear that he has a disabled son of twenty-three.

Martha Beck is cautious not to leave us with too rosy impressions, however. For every farmer who invites her to smell the bushes because of Adam, there are at least three other salespeople complimenting her for her cute little girls, while looking past her son as if he is not there. But along with the pain, Adam teaches her to see the beauty of things too by paying attention to what is most common. "It is a quality of attention to ordinary life that is so loving and intimate, it is almost worship."[28]

Paying attention to the little things surrounding her is hardly what she learned at Harvard, because there only the intellect is worshiped. Earlier we came across the discussion Martha had with her husband John when they were considering the question what humans do to live, the way horses live to run. Adam makes revising her conception of "human" a major task of parenting him.

When he is three years old, Martha begins to lose faith that he will ever be able to speak. The frustration that he cannot say anything is hurting him. To have to watch this breaks Martha's heart. She tries and tries, but there is no real progress. One day she takes the kids out to the grocery for a treat, as a way to overcome endless hours of unsuccessful speech therapy. Each of them can pick a piece of candy. The girls are already at the candy stand near the checkout corner, when Martha notices her son wandering in the wrong direction. Returning with a rosebud his mother explains that a flower is not candy. Adam says he wants it anyway. So they leave. The girls unwrap their candy and start nibbling at it, while Adam holds his flower with both hands all the way home. When they get there, Martha is busy with groceries and completely forgets about the rosebud.

Then, the next morning, when John is off to work early, she hears Adam paddling toward her bedroom. The door opens, and there he is, in his small hands a vase with the rose in it. He walks over to his mother's bed, and with a clear, calm voice, he says, "Here."[29] Martha stares at him, not knowing what to say. He looked at her with steady eyes, making her see that he is trying to make up for her pain in trying to change him into a 'normal' child, and that he loves her despite her many disabilities. "Then he turned around, his little blue pyjamas dragging a bit on the floor, and paddled out of the room."[30]

In view of the shifts in their worldview that came with Adam's arrival, Martha remembers how it dramatically changed their relationship to work. Before that time, the Becks, like so many other people, had shared the strong belief that hard and disciplined work was the only path to success regardless of whether one likes it. Now they discard this view as just silly. Living with someone who does not care for a single moment about getting ahead, you learn a very different attitude toward spending time. Adam teaches his parents what they are tempted continuously to forget:

> After spending the first decades of my own life in desperate attempts to pass every arbitrary test placed before me by the educational system and the rest of society, I have to be constantly reminded that the end goal of all this striving is to live joyfully, and that there are often more direct ways of achieving this than conforming to rigid standards set by social custom.[31]

"Aggabies!"

Adam's capacity to arouse his family's sense of wonder comes out lovely in another episode that also brings out Beck's ability as a writer. In this case particularly, the placing of the story in her book is important; it follows right after Martha has received the message about the diagnosis of her baby. The theme is "disappointing gifts."

Preparing for Christmas, John and Martha are busy doing what most parents do at that time: running around stores to find the select items their kids have written down in their letters to Santa. When the moment of wonder is there, Katie first unwraps her present, a set of birdcalls. The one she had found in the catalog was several hundred dollars, so Martha and John had decided upon what they thought was sufficiently similar. Katie's face falls when she sees it is not what she wanted. With a trembling lower lip she barely manages to say she likes it. When Lizzie gets to unwrap her present, a doll, the result is the same. It is not exactly what she wanted because the doll has pink instead of purple jewels. The comment following this scene is a fine example of Beck's sense of humor:

> Within minutes, both the girls had reconciled themselves to their gifts. Like their pioneer ancestors, many of whom had died crossing the Great Plains on foot in the dead of winter, dragging their possessions behind them in handcarts, my daughters were able to steel themselves to the brutal realities of an imperfect world. This was good, because I had been on the verge of sending them both to military school.[32]

Then it is Adam's turn. Adam, the reader must know, regularly gets spoiled by Martha's friend Annette, who considers it her prerogative to give him the most obnoxious gun toys that she can find: lots of noise, flashy colors, and an exotic, deadly appearance are among the most preferred features. Aunt Annette is pleased to indulge—as Beck puts it—"the kid's most violent, macho, antisocial tendencies."[33] It is needless to say that Adam's parents do not surprise him with gun toys. Annette is so conscientious about her responsibility to spoil their son that she never forgets to wrap up a stack of batteries, to make the gun blast for weeks.

Adam fishes under the Christmas tree to get something sufficiently attractive to be his present, and from the shape of it, Martha knows what he has got. She tells him to look for another because the one he has found is not his real present. Adam does not listen and tears the paper off and stares at the batteries as if he cannot believe his eyes, so magnificent a gift! *"Oh, wow! Mom, ook! Aggabies!"*[34] Without considering the possibility of another gift, Adam jumps up and goes to try every tool, toy, and appliance in the house that runs on batteries, pointing out all the things one can do with this gift. They watch him completely astonished about the qualities of a Christmas present that makes all kinds of objects in the house move, sing, even dance, or lighten up an entire room! "Something about Adam always manages to see straight past outward ordinariness of a thing to any magic it may hold inside."[35]

Martha admits that from the day she found out about her baby's diagnosis, her journal indeed reads as coming to terms with a disappointing gift. When Adam was born, she soon found out that his presence could not be mentioned at Harvard once the word was out that there was "something wrong" with her baby. "Harvardized" people did not know of anything as disappointing as a "retarded" child: Apart from friends, the only exception is the homeless man on Massachusetts Avenue, whom we already met when he greeted her on that winter's day and congratulated her with her swollen belly.

Apart from her account of how parenting Adam changed their lives for the better, Martha Beck keeps repeating that the pain and the frustration never go away. But even though the lessons she had to learn did hurt her more than just about anything else she ever felt, she concludes, "It has been worth it, a thousand times over."[36]

Evaluating Providence

There is a sense of divine providence that takes the form of supernatural intervention. Many people actually share this view—presumably also the Mormons known to the Becks when they lived in Utah. Martha remembers a friend with a daughter with Down syndrome, who comes from a very religious family. This friend told Martha that her own mother had blamed her for not miraculously changing her little girl into a "normal child."[37] The logic was, presumably, that if this friend would have had enough faith, then God would have removed the extra chromosome.

Martha does not seem to notice, however, how close she was during her pregnancy to believing something very similar. If the Bunraku puppeteers as her "miraculous helpers" came invisibly to rescue her on the night she was nearly passing away, and stopped the bleeding, then why should God not be able to remove the extra chromosome? Both kinds of interventions would classify as suspensions of the laws of nature of modern science in exactly the same way, which is why the Becks had such a hard time allowing them into their cognitive system as "supernatural" interventions.

I have read *Expecting Adam* as a story that entails two alternative accounts of providence, however. There is another way in which God's providence may be seen to work. It has little to do with natural causation, because it is about transformation. Living with Adam helped Martha to overcome her fears, but not by means of supernatural intervention. In the end all her fears came true, nonetheless what she came to discover *and enjoy* was a very different story about Adam's life, unexpected and unanticipated, but as real as his Down syndrome.

This was the story of how living with Adam transformed their lives—to its very core—as well as their conception of what is the point of living. This story is no less of a miracle, I would argue, since it contradicted all the beliefs Martha held about herself before Adam was born. Only, this miracle is of a different kind. Martha was afraid she could not do it, but what most needed doing was actually done by Adam, simply by being the loving and lovable person he turned out to be.

With her book Beck has provided us with a most important clue for how we might think theologically about the "why" question, as described in the first two chapters. She does not believe in "cheap theology": the kind of theology that uses simple formulas to explain—in her own colorful language—"why some people get help from angels and some get lobotomised by flying debris from freak wheat-threshing accidents."[38] Cheap theology is a theology that claims to know why some people are saved in situations where others are destroyed. Its formulas explain how God distributes favors and disfavors among human beings—for example, the formula like "your faith is too weak," or "you must pray harder," or "you're cursed," or "it is a special blessing," or "consider yourself lucky," or "it's an opportunity to grow," and so on. The problem with such formulas is that in real life, they do not add up, whichever way you turn them.[39] As I said before, the book of Psalms would not exist if such formulas had a glimmer of truth in them. "God where are you?" is not the cry of someone who knows why what happens, happens.

Praying to a providential God, then, is what you need when God seems further away than ever. This suggests that the question of God's providence is a question about God's abxence rather than about his presence. "Why do you hide yourself in times of trouble?" is the question that points us in the right direction.

4

DOES THE COSMOS CONTAIN KEYS?

Accidents divide things into the great Before and After.

—*Cathy Crimmins*

Introduction

By looking closely at Martha Beck's *Expecting Adam*, I intended to bring to the surface two different readings of her story. One reading proceeds from her fearful anticipation of giving birth to a "retarded" child with Down syndrome—the other proceeds from how such a child may transform the life of one's family. It is the latter reading that explains the "rebirth" in Beck's subtitle, which indicates the transformation that enables her to see her son Adam as a true gift rather than merely a disappointing one.

We have seen how such different ways of seeing him are related to the interplay of different time frames. In Beck's narrative, there is a rivalry between two such frames: one is the time frame of her pregnancy; the other is the time frame of living with her son Adam. The two time frames are divided as a "before" and an "after." This is a feature of her story that appears in many first-person accounts of the experience of giving birth to a child with a disability.[1]

The point to be explored in this chapter is how people negotiate the connection between both these time frames. Whatever the incident dividing their particular "before" and "after" may be, it is an event within one and the same life, which creates the task of negotiating a connection. The "before" and "after" are separated by a chasm: a deeply emotional disruption that needs repairing. The wound needs to be healed, and life wants to be made "whole" again.

In looking at stories that people tell about life-changing experiences, there is one particular kind that stands out as exemplary in this connection, at least insofar as disability is involved. This is the experience of traumatic brain injury (TBI). There is no example that I have seen that does not deal extensively with the task of negotiating different time frames. As virtually all accounts testify, there is no TBI survivor who is not struggling with the gap between the "before" and "after."

Before looking at a few stories about this struggle, there is one issue that I want to address in advance. The issue is suffering. The reason for bringing it up has to do, again, with the doubts about the "why" question. It regards a conviction that we discussed before, and that is often represented by the medical profession—namely, that people need to look forward in order to be able to get on with their lives.

Taking Suffering Seriously

Going through the experience of some kind of loss, people often feel they have to get on with their lives, sometimes at the expense of taking sufficient time for their own mourning. They report that this is due to what their social environment expects, particularly in the context of being in "rehab." They are there for recovery, which makes looking back on their previous lives a waste of time. At least that is what they are told. In other words, the advice is not to turn back to "before," because "before" does not exist anymore. So the "rehab" mindset is attuned to what is possible rather than to what is impossible; there is no returning to the life one has lost. Recall the earlier quote by a TBI survivor who became a "motivational speaker" on overcoming brain injury:

> Many folks ask "why me?" and the answer is likely "why not me?" Nobody "deserves" to fall and sustain a serious head injury . . . but those things happen. You can either respond—which is positive, or react—which is negative. When you respond, the results are better by far. Being

hotheaded and self-centered, or seeking to place blame never leads to
a positive outcome.[2]

No doubt, being "hotheaded" and "self-centered" are not going to do
much good, but under the circumstances it is important not to be mistaken about *how to name* people's experience. This is particularly relevant
in connection with TBI, where people are encouraged to always look at
the bright side of life. Every cloud has a silver lining, does it not?

In encouraging people to overcome the experience of loss, there is the
risk of renaming the experience itself in a utilitarian fashion: "They saved
your life, it could have been worse," "Look at the positive side of what you
can do, instead of what you cannot do," and so on. Recovery is the name
of the game, not mourning, let alone suffering. Consequently, people feel
sometimes discouraged in their lament. Reflecting upon their suffering
allegedly distracts them from positive goals.

There is a point in taking people's suffering very seriously, however,
and in not letting it be pushed aside too quickly by being attuned to a new
future. The great divide between "before" and "after" implies rebirth, and
therefore death. There is always the loss of the "old" person to be lamented.

In connection with TBI, there is a frequently noted tendency toward
false optimism, which presumably has to do with a need to believe in the
possibility of recovery. Without this possibility, there is no hope. But with
the need to believe in recovery comes the need to believe in the powers of
medicine and technology:

> The miracle working of medical science and technology is the first stop
> for hope. But this source of hope fades quickly when the medical com-
> munity can offer no better than support for the rest of the body while
> waiting anxiously to discover to what extent the brain heals itself.[3]

"Waiting" appears to be key in this connection. When people have
suffered an accident that puts them in a state of unconsciousness, or semi-
consciousness, there is not much that can be done but to wait. This is particularly true in the case of TBI—or "closed head injury," as it used to be
called—when the powers of medical technology turn out to be frustratingly diminished. The late Cathy Crimmins—award-winning author of

Where Is the Mango Princess?, a story about her husband's recovery from traumatic brain injury—describes the experience as follows:

> Since neurosurgeons are a macho breed, inoperable brain injuries often frustrate them. They are in charge of tracking such injuries, yet there is little they can do but wait along with the family and check the CT scans to see how the bruising is developing.[4]

This experience must be widespread indeed, given its appearance in the name of a website with information on brain injury: "Waiting".[5] Apparently, what you are waiting for is "recovery."

In this context, "recovery" is clearly an ambivalent concept—not only because medicine cannot do all that much except stabilize the patient in order for the brain to begin healing itself, but also because it puts a premium on restoration. However, the fact of the matter is that when the patient has recovered from being comatose, the worst is yet to come. "The chasm between the old life and the new is wider than you think."[6] Whatever else may be true about recovery, the people involved will always be referred to, and also see themselves as "survivors" of TBI. The effects of TBI may result in the birth of a new person, but that person is different from whom he or she was before:

> The "old" Alan died on July 1, 1996, and a new one arose, created by the rivers and lakes of bruises that coursed over his brain, as he lay unconscious in the days after his injury. He is a man with different frontal lobes, and a different personality to match.[7]

As testified by patients and their families, "recovery" is directed toward going back to their previous lives, at least initially. Quite frequently it turns out that this is impossible. The chasm cannot be bridged, as Cathy Crimmins put it. There is "old" and there is "new," but the two will not merge, mainly because there is no transition. The reason is named coma. The person of coma is in a state in between being and non-being. What happens during this "in between" will not be recovered. "The comatose person is living a narrative that he will have to take on faith from other people, once he wakes up."[8]

Even when climbing back at a later stage, TBI patients will not know they have been hit. They will never know from firsthand experience what happened, because that part is missing. Put differently, the goal of recovery implies overcoming the experience of living in two radically separate time frames. This is often a bridge too far because the TBI does not go away, which implies the difficult task of negotiating the connection with the other side of the chasm.

In what follows, we will be looking at two stories about living with TBI that deal with this task in quite remarkable ways. One, I have been quoting already—namely Cathy Crimmins' book *Where Is the Mango Princess?* The other, with which we will start, is Jean-Dominique Bauby's book *The Diving Bell and the Butterfly*.

Locked-in Syndrome

At the age of forty-five, Bauby suffers from a massive stroke that results in a condition known as *locked-in syndrome*. Completely paralyzed, he communicates with the outside world through blinking with his left eyelid, which is what allows him to write his book. The author is painstakingly honest about his excruciating condition and in unadorned language he describes the situation he finds himself in. It is devastating.

Given its irreversibility there is very little expectation that there will be a life "after" his accident, which leaves Bauby in a condition too horrific to contemplate as the final truth about his life. In his case there appears to be no time that will heal all wounds. In order to appreciate what the author is doing with time, the first thing to notice is that he takes his present state of suffering seriously, not in order to complain, but in order to take his condition for what it is: "Paralyzed from head to toe, the patient, his mind intact, is imprisoned inside his body, but unable to speak or move. In my case, blinking my left eyelid is my only means of communication."[9]

One day, when Bauby is still in the dark about whether he will regain his abilities, the medical staff decides it is time to bring him back into the world again. Two of his attendants lift him out of his bed and put him into a wheelchair, promoting a patient with a lethal condition to the official status of a quadriplegic. They chase him through the hospital in his upright position to find out whether his body will respond with uncontrollable spasms, and are thrilled about their success. "They didn't quite applaud, but they came close."[10] The patient has very different feelings about the experiment, however: "I was too devastated by this brutal downgrading of my future hopes to take much notice."[11]

What advanced medicine considers a success does not apparently always match the feelings of its beneficiaries. An unshakable faith in its results often prevents its supporters from recognizing the possibility that medicine occasionally produces harm. From the medical point of view, there is no harm, short of death, however, because the preservation of life trumps all other outcomes. As a result of this utilitarian view, the unanticipated failure to restore life to what it was before is not named for what it is, but is presented as the lesser evil of disability, outweighed by the greater good of life.

In view of this tendency to subject harmful outcomes for the good of preserving life, it may be noticed that it is in fact analogous to the ancient view of evil as *privatio boni*. Ending up as a quadriplegic is an "evil" that has no standing of its own, on this view, because compared with the ultimate defeat of medicine—death—it is only relative. The result could have been worse, because life is preserved and can go on.

Bauby is not convinced, for that matter. When the occupational therapist predicts that some day he will handle his wheelchair, the patient does not receive it as good news, but rather as a life-sentence. It is a truth "keener than a guillotine blade."[12] For Bauby, "life" in any true sense of the word is lost, completely and for good. He experiences the consequence of naming evil as relative to good in the same way that it was explained before by John Swinton: it renders evil nonexistent.[13] It cannot be named for what it is, at least not by those who see it as their task to work for progressive recovery. From their point of view, only the prospect of *improvement* can be named. Bauby, however, has no intention to comply. Noticing the comfort of a bath to ease the pain of his limbs, he immediately connects it with memories of extensive bathing as one of the greater joys of his previous life. "Armed with a cup of tea or a Scotch, a good book or a pile of newspapers. I would soak for hours."[14] Rarely does he feel his present condition as cruel as when remembering these hours.

When he introduces his readers to the hospital, the author mentions the various departments where they keep different categories of patients: people of old age in geriatrics, broken in both spirit and mind; orthopedic patients, survivors of all kinds of accidents—highway, sports, domestic; "tourists," he calls them, who will leave as soon as the doctors have put their limbs together again.[15] And then there is this place that everybody knows exists, the section of the hospital with comatose patients, "poor devils at death's door, plunged in the face of an endless night."[16] These patients never leave their rooms. Everyone knows they are there; nobody ever mentions them. But "they weigh strangely on our collective awareness, almost like a guilty conscience."[17]

What exists merely on the brink of nonexistence cannot be named, because it defies the very point of advanced medicine. People prefer to turn away, into the light, in the positive direction, where there is still the projection of a future. The fake optimism of Bauby's neurologist is telling: "We need to be very patient."[18] Despite the fact that his patient has not used his palate for months to enjoy the taste of food, the nursing aid—who wheels him to his room after his daily exercises—nonetheless wishes him "*bon appetit*" every single day, as if the liquid fluids dripping through his feeding tube to satisfy his calorific needs have anything to do with food.

Once your body is changed into a cocoon, the one possibility left is to wander around in your *mind* and have all sorts of imaginative experiences. Bauby's hospital has a patroness from the nineteenth century: Empress Eugenie, spouse of Napoleon III. Her remembrance is kept alive by her image on a stained-glass window in the main hall, supported by a white marble bust showing the glory of her youth. Bauby loves to visit her, because she is his consolation. On one occasion when he confides his sorrows to her likeness in the stained-glass window, the patient is looking into an unknown man. "His mouth was twisted, his nose damaged, his hair tousled, his gaze full of fear."[19] Bauby stares him in the face for a few seconds, before he realizes it is his own.

Not only does the author find himself exiled, paralyzed, mute, and half deaf, but on top of all this is his appearance, which is too horrible to behold. Now he understands: no wonder that his visitors are confused and shocked. They probably need a firm resolve not to turn away from him when entering his room. At least they hesitate a moment to step in, and then take a deep breath to confront him: "When they finally come in, they are gasping for air like divers whose oxygen has failed them."[20]

Substitute Destinies

Given the condition of surviving TBI as a quadriplegic without much of a future, how does one manage to survive both mentally and spiritually? Bauby answers this question through his rendezvous with the empress: he lets his mind wander away in memories and dreams.

He recalls a schoolboy from the days of his youth, Oliver, who made up the most incredible stories to impress Jean-Dominique and his friends, for example that he had met Johnny Hallyday, or just had been to London to see the new James Bond. The boys at school loved him. His imagined adventures embodied an entire movie theatre, providing his friends with the best seats in the house. Bauby confesses to envy the gift of such capacity for storytelling. But his present condition motivates him to the art of forging "glorious substitute destinies" like racing the track of Monza or Silverstone as a Formula One driver. [21]

During his inspirational pastime, Bauby sees himself in an impressive array of mainly military characters: fighting Caesar alongside of Vercingetorix, or helping Napoleon to victory, or surviving both Verdun and D-day in Normandy, soothing his aching soul with these successes. Creating imaginary stories is a way of escaping the inevitability of his actual story. Bauby celebrates his schoolmate Oliver the mythmaker for his ability to do just that. He was an incredible inventor of "runaway mythomania."[22]

But of course, inventing substitute destinies is just another way of telling his readers that he does not see a way to negotiate the connection between "before" and "after." Given his irreversible locked-in syndrome, there is no intelligible transition to explain how they are related, other than by keeping his imprisoned soul alive with imagination.

This comes out very strongly in another episode, when Bauby tells us about a trip to the beach in the company of two people who each belong within a different time frame: Brice—"my partner in crime"—who has been his friend for twenty-two years, and Claude, the young woman to whom he is dictating his book. Unlike Brice, Claude hardly knows anything about the author's previous life, because she has only known him for two weeks. Pushing Bauby's wheelchair to the beach, Brice talks with Claude and tells her all sorts of things about his friend, his quick temper, his love of books, his red convertible, and so on. The episode illustrates the gap in the sense that Claude is most intimate with his thoughts in the present time—given her role in writing his manuscript—but she hardly knows anything about the "old" Bauby.[23] There is no traverse between his life "before" and "after." It will henceforth be divided between those who knew him before, and all the others. "What kind of person will those who only know me *now*, think I was?"[24]

There are two accounts of Jean-Dominique Bauby's life, then, that are separated by the chasm of a massive stroke. These accounts are construed within two unrelated time frames that are nonetheless part of a single life. This is most painful. Bauby's present condition does not reflect in any way the person he takes himself to be. Proof for this claim comes in a very moving episode with highly symbolic significance: the celebration of Father's Day.

It is the second Sunday in June, and Bauby's wife and their two children, Théophile and Céleste, come to visit him. Watching his children brings him the greatest joy, but also the greatest sadness. He has become their "zombie father," a fact they try very hard to ignore. But they are inadvertently betrayed by their loyalty, as when his son wipes a thread of saliva from his father's mouth with a Kleenex, or when his daughter Céleste cradles her father's head in her bare arms, covering his forehead with noisy kisses while repeating over and over again: "You're my dad, you're my dad," as if in incantation.[25]

Bauby is painfully aware that the reason for his family to celebrate Father's Day—something they never felt a need to do before—only confirms that what remains of him is but a "rough sketch, a shadow, a tiny fragment of a dad."[26] Bauby is torn between the joy of looking at his children and the fear that the sight of his suffering is unhealthy entertainment for children their age. At the moment they are about to leave, Bauby asks himself what they will take home from this "field-trip into his endless solitude?"[27]

Finally, another remarkable episode appears close to the end of the book. It is about a dream that shows the wax museum in Paris, the Musée Grévin, which the author Bauby knows quite well. The episode receives its strength from the awareness of what a wax museum actually is: a place to commemorate celebrities, represented in a scene that reflects how they are remembered.

Upon entering the museum in his dream, Jean-Dominique notices that the galleries with contemporary figures are gone. In other words, the room where he himself would be represented as the glamorous editor of

Elle is empty. The next room shows figures in white clothes, indicating the hospital, after which he enters room 119, his own room, reproduced to the last detail.

When he comes closer, he finds the drawings and photographs on the wall—as memorabilia of his former life—blurred, "like impressionist paintings." The bed itself is empty, the patient is not there, but Bauby recognizes the wax figures surrounding it. They want to be some of the people who have been with him from the beginning of his stay, which he describes with unexpected delicacy:

> Michel, seated on a stool and conscientiously scribbling in the notebook where visitors set down all my remarks. Anne-Marie, arranging a bouquet of forty roses; Bernard, holding a memoir of diplomatic life in one hand, while with the other executing a theatrical barrister's gesture that is pure Daumier. His steel-rimmed glasses, perched on the end of his nose, complete the picture of a courtroom prima donna. Florence, pinning children's drawings on a corkboard, her black hair flaming in sad smile. And Patrick leaning against the wall, apparently lost in thought.[28]

At the depiction of this scene, the author comments how this group of wax statues represents the tenderness and shared sorrow of his closest friends whenever they come and visit him. What makes this scene remarkable is that it does not depict Bauby in his *former* life, say behind his desk as the editor of the famous women's magazine *Elle*. It depicts the world that is now his. At the end of the book, he also seems to have accepted it as such. This state of mind is revealed by the penultimate episode, which is named "Season of Renewal":

> The start of my first autumn season at the hospital has made one thing very plain—I have indeed begun a new life, and that life is here, in this bed, that wheelchair and those corridors. Nowhere else. September means the end of holidays, it means back to school and to work, and here at the hospital it's time to start a new season.[29]

Describing his life in terms of a "before" that represents who he really is, and an "after" in which he is but a shadow of that reality, the author indicates an unbridgeable gap between the two. This results in the conclusion that the "here and now" has no meaning other than disaster. Read in this light, the above reference to a *new* season is quite remarkable and unexpected. It suggests a different conclusion, one that the author confirms in the very same episode: "For the first time in a long while I don't have that awful sense of a countdown."[30]

In the introduction to the present chapter I said that the point to be explored in it is how people negotiate the connection between the "before" and "after," so that their wound is healed and life is made whole again. I will refrain from reading something into Bauby's story that the author does not explicitly explain to his readers, but it is clear that the foregoing account leaves us with a suggestion as to how to answer this question in his case. Throughout the book Bauby exhibits that the story he lives by is the story of his past. As the episodes about his present condition show, the dominant picture is one of loss and grief about the prospect of a life with locked-in syndrome. In the end, however, there is the image of a season of renewal, not as part of a "runaway mythomania," but here, "in this room," and "nowhere else." Also Jean-Dominique Bauby seems to have faced the question that many people with TBI and their families face: how do I make this "new" life my own? In his case we do not know the answer to this question, however. Bauby died shortly after his book was published.

The Mango Princess

Cathy Crimmins' *Where Is the Mango Princess?* is the widely acclaimed story of the traumatic brain injury of her husband, Alan Forman, in which she tells how they learned to live with it. It is a wry and humorous account of the episodes following a horrific accident in which "Al" got hit by a speedboat on a Canadian lake. After being hospitalized in a foreign country, Al has to be transported back to their hometown, Philadelphia, which turns out to be quite an ordeal. The HMO that has to pay for the air ambulance manages to make the arrangement of this trip as miserable as possible, which drives Cathy crazy. When Al is recovering from his coma, she gets permission to arrange what is necessary for a safe transport.

If I were to mention one particular feature that stands out in Crimmins' book, it should be her account of how she seeks to stay connected with her husband, by learning as much about TBI as she possibly can. In this way, she manages to convince herself that Al's occasionally outrageous and crazy behaviors are not untypical of TBI patients. Not only is he a different man from who he used to be, but Cathy also feels strongly that she does not know this man, so that the most important reason for accepting her situation is "he can't help it."

When Al has recovered from his coma and starts to regain his speech, the first sign that Al is no longer Al comes with a question he raises: "Where is the Mango Princess?" At that point he has awakened from his coma for two and a half days. His wife does not understand the question, so Al repeats it: "Where is the Mango Princess?" Cathy gives it a try and asks if he means his nurse. "No, the Mango Princess."[31]

Cathy tries to figure out who might be intended by this title, but does not succeed, which makes Al's blood pressure beepers go up, as he keeps repeating the question. His wife fails to understand. "I spoke with her earlier today," he says softly, drifting back to sleep. His wife ponders where he goes at these moments. Where has Al been during his coma? Perhaps the Mango Princess is there, in that other place.[32]

There seems to be a blank space in time, a space of which her husband does not know anything, that seems to have affected not only his brain but also his mind—Cathy's greatest fear. Where is Al when he wanders into that space? This question persists in the next days when the first bits and pieces of conversation are exasperating Cathy.

At some point during this time Al wants to know who is in charge. He repeats the question over and over again, reminding his wife of a demented version of Abbott and Costello. "I'm in charge," she says, upon which Al asks her, "So when are we going to have the meeting?"[33] When she asks him what he means, her husband gets impatient. He says that as soon as the person who is in charge shows up they are going to have a meeting. Cathy decides to put him straight and tells him she's the one in charge, there is not going to be a meeting. "That's what I was afraid of," Al responds dryly.[34]

Unfortunately there are also less funny exchanges. Cathy expects more confusion from Al, but it turns out he is not even close to being confused—"oblivious" would be the better term. Their short conversations have little or no relation to what is actually happening. Al does not even know that they are in Canada, even though this has been communicated to him dozens of times. It appears that he does not take an interest in his surroundings whatsoever. Cathy is afraid of what is to come. She admits his coma has been easier to handle than this lack of self-awareness.

During long days and nights in the ICU, fond memories about the former Alan Forman are coming back again and again. Cathy tells her mother that she is beginning to understand what the phrase "lack of companionship" means, referring to a piece of information she has picked up from the literature on TBI. Partners of TBI survivors report a lack of companionship, which is another way of saying that their partners are not "partners" any longer. "He's not here," Cathy worries. "He might never be here again."[35]

After Al has had a major seizure, he is put on heavy medication to prevent this from happening again. It is recommended that he stays on this drug for at least a year. Cathy anticipates that recovery may be a very long process. The doctor speaks of six months to a year, but there is a "catch": the patient might get stuck in any phase, and only very few patients recover fully. He prepares her for the worst, mentioning that Al could stay the way he is now.[36]

There are more signs that her husband is far out from who he used to be. Some of the more exasperating features of TBI are kicking in, of which confusion and agitation are not even the worst. Part of Al's frontal lobes are lacking control, which leads to an embarrassing lack of inhibition. He develops the habit of masturbating in front of visitors, even their daughter Kelly. Apart from this, he swears while yelling obscenities at them.

One afternoon, when she enters Al's room, a nurse approaches Cathy to tell her that he has been pretty wild. "He's a wild thing," she says. His wife jumps on that phrase because of the dear memories attached to it. It is the title of a song Al sang for her on their wedding. She asks him if he remembers the song "Wild Thing." Not only does Al fail to remember, he even denies there is such a song. Cathy is exasperated. He couldn't have hurt her more than denying one of her most cherished treasures from their marriage: "Oh, God, to lose 'Wild Thing'! It is tantamount to saying that our past together doesn't exist, and right now that's all we have."[37]

The comment is heartbreaking, of course. Cathy does not know how to negotiate the connection between "before" and "after"—not only because she is strongly attached to her past, but also because she does not see any future. There is nothing to negotiate. Right now, there is only the dreaded loss of what they shared together. Gradually, this will turn out to be Cathy's biggest problem. As we will see, Al will recover slowly but gradually. Hanging on to her memories of "old" Al, however, his wife has a hard time to enjoy the "new" Al who is taking his place.

Creation Business

In Jean-Dominique's story we encountered the notion of "substitute iden-tities," which indicated his strategy of negotiating the connection between the "before" and "after." So we find him as a Formula One driver, as Napo-leon's *Aide-de-Champ* and so on. One way to the bridge the gap apparently consists of imagining things that somehow suggest one is still in the driver seat of one's life.[38] Something comparable is going on in Cathy Crimmins' book. It is one of its most moving and fascinating episodes. I will resist the temptation just to copy/paste the entire episode, but summarize it, hope-fully without losing too much of Crimmins' skillful writing, I hope.[39]

Back in Philadelphia, Al enters a rehab hospital. One day, Cathy enters his room. Al is entertaining a bunch of people who happen to be with him when she arrives. He is showing off with his mastery of sports statistics, which, incidentally, Cathy discovers he has retained. Suddenly the merriment of the moment is interrupted when Al announces that he wants to call Cathy. She responds he does not have to. "You don't have to call me Al, I'm right here."[40] Her husband insists: "No, I want to call Cathy. The Other Cathy. The one at home."[41] The visitors fall silent, as if realiz-ing that they now have entered the real world of TBI. Persistent as he is, Al does not let go, so eventually Cathy hands him the phone. The entire atmosphere in the room breathes uneasiness. Curiously, Al dials their home number without hesitation and leaves a message on the answering machine. When Cathy gets home later that day, she plays it back. "I realize how appropriate it is that he wants to talk to the Other Cathy; after all, he is now Another Alan."[42]

What strikes me in this passage is not what it tells us about Al—a bit more on this in a minute—but what it tells us about his wretched wife. She is in his room, but he does not recognize her as the one she is, so she is locked out. And then, why in this episode is the "Other Cathy" written in capitals?

From this moment on, the "Other Cathy" begins to appear as a mythi-cal figure, the imagined *enviable* spouse that knows how to be happy with the new Al.[43] In the meantime the real Cathy is left hanging at the other side of the chasm, not knowing how to jump. What she *does* know is how to handle medical information about this new phenomenon in Al's behavior. It turns out the strategy of imagining alternative worlds where life continues to be under control somehow is a well-known phenomenon among TBI experts. They even have a name for this: "reduplicative paramnesia." It has been described in the medical literature as part of the condition of TBI. Cathy calls a befriended neurologist, Andy, to consult him about this. He tells her Al's case is an exceptionally clear example. "He's really a cool TBI person," Andy says.[44]

There is more to come, however, for Al is not done yet with making "doubles." This time it is related to their daughter Kelly. One night, in the presence of two of their closest friends, Al has a question for his wife: "What are we going to do about the Kelly device? Should we keep it or get rid of it?"[45] The three women are stunned, totally speechless. Al then continues, "Because we could create another Kelly device, one that would fit better into everything." After a few moments of silence, Cathy finds words to respond, and asks him about "the Kelly device." What does he mean? Her husband does not answer, but continues in his own imaginative world.

> "Maybe we shouldn't *have* the Kelly device," Alan says. "What is the Kelly device, Al?" He's upsetting me. "Ummm. A plant?" says Al. "No. She is a child. Kelly is our child. We can't get rid of her." "But maybe we should create a second Kelly. The character Kelly," says Al, "One that could fit better into our lives."[46]

Al's question is incredibly cruel, both because the man she loves is denying the child they conceived together in love, *and* because he does not know what he is doing. Cathy makes an attempt to save the situation by joking that they have a hard time handling one Kelly already, let alone two. But again, Alan does not let go: "So what are we going to do?" No one responds. "Okay, let's just keep the Kelly device." Then he appears to give up. "Gee, this creation stuff is really exhausting."[47]

Sometime later, in the presence of one of their woman friends and Al's brother, there is more of this "creation stuff." Al has a stunning question for his visitors. "The defective Alan Forman versus the second Alan Forman that we could create, what do you think?"[48] Of course, they do not know what to say. Al gets impatient and tells them he is talking about a second Alan Forman who could replace the first. What do they think of the defective Alan Forman? "Should he really have a right to exist in the universe?"[49]

This episode reminds one of the story we will encounter in the next chapter. It is as if we are witnessing the heavenly court where Satan is questioning God about his servant Job. What to do with the poor sucker? Let him hang? Restore him to his previous life?

Cathy, typically, is the first to compose herself. "How do you think Alan Forman is defective?"[50] Al responds that he does not know. The friend says that since he cannot think or move the way he could before, Alan Forman may *feel* defective. Al agrees, but then comments: "But *he* could decide if the defective Alan Forman still had a right to live in the universe."[51] Cathy senses there is another player involved in Al's mind, so she asks him, "Who's '*he*,' Al?"

Without any hesitation Al responds he is talking about Mr. Finkelman. Cathy wants to know, of course, who Mr. Finkelman is. Again, the answer is stunning: "He creates the Al Forman and Kelly characters."[52] His wife understands that Mr. Finkelman is a playwright who writes characters. She then raises a question that is as telling as it is heartbreaking because it indirectly invokes the "Other Cathy" figure again:

> "Does he write my character too?" I ask anxiously. Alan looks grave. Professorial. He sighs and then explains the situation patiently: "Oh, no. Mr. Finkelman could *never* write the Cathy Crimmins character. He could not write that character at all. That's not to say that the character doesn't have a right to exist, just that Mr. Finkelman could never create her."[53]

Naturally, Cathy is devastated. Later that night, at the dinner table with her friend and Al's brother, she keeps asking again and again why the Alan and Kelly characters get to be part of the play, and she is not. How is she going to find her part in the new script, the script that has the "new Alan Forman" and the "Kelly device" in it? How is she going to fit in? What part has Mr. Finkelman in store for her?

The day comes for Al to move to a rehabilitation facility. The night before the transition is going to take place, Cathy intends to have a serious conversation with her husband to make sure he understands what he will be up against. She tells him this will be the biggest challenge so far. Al looks at her with dull eyes, but there is a smirk around his mouth when he responds, "Yeah. I think I would do okay in rehab. *If* I had another wife."[54] Cathy recognizes the smirk and asks him whom he would want for a wife. Al picks their friend Kay; she has been visiting him almost every day since their return to Philadelphia. Cathy thinks Kay is a great choice, as she herself is fed up with making all the decisions. Let someone else do it. Being the wife of a TBI survivor is a bad role for her, as Al lets her know in his inhibited phase. Cathy feels guilty by dissociation: she rather would wish him another wife too. She has in fact been worn out in the weeks since the accident, and does not seem to realize that her biggest challenge lies still ahead.

Al's Recovery

"Rehab" turns out to be a leveling experience. People usually draw a large part of their social identity from what they do, but not at the rehab center. What they did in their previous life does not matter all that much. The only thing that matters is to learn to live independently again. So Cathy has to get used to the ways people are busy adjusting. For example, a middle-aged man perched on his stomach playing poker with his friends in the roof garden is unremarkable, as are the giant buzzers announcing the floors to the blind. The truth turns out unadorned at "Magee," as Al's rehab center is called.

There is a great difference, however. Al is no longer approached as a patient. He is now the active participant in his process of recovery. After a few days, Al tells Cathy that he is going to a baseball game. She assumes he must be confused, but it turns out she is mistaken: her husband has been selected with a few other paraplegics to go and see the Phillies. While waiting for the bus, a young man with slurry speech addresses Al. When he asks whether Al has TBI, Cathy confirms. "Me too," is his response. "Motahcycle accident. Six yeahhs ago. Drunk. Ma-a-a-an. Dey had to teach me everything all ovah again."[55]

Cathy begins to see a scary future. Six years of rehab, and then this! In her view the guy is a walking poster child for frontal lobe damage. Is this what lies ahead? "A wave of pity hits me, but it is not pity for the young man, it is pity for myself. Is this what my husband will be like forever?"[56] Rehab brings a lot of challenges indeed. There are group meetings, speech therapy, recreation therapy, physical therapy, and psychology sessions with the neuropsychologist. These are just the items on his daily program.

Al also has to keep a logbook—to help him remember what he has done. At first he can only scribble a hardly readable word or two, of course, but that's fine. More difficult to handle is the fact that Al does not think he needs help to train his short-term memory, because he does not think he has a problem. He keeps telling everyone that he knows very well what he has done this day, but when Cathy puts him on the spot, he cannot remember a single activity.

The opening section of his logbook contains autobiographical information, where Al tells about himself. Cathy has provided this information, of course. She went through it with Al's case manager, a woman who is sensitive to what family members go through. Understanding that Cathy wants people to know that Al is a very high-IQ-patient, the case manager has noted this in the logbook too. But there is more that Cathy wants her to know. She tells the woman about how they share responsibilities in their household, so as to make sure Cathy is not just a typical female. She and Alan are equals. "I sound like an asshole, defensive and elitist."[57] The case manager tells her she is there for Cathy and their daughter too.

In the meantime Al's recovery goes remarkably well, given the seriousness of his injury. Only a few weeks after the accident, he starts walking again. He starts to control his incontinence problems, which is another large subject for TBI patients. But his cognitive problems remain, of which there are many telling examples. One afternoon Cathy comes in to find Al talking to a visitor about a girl he saw outside in the street. Supposedly, the girl was the person who caused Al's accident. "She told me she was sorry that she ran me over." When Cathy interrupts to ask what girl he is talking about, he says, "The girl. The girl who hit me, I saw her in the street, and she told me she was sorry."[58]

Cathy does not say anything, but when the visitor has left, she asks her husband to tell that story again. He tells it exactly the same way, and then Cathy contradicts him. He could not possibly have seen this girl, because he was hit in Canada, but Al is convinced he met the girl and sticks to his story.

The Pod Person Theory

Despite Al's unusually quick recovery, Cathy is worried. When she explains to the case manager how she really feels, Lisa's response is wonderful: "Of course you feel that way. You're experiencing grief. You're in mourning." Cathy is grateful for these words. She admits that she should feel more ecstatic about Al's progress than she actually does, and that she should be overjoyed that he is alive and doing so well. It is not enough for her; however, she wants him uninjured. She wants to turn back the clock to make sure the boat accident never happened. The fact that Al survived at all and is recovering should make her feel happy, but it does not. It makes her scared. "Each day just seems to emphasize that I am alone, that Al is never coming back—or at least not the old Al."[59]

During the next episodes, there is a lot of information on the various signs of TBI that Al is overcoming, but Cathy remains skeptical about all the excitement on his progress. She tells his case manager about Al's parents, who believe that everything is going to be okay, but who—according to Cathy—do not want to be informed about what is truly happening, particularly not when it relates to Al's cognitive problems: "God forbid their brilliant son might now be an idiot. It is unthinkable, so they choose not to think about it. But someone has to."[60] Cathy resents that this person is herself, while his family is in denial. Yet she recognizes that her husband is improving.

Soon afterward Al is ready to make a visit to their home. Cathy expects too much. Al is not very excited, and wants to go to bed because he is tired. When he gets into the bed, he chooses the wrong side. When she asks him about it, he says he does not know, even though he has been sleeping on the left side for eighteen years. Even though she knows Al has bigger problems than this, Cathy is greatly disturbed. It brings to her mind what she calls her *Pod Person theory*. It looks like she has brought her husband home, but he only looks like her husband. In fact the one who inhabits his body is an alien, like in those bad sci-fi movies about people whose brains have been taken over by creatures from another planet.[61]

There is a lot more to Crimmins' book than what I have presented here—in particular, the many episodes dealing with the fear that their daughter Kelly has developed with regard to her father. As a matter of fact, Kelly has reason to be afraid of her father, because he is yelling and cursing at her, mainly because he is irritated so quickly, especially when he gets tired. Eventually, however, this episode comes to an end, and the two of them start bonding again, united by the fact that they are both big sports fans.

Al's time at Magee rehabilitation center comes to an end, and he returns home; he even returns to his job for a while—before he gets fired on very disingenuous grounds—but Cathy is still in mourning. The "Pod Person theory" she presents her readers with is quite convincing when it comes to understanding her feelings. The old Al died in the accident, but the new Al does not really exist. He exists in the same body, all right, but his mind is that of a stranger. Cathy envisions that for the rest of her life she has to share the life of intimacy with a man she does not know.

The Stories We Find Ourselves In

Readers who happen to know the books I have presented in this chapter will be surprised to find them in a study on providence, since that is not a subject the authors seem to have any interest in at all—that is to say, they do not articulate the issue in a religious manner. But on the other hand, providence is very much the point of their stories, at least as I have read them. To explain why is the burden of this final section. Lest this be misunderstood, let me point out that I do not assume that either Bauby or Crimmins had hidden religious inclinations. At any rate, their books do not show any sign of it. So I am not in any way interested in claiming these authors as some kind of "anonymous believers."

The stories we have been reading are about radical disruptions. Whether we look at Martha Beck's, or Jean-Dominique Bauby's, or Cathy Crimmins' story—or many other first-person accounts of similar experiences for that matter—they all are about evolving lives that all of a sudden get disrupted, quite dramatically. In each case the question arises inevitably of how to continue one's life—or, as I put it earlier, how to negotiate the connection between the time frames of the "before" and "after."

Martha Beck, for example, seems to evaluate the connection in her own experience of the "before" and "after" in moral terms: "remaining closed" as an indication of a fixed frame of reference, versus "opening up" as an indication of open-mindedness toward an unexpected and unwanted future. When she learned that her child would be born with Down syndrome, she was horrified by "the little monster" inside of her. Once Adam was born, however, she began to see her past with this dreaded future in a different light. Somehow she manages to trust her love for this child, despite her initial disappointment and fears about the prospect of raising a kid with Down syndrome.

The main characters in the foregoing chapters demonstrate different answers to this question[62]—each in his, or her, own way. In Bauby's case he is trying to stay connected to his previous life by creating imaginary extensions of it. He struggles to keep his soul alive by inventing "substitute identities," which is about all he can do. There does not seem to be much prospect left for any kind of "after," given the irreversible nature of his locked-in syndrome, so he reinvents himself as a character in various glorious dramas.

Even so, things change with his dream of the wax museum, when he begins to understand that his lifeline after his accident has been the friendship and love he has received from friends who have been there for him all along the way. It is at that very moment that he writes about a "seasonal renewal." Despite this incredibly brave attempt, however, the disruption of his life turns out to be final: he dies quite soon after he finishes his book.

Cathy Crimmins' example is again different and more complicated. My reading of her book strongly focused on her response to Al's condition. She is struggling to connect to the new Alan Forman, but she fails to convince herself that there is a new Alan Forman. Cathy wants him to be the man who sang "Wild Thing" for her at their wedding. Her Pod Person theory suggests that "old" Alan Forman is gone. He is replaced by a new character all right, but it is not a character she can identify as connected to her husband. Cathy is not even sure she wants to get to know him.

In a sense this is sad, because when Al tells her he is much happier now his wife admits he is right. He is much less pent up and restrained than he used to be. Nonetheless Cathy cannot wholeheartedly rejoice in this renewal. After they spend a holiday in Key West in Florida, a neighbor asks her if she feels that their old life is back. "What we have," she responds, "is a reasonable facsimile of our old life."[63] For Cathy Crimmins the decisive question is to what extent her husband is recovered as the person he was before the accident. It is understandable from her point of view, but it is sad nonetheless.

In what sense is providence the point of these stories? The answer lies in the "why" question. The "why" question—I have argued, following John Swinton—is a question of lament. What is lamented is the loss of being connected with the life one used to live, which in the case of disability experience takes a particular form. For persons with TBI, it is the loss of a previously existing self. For their relatives, it is the loss of the one they used to know. For families in which a child with a disability is born, it is the loss of expectations and future plans. This sense of loss creates the gap between a past that was familiar and a future that is dreadfully uncertain, in the midst of which is the abyss of a bewildering present.

In view of this bewilderment, "providence" is the notion that God will provide what is needed to bridge the gap. Providence entails the promise that somehow and someday life will be good again, that life's purpose will be uncovered in ways that only God knows. Whether this promise will be delivered, and when, and how, nobody knows. When the moment has come, however, *that* is when people will know—*in hindsight*, that is to say. Then they will know how their story has continued, how life has taken its course again, and, therefore, what the connection between the "before" and "after" has turned out to be. Providence is about the way God sustains people to make them succeed in doing so.

The stories we have read present us with mixed messages in this regard. Martha Beck knows in hindsight what it is that healed her wounds. It was Adam's love that made her realize what she had known—and should have remembered—all that time: that "this flesh of my flesh" loved her, despite her many mistakes and inadequacies, and that he was sorry for the pain she felt in trying to turn him into a "normal" child. For Jean-Dominique Bauby, there was no hindsight, because he was not given the time to live and discover it, but there was the glimmer of light, the loving friendship of his companions that made him anticipate a "season of renewal." In Cathy Crimmins' story, there are signs of reconciliation, but they seemed to have been blocked from her view. What she saw in hindsight was a "reasonable facsimile" of their old life. The presence of new Al as the remaining stranger kept her from reaffirming that life was good again. I cannot help but think about hers as a sad story, therefore, even though there were signs he was a happier man than he used to be.

As indicated, however, all this is hindsight. Before that, there is only the gap, and nothing suggests a reason to be reassured that all will be well. The road ahead is empty. Life's purpose—as it was known—is gone without leaving much of a clue as to what will replace it. Each of the stories that we have been close-reading, in its own way, testifies to the fact that this is what we do as human beings. In times of hardship, we are constructing stories that enable a transition from "old" to "new." Since we cannot know ourselves *outside* of these stories, however, there is no escape from uncertainty. The loss of connectedness is acutely felt, as when Cathy Crimmins asked herself in which play she was one of the leading characters. Similarly, Martha Beck sensed that she was part of some kind of plan that her son Adam and the "Being of Love" had together. In the same vein, Jean-Dominique Bauby asks himself whether the cosmos contain keys for opening up his cocoon. Each of these statements expresses the same idea:

there must be a way to make sense of it all, but the main character does not know what it is.

So what they are left with at the time of their ordeal are unanswered questions about how to reconnect the shattered parts of their lives and, particularly, about what their future is going to be, and how they themselves will fit in. Will the defective Alan Forman be the new Al? Does he have a right to exist in the universe? How is the locked-in soul of Jean-Dominique Bauby connected to the glamorous editor of *Elle*? Does the cosmos contain the keys to unlock it? What is the story that negotiates the connection? Is there a script? What does it say? Is there a writer at all? Who the hell is Mr. Finkelman?

For the time being, there is no way of answering any of these questions with any degree of certainty. The most that can be said is that we see people figuring out what is happening in their lives, such that they do not fall apart. Supposedly, talking about these lives in terms of a "story" means retelling their past, as a way of finding out how to continue. They have become who they are, because of the story they have found themselves to be part of. How they will continue, therefore, depends on the kind of people they have become.

All this is to say that people's stories are by definition unfinished business, which implies that their lives are also unfinished business. In the next chapter, we will adopt the same perspective once again, this time in order to read a story from the Hebrew Bible, the story of a man called Job.

5

A MAN NAMED JOB

*A pawn in a contest of which he knew nothing, the beneficiary of "friendly"
advice he refused to accept, the target of suffering he could not understand,
and a victim in a universe that threatened to overwhelm him,
Job has been a man for all ages.*

—*Susan E. Schreiner*

Introduction

The last chapter ended with a somewhat skeptical claim. As human beings
we always find ourselves in circumstances that can be "read" in any number of ways. Such "readings"—stories—present different ways of seeing
how the things that are happening in our lives may fit together. In the
midst of these events, however, there is no way of "knowing" which of
these stories will survive the test of time.

In the case of catastrophic events that create the gap between the
"before" and "after," the story that people believed was running through
their lives, breaks down. This is when the "why" question arises in their
souls. Particularly when people are hit hard by life's contingencies, the
response is one of bewilderment. There does not seem to be any coherence, and no apparent link, between the "before" and "after." "*Why this, O*

Lord?" is the lament of the believer that expresses this lack of coherence. The "why" question signifies the gap.

In this chapter we will read yet another story about this experience, which is a story that is truly a world classic in religious imagination. The story I have in mind is from the Hebrew Bible. It is told in the book of Job. It is a story that opens with a heavenly court in session. The court deliberates the fate of someone who was once a wealthy and prosperous man but is now swept off his feet by the evil that has come over him. Of course Job does not know of God's contest with Satan concerning his character. He suffers his misery without understanding why. So he sits down in total desolation when his friends call upon him. As they speak their words of comfort, they discover a serious disagreement about how to make sense of Job's fate, which leads to their alienation as friends.

In Christian circles, the story of Job is often invoked in a pastoral context, particularly when people are going through rough times in their lives—for example, because of an illness they are suffering from. There are always religious people around who are willing to explain the meaning of that experience: "You must have done something wrong," or "God must have chosen you to bear this cross," and so forth. In other words, there are always people around who are willing to administer to the sufferer what I have called "cheap theology."

In this context the story of Job is brought up frequently as the classical example of false comfort. Job is grieving because he has lost almost everything, but particularly because of the killing of his children. His friends arrive to join him in mourning their death, but instead of being offered consolation, he finds himself lectured and questioned about the real cause of his misery. Such is the common reading.

While false comfort is certainly part of it, I do not think this common reading of Job's story adequately addresses its main concern, which regards the nature of divine providence. Job is a man who has lived a life of exemplary virtue, but nonetheless he gets blasted away by misfortune. While seeking understanding in the midst of all of this, Job and his friends are "testing" the truth of the traditional view on why bad things happen to good people, as Rabbi Kushner's felicitous book title has it.[1]

In this respect, the story of Job has remarkable similarities with the stories we have been reading thus far—notwithstanding the fact that strictly speaking it does not address disability, even though the seriousness of his skin disease would nowadays probably register as a disability.[2] In order not to jump ahead of my reading, I will postpone pointing out these similarities until the end of this chapter. One of them can be mentioned in advance, however, which is that Job and his friends are trying to find out how to make sense of it all. The stage setting is the same. There is a catastrophic discontinuity in Job's life that divides his life into a "before" and an "after." We also find the gap between different time frames, particularly when his friends are pushing the question of whether his previous life may not have been the life of exemplary piety that they thought it was. The underlying question they are attempting to answer is this: what is God doing, in the way God is dealing with Job, in this catastrophic episode of his life?

I have two remarks before we turn to reading this story. The first regards the way to approach this question. In chapters 2, 3, and 4, we have been listening to first-person accounts of people's experience, which explains the emphasis on narrative. In the last three chapters (6, 7, and 8), we will enter a new genre—namely, that of theological analysis. We will focus mainly on John Calvin, on all counts a classical voice on the theology of providence. Suffice it to say that Calvin is usually regarded, rightly or wrongly, as the main source of the conception of providence I am struggling to leave behind in this inquiry.

The present chapter forges the connection between the two parts, representing in its own way a bridge between a "before" and "after." To forge this connection we will be close-reading the story of Job. There will be quite a few references to Calvin, however, who was an ardent reader of the book of Job, which is demonstrated by his about 150 sermons on Job, delivered within the course of only two years.[3] As we will see, Calvin's opinion was that Job defended a good cause, but handled it badly, whereas the opposite is true of his friends.[4] Thus, there are two aspects of the story that need to be separated, according to Calvin: what Job believes to be true of God, on the one hand, and how he speaks to God, on the other. Taking Calvin's reading of the story into account will enable us to prepare for the next chapter, where we will be looking at his own doctrine of providence.

My second remark regards the question of how I have read the book of Job as a biblical text. To answer it will take more space, given abundant academic scholarship on this text. This scholarship has resulted in a number of commentaries, particularly in the nineteenth century, in which both the history and the text of the book are explained, and verse-by-verse comments are offered.[5]

Following a basic rule of nineteenth century biblical scholarship, these commentaries set out to reconstruct the text from what are presumed to be its original sources. The aim is to figure out what each of these sources had to say. In this way scholars hoped to identify the authentic voice of the text as part of the so-called Old Testament. For example, the first two chapters of the book of Job, together with the last five chapters, frequently have been noticed to be very different from the dialogues between Job and his friends (Job 3–31); wherefore, many authors have concluded that these parts must originate from another source. In this particular case, a common suggestion is that of a much older "folktale." Apart from language and style, the Job of the "prologue" is very different, commentators say, from the one in the later chapters—much more docile and patient—and holds a different theology. This means that this part does not really belong to the same text, but is a later addition.[6]

Historical critical scholarship had not much interest, however, in the question of what the idea behind particular "additions" might have been.[7] It did not consider the possibility that biblical texts, as they have been handed down by tradition, represent ongoing and unfinished debates on important theological questions. The procedure of distinguishing what different parts of the text said, in order to find the most reliable source from which they originate, might have been the best way to miss what is actually going on in these texts. For all the rigor of the historical criticism of biblical sources, the underlying assumption was that somewhere there had to be an original voice, uncontaminated by the comments of later generations. Consequently, its aim was to get as close as possible to this original source.

In view of this historical approach, biblical scholarship in recent times tends to be much more interested in the intratextual dialogue of the biblical sources as such.[8] This is how I suggest reading the story of Job, as it unfolds. It consists no doubt of material from various sources, but the question is not which of these sources is more authentic than another, but what they have to say to each other.[9] God's word is not spoken univocally, but comes to us through different languages, for which the book of Job provides ample testimony.[10]

Job's Lament

The story begins as follows:

> There was once a man in the land of Uz whose name was Job. That man
> was blameless and upright, one who feared God and turned away from
> evil. There were born to him seven sons, and three daughters. He had
> seven thousand sheep, three thousand camels, five hundred yoke of
> oxen, five hundred donkeys, and very many servants; so that this man
> was the greatest of all the people of the East. His sons used to go and
> hold feasts in one another's house in turn; and they would send and
> invite their three sisters to eat and drink with them. And when the feast
> days had run their course, Job would send and sanctify them, and he
> would rise early in the morning and offer burnt offerings according to
> the number of them all; for Job said, "It may be that my children have
> sinned, and cursed God in their hearts." This is what Job always did.
> (Job 1:1-5)

The story is about a God-fearing man, then, who is rewarded presumably for his serious and consistent attempts to lead an observing life. If *this* story tells us anything, it is that God rewards piety. Job's fortune has been piling up; wherefore God must have recognized his righteousness.

But after a while, Job's fate changes dramatically. His life gets turned upside down when one day a messenger arrives at his doorstep. It is the start of a chain of disaster instigated by rival clans. A band of robbers has assaulted his herdsmen in the field. The robbers killed his servants and took his donkeys and oxen. This messenger has not yet left Job's place, when another one arrives to inform him that his sheep and the shepherds who were guarding them have been killed by a stroke of lightning. And as if this is not enough bad news, a third one arrives with the message that another clan has taken his camels and killed their guards with the sword.

Throughout these tidings, no word of complaint is heard from their master. But then the fourth messenger arrives and reports: "Your sons and daughters were eating and drinking wine in their eldest brother's house, and suddenly a great wind came from the desert, struck the four corners of the house, and it fell on the young people, and they are dead; I alone have escaped to tell you" (Job 1:18-19).[11] This time, Job is really grieving about the loss:

> Then Job arose, tore his robe, shaved his head, and fell on the ground and worshiped. He said: "Naked I came from my mother's womb, and naked shall I return there, the Lord gave, the Lord has taken away; blessed be the name of the Lord." (Job 1:20-21)

At this point still not a word of complaint comes from Job's lips. In all his misfortune—the author of the text comments—Job neither sinned nor charged God with wrongdoing. Having lost first his fortune and then his children, he himself is afterwards attacked by a skin disease. His entire body is covered with sores. This is when his wife turns away from him. She has had enough. There is no point in keeping his integrity, she argues, he may just as well curse God and die. Job responds to his wife's lament, however, in a manner we have heard before: why not me?[12] People who are aware of the fact that they have been blessed in their lives may as well be prepared for their share of misfortune: "Shall we receive the good at the hand of God, and not receive the bad?" (Job 2:10).

This is the story from the perspective of Job and his friends, who now appear on the stage. As was indicated above, the responsive behavior of Job's friends has been thoroughly discredited in the Christian tradition as an outstanding example of pious fraud. Instead of offering Job their consolation in his suffering, they are in fact confronting him and questioning his loyalty to God. Such has been the common reading of the book.[13] In view of this reading, however, I want to suggest a different emphasis. To start, Job's friends are not lecturing him at all. What they are actually doing is something quite different:

> Now when Job's three friends heard of all these troubles that had come upon him, each of them set out from his home—Eliphaz the Temanite, Bildad the Shuhite, and Zophar the Naamathite. They met together to go and console and comfort him. When they saw him from a distance, they did not recognize him, and they raised their voices and wept aloud; they tore their robes, and threw dust in the air upon their heads. They sat with him on the ground seven days and seven nights, and no one spoke a word to him, for they saw that his suffering was very great. (Job 2:11-13)

There are no lame excuses that they were held up from being with him, no false comfort, not a word; there is only silence during the full term of the habitual practice of mourning. Then Job speaks. Cursing the day he was born, he laments, "Why is light given to the one who cannot see the way, whom God has fenced in?" (Job 3:23). In various ways Job contends that it would be better if he had never seen the light of day (Job 3:1-19). Only when Job has spoken do his friends take the liberty to respond. Given what they know about the kind of life he has been living, their response makes perfect sense: the curse in Job's opening words belies everything he has believed, and stood for, in his life so far.

His friend Eliphaz the Temanite, who appears to be a sensitive man, is the first one to speak. Eliphaz finds himself compelled to respond, but he does so very gently: "If one ventures a word with you, will you be offended?" (Job 4:2). Those who in their time have known false comfort often have been addressed in much less gentle ways. Eliphaz then continues, not in order to rebuke Job, but to suggest that Job remain faithful to *himself*, and not betray his own example:

> Your words have supported those who were stumbling, and you have made firm the fable knees. But now it has come to you, and you are impatient; it touches you, and you are dismayed. Is not your fear of God your confidence, and the integrity of your ways your hope? (Job 4:4-6)

Eliphaz is not lecturing Job, at least not at this point, but he is encouraging Job not to give up on his own integrity.[14] In view of the traditional reading of the story, Eliphaz' comment seems to be quite adequate, does it not? Telling people who suffer not to lose confidence in themselves: is this not precisely what conscientious ministers and priests do instead of imposing their views upon the sufferer? Trying to sustain him in remaining faithful to himself, Eliphaz reassures Job of the fact that he is a God-fearing man, as everybody knows, so he must trust that his faith and his integrity will restore him in God's grace. Has it not been Job's belief that those who are upright will not perish, and that those who plow iniquity and sow trouble, will reap the same? If so, then surely his integrity must be a source of hope (Job 4:7-10).

God's Unsearchable Majesty

Having arrived at this conclusion, however, Eliphaz is struck by a deeply disturbing thought: "Now a word came stealing to me, my ear received the whisper of it" (Job 4:12). Most commentators read this passage as the report of a vision Eliphaz had during the night that revealed to him that Job must have sinned.[15] In contrast, I have read it as a way to express what I take to be Eliphaz' second thoughts, which came to him in the still of the night, when he was pondering what they had been speaking of. Reminding himself that they were speaking of the Lord who induces fear and trembling in the reverend soul, Eliphaz cautions Job:

> Amid thoughts from visions of the night, when deep sleep falls on mortals, dread came upon me, and trembling, which made all my bones shake. A spirit glided past my face; the hair of my flesh bristled. It stood still, but I could not discern its appearance. A form was before my eyes; there was silence. Then I heard a voice: "Can mortals be righteous before God?" (Job 4:12-16)

In encouraging Job to trust his integrity, as Eliphaz had been doing in his first response to Job, he has been suggesting in fact that Job assert his righteousness *before God*! But the question posed before him—can mortals be right before God?—indicates that this is a profound mistake. Acknowledging the unfathomable difference between Creator and creature, any suggestion of God's accountability must be blasphemous! This is what Eliphaz now realizes and wants Job to acknowledge too: no human being may assert his or her righteousness before the Almighty. Thus he repeats, "Can mortals be righteous before God; can human beings be pure before their Maker?" (Job 4:17).

When everything is said and done—that is, on the day of the last judgment—is there anyone who can stand upright untainted? This rhetorical question is hyphenated by Eliphaz' remark that God even charges angels with error (Job 4:18). Even though not fallen to sin, the angels are still not free from imperfection. If this is true of unfallen creatures like angels, Eliphaz is implying, how much more must it be true of human beings? He suggested that Job should hold on to his belief in God's retributive justice, but now sees that to do so is to ignore the creaturely imperfection of any mortal before the Creator!

This notion of creaturely imperfection suggests an important distinction. What Eliphaz draws Job's attention to does not regard his sinfulness; it regards human creatureliness.[16] Even though the angels have not been

separated from God in the way that other creatures are, their state of perfection is nonetheless diminished. The reason is not sin, as it is in fallen
human beings, but the ontological difference between Creator and creature, a difference that—if maintained—must transcend the possibility of
sinfulness.[17]

With regard to Eliphaz' second thoughts, then, the difference between
Creator and creature opens up the question that he wants to put before
Job. Note that Eliphaz still does not name Job a sinner at this point. His
point is that rather than standing in awe before God's majesty, Job must
lower his voice and turn to the Holy One, in becoming humility:

> As for me, I would seek God, and to God I would commit my cause.
> He does great and unsearchable, marvelous things without number. He
> gives rain on the earth and sends waters to the fields; he sets on high
> those who are lowly, and those who mourn are lifted in safety. (Job
> 5:8-11)

Job is charged with displaying lack of reverence. "As for me, I would
seek God. (Instead of opposing God)." Eliphaz speaks elliptically. So we
begin to see the argument that he is developing. The problem with Job is
not that he mistakenly assumes his own innocence. After all, God even
confirms Job's judgment in this respect (Job 1:8; 42:7). The problem is
rather that his tone of voice—and his language—is completely out of
bounds with regard to the creaturely reverence that imperfect human
beings owe their Maker. The reason is not some grand scheme of just retribution, but lies in God's *unsearchable* majesty. From a religious point
of view, human beings have no ground to lay claim against the Almighty
God, as he has no obligations toward his creatures. "We are not discussing
the scales of justice here," Eliphaz seems to be saying. There is no comfort
in our innocence; there is only hope in God:

> How happy is the one whom God reproves; therefore do not despise the
> discipline of the Almighty. For he wounds, but he binds up, he strikes,
> but his hands heal. He will deliver from six troubles; in seven no harm
> shall touch you. (Job 5:17-19)

So, the prime advice of Eliphaz is not that Job should reconsider his
claim to innocence, but that he show the humility that is becoming of

human beings when they approach God in their affliction. This reading reflects Calvin's view that Job had a good cause but handled it ill. He had a good cause in that he knew that "God does not always punish man to the measure of his sin," but he handled it ill since "because of the outrageous talk he used he was out of bounds."[18]

To sum up Eliphaz' point, human understanding is in any case limited when it comes to grasping divine justice. It only knows justice as revealed by divine law. This is justice in respect of the law. It addresses transgression and therefore pertains to human sinfulness. Apart from this, there is another justice, however. It resides in the majesty of the Creator, in whose light none of the Creator's creatures can stand the test of perfection.[19]

In the meantime, Eliphaz continues to assure Job that things will change for him. Even when God strikes, he will prove to be merciful in the end. Eliphaz again attempts to convince Job of the truth of this insight, in the light of his *own* beliefs: "See, we have searched this out; it is true. Hear, and know it for yourself" (Job 5:27).

It is at this point that the dispute between Job and his friends takes off. If Job has previously believed in God's retributive justice, he now appears no longer convinced of the matter. He refuses to accept Eliphaz' advice to turn to God and pray for his mercy. While his friend continues to argue that God's justice shows itself in his mercy, Job is not prepared to accept this as a consolation. First of all because he has turned to God again and again but there has been no answer, and second because Job does not want mercy. He wants justice. In view of the violence he has suffered, he justifies why he has spoken rash words:

> O that my vexation was weighed, and all my calamity laid in the balances! For then it would be heavier than the sand of the sea; therefore my words have been rash. For the arrows of the Almighty are in me, my spirit drinks their poison; the terrors of God are arrayed against me. (Job 6:2-4)

"Do not despise the discipline of the Almighty," Eliphaz has said (Job 5:17). Job, however, does not see discipline; he only sees terror. If God is the source of comfort, as Eliphaz suggests, how can it be that he has ignored Job's supplications? Now that the Almighty has turned against him, he might as well strike him down for good!

O that I might have my request, and that God would grant my desire; that it would please God to crush me, that he would let loose his hand and cut me off! This would be my consolation. (Job 6:8-10)[20]

If God's majesty is Job's hope, why then does not God take him out of his misery? Why should he hang on? Grounded in what strength? "In truth I have no help in me, and any resource is driven from me" (Job 6:13).[21] Pushing his argument to its logical end—"I would rather be dead than be without God"—Job distrusts Eliphaz' retreat. Eliphaz wants him to give in, Job suggests, for no other reason than fear: "You have seen my calamity, and you are afraid" (Job 6:21).

Job is not asking to offer God a bribe to spare a friend, however. There is no reason to bargain on behalf of someone who has done nothing wrong. His friends implore that he makes peace with God, but he refuses. He did not ask them to try and rescue him from his opponent: "Have I said: from your wealth offer a bribe for me? Or: save me from my opponent's hands?" (Job 6:22-23). In playing out God's majestic inscrutability, his friends are corrupting themselves, Job is suggesting. There is no reason to bargain for sins not committed. He scorns them: "You would even cast lots over the orphan, and bargain over your friend" (Job 6:27). Casting the issue in terms of God's unsearchable majesty puts it beyond the scales of justice to which he has always held himself accountable. That is unacceptable to Job.

"Does God Pervert Justice?"

It appears, then, that the unfolding controversy regards two different conceptions of how God's majesty is related to his justice. On Eliphaz' view God's unsearchable majesty rules out applying the ultimate principle of justice—*suum cuique*—to the Almighty. God is too great and too powerful to be held accountable by human understanding of what is deserved and what is not. There is no just cause before God, at least not one that can be measured up by God's creatures. Even when the things happening in our lives cannot but appear as arbitrary from our human perspective, Eliphaz implores Job not to turn against God, who heals those that he wounds.

Job resists this move because he regards it to be equating divine justice with fate. To separate God's justice according to the law from his justice according to his majesty is unacceptable, because it threatens to pervert divine justice into arbitrariness. God is not like the goddess Fortuna administering good and evil according to chance. If that were all there was to it, then Job would rather be dead: "Therefore I will not restrain my mouth; I will speak in the anguish of my spirit; I will complain in the bitterness of my soul" (Job 7:11). Not only does he refuse to give in, but, in fact, he makes things worse—in the eyes of his friends—when he straightforwardly scorns the Almighty:

> Will you not look away from me for a while; let me alone till I swallow my spittle? If I sin, what do I do to you, you watcher of humanity? Why have you made me your target? Why have I become a burden to you? Why do you not pardon my transgression and take away my iniquity? For now I shall lie in the earth; you will seek me, but I shall not be. (Job 7:19-21)

The sarcasm of these words ("what do I do to you, you watcher of humanity?") goes a long way to explain why Calvin did not like how Job handled his case. In rejecting his friends' advice to speak with becoming humility, Job is in fact in defiance of everything that Calvin has been trying to argue. But Job is simply not buying into this concept of a "hidden" justice. Compared with Calvin—who in this regard takes sides with Job's friends—the lack of reverence indicates a negative regard for the *deus absconditus*. When Job later in the book proclaims to know that his redeemer lives, it seems as if he is challenging the very conception of a hidden God. His language at this point is very direct, and very personal, almost like that of a rejected lover: when you finally decide to come looking for me, you will not find me anymore, for in the meantime your abuse will have killed me![22]

Then Bildad the Shuhite steps in. Also contrary to received opinion, Bildad does not suggest that because of what has happened to Job, he must have sinned against God. Nor does he suggest that Job cannot appeal to divine justice. On the contrary, Bildad asserts merely what Job has believed all his life; he only adds the advice to exercise more patience. As he sees it, the rashness of Job's words against God makes Job sound like a windbag:

> How long will you say these things, and the words of your mouth be a great wind? Does God pervert justice? Or does the Almighty pervert the right? (Job 8:2-3)[23]

Bildad maintains that if Job puts his trust in God, he will surely be heard in due course, because God will not let down a blameless person—things look very dim in these days, but there will be sunshine in the days to come, and Job will be restored to his former life:

> He will yet fill your mouth with laughter, and your lips with shouts of joy. Those who hate you will be clothed with shame, and the tent of the wicked will be no more. (Job 8:21-22)

Job has not been mistaken in his original view on retributive justice, then; he is just presumptuous in his impatience now that he is suffering, at least according to Bildad. So Bildad's advice to Job is to hold on to his belief even though his current experience seems to contradict it. When Job responds, however, he seems to have taken in Eliphaz' warning—it does not become God's creatures to question their Maker: "How can a mortal be just before God?" (Job 9:2).[24]

From here on, a new thought slowly emerges for Job. He begins to think of this question as an issue of representation. Considering that there may be a side to God that he does not know, his only hope is to rely on the God he *does* know. Eliphaz' question (how can mortals be just before God?) then becomes a very pertinent one: How does one approach the Almighty? Who dares to sepak up before his throne? "How then can I answer him, choosing my words with him? Though I am innocent, I cannot answer him; I must appeal for mercy to my accuser" (Job 9:14-15). When human beings simply cannot be just before the Almighty, then indeed there is no defense:

> If I summoned him and he answered me, I do not believe he would listen to my voice. For he crushes me with a tempest, and multiplies my wounds without cause, he will not let me get my breath, but fills me with bitterness. If it is a contest of strength, he is the strong one! If it is a matter of justice: who can summon him? Though I am innocent, my own mouth would condemn me; though I am blameless, he would prove me perverse. (Job 9:16-20)

Clearly Job is still thinking here of God's majestic inscrutability. Even though he is blameless, it will not make a difference. The Almighty is about to crush him, so what chance does he have? Having this conception of the hidden God now firmly on his mind, Job appears ready to admit that with the Almighty as his opponent, there is no ground for adjudication. One cannot have a trial with one's Creator, can one? "For he is not a mortal, as I am, that I might answer him, that we should come to trial together" (Job 9:32).

When the heavenly court is presided over by this incomprehensible God, Job now begins to realize, then his case is indeed doomed, because there will be no *overriding* justice. There will be no impartiality, because "there is no umpire between us, who might lay his hand on us both" (Job 9:33). In other words, if God is both the prosecutor *and* the judge, then how is the defendant to be represented? Who will speak up for Job? The emerging answer is that the human being standing accused for the Almighty is in need of an intercessor, an "umpire," someone that can represent a "mortal" in the heavenly court and argue his case. [25]

This thought will return several times in Job's plea. It is rooted in the observation of an unbridgeable gap between Creator and creature, which leads Job to seek an ally. When the Almighty is testing Job's iniquity and searches his sin, Job feels he does not stand a chance, regardless of his innocence: "Your hands fashioned and made me; and now you turn and destroy me" (Job 10:8). There is no alternative left but to call on God's own integrity as his Maker: "Remember that you fashioned me like clay, and will you turn me to dust again?" (Job 10:9). As the Almighty, whose inscrutable verdict is beyond human comprehension, God has turned against him. But Job knows God better than this!

> You have granted me life and steadfast love, and your care has preserved my spirit. Yet these things you hid in your heart; I know that this was your purpose. (Job 10:12-13)

There is the other side to God that Job holds on to, because he knows it and has known it all his life! On the other hand, if that were true, why then is there no response? So Job finds himself stuck, and we find him where he started:

> Why did you bring me forth from the womb? Would that I had died before any eye had seen me and were as though I had not been, and carried from the womb to the grave. (Job 10:18-19)

Since God is relentlessly pursuing him—"you bring fresh troops against me" (Job 10:17)—when there is no intercessor to step in for him, Job's fate is sealed! Had he known that this would be his fate, he would rather never have seen the light of day!

Job's Innocence Questioned

It is at this point where the third friend, Zophar the Naamathite, begins to lose his patience. It is about time that the ongoing complaint against God is silenced! Zophar says, "Should a multitude of words go unanswered, and should one full of talk be vindicated? Should your babble put others to silence, and when you mock, shall no one shame you?" (Job 11:2-3). Not only does he react in anger; he is also the first to openly question the claim of Job's innocence:

> For you say 'My conduct is pure, and I am clean in God's sight,' but oh, that God would speak and open his lips to you, and that he would tell you the secrets of wisdom! For wisdom is many-sided. For know that God exacts of you less than your guilt deserves. (Job 11:4-6)

Job may think he is blameless, but what does he know? There may be another side to his story, so that if God were to speak, he surely would lay bare Job's guilt. Like Eliphaz before, Zophar also points to God's majesty, but he brings it up not in order to point to reverence as the appropriate way of responding, but to question Job's innocence. When God summons the guilty into his courtroom, who is there to stop him? Zophar continues, "For he knows those who are worthless; and when he sees iniquity, will he not consider it?" (Job 11:11).

Unlike Eliphaz and Bildad, then, Zophar attacks Job's presumption of innocence. The reason is that Job forgets the limits of his own judgment in view of the depth of God's wisdom. His apparent lack of reverence for the Holy One puts him at fault.

Job is not prepared to retreat from his defense, however: "I have understanding as well as you; I am not inferior to you" (Job 12:3). But instead of boasting about his knowledge of divine wisdom, he tells Zophar to consult the animals in the fields and the birds in the sky. Even the fish in the water will declare "that the hand of the Lord has done this" (Job 12:9). So Job lashes out and makes the wisdom of Zophar, and the likes of him, look ridiculous. In God is wisdom and strength, Job argues, and God's counsel is no match for earthly counselors, judges, and kings, whom he leads away stripped naked and makes to look like fools. (Job 12:17); God "deprives of speech those who are trusted, and takes away discernment of the elders" (Job 12:20). Apparently, Job no longer trusts the words of these dignitaries, and this verdict includes Zophar as well: "As for you, you whitewash with lies; all of you are worthless physicians. If you would only keep silent, that would be your wisdom!" (Job 12:4-5).

Job is done with his friends, then, and turns away from their dispute. His desire is to argue his case before God, wherefore he is asking for two things, and two things only: first, that God will withdraw his hand from him, and then, second, call upon him as God's servant. If God does, Job will not hide away from his face:

> Oh that you would hide me in Sheol, that you would conceal me until your wrath is past, that you would appoint me a set time, and remember me. If mortals die, will they live again? All the days of my service I would wait until my release should come. You would call, and I would answer you. (Job 14:13-15)

Acknowledging his position as a fallen creature before God, Job nonetheless addresses him as his equal in their unequal relationship. He is more than ready to accept God's judgment, but he wants to be treated with fairness. What does fairness mean in this connection? "Fair" means precisely that God recognizes that, as a human creature, Job can never measure up against the Almighty:

> A mortal born from woman, few of days and full of trouble, comes up like a flower and withers, flees like a shadow and does not last. Do you fix your eyes on such a one? Do you bring me into judgment with you? Who can bring a clean thing out of an unclean? No one can. (Job 14:1-4)

Here we see confirmed how Job's thought is developing. He does not doubt his judgment regarding his innocence, but recognizes his limitations as a "mortal." God's majesty puts him at immeasurable distance from any creature. This explains, I suggest, whence comes the notion that there must be an intercessor, someone who may argue his case before

God and speak a word for him as a human being. This notion of representation develops into a climax when for his defense Job calls upon God against God!

The Case of God Against God

With his outburst against Zophar the Naamathite—"You whitewash with lies; all of you are worthless physicians. If you would only keep silent, that would be your wisdom!"—Job has changed the tone. But due to this tone, he now faces a similar rebuke from Eliphaz, who previously was much more delicate in his response. He says that Job's speech belies his claim to blamelessness: "Your own mouth condemns you, and not I; your own lips testify against you" (Job 15:6). Most of all, however, Eliphaz is irritated by Job's words questioning them in their religious understanding:

> Are you the firstborn of the human race? Were you brought forth before the hills? Have you listened in the council of God? And do you limit wisdom to yourself? What do you know that we do not know? What do you understand that is not clear to us? (Job 15:7-9)

Eliphaz does not add new thoughts to what their friends already have put forward, however. He now also accuses Job of standing against the Holy One, which itself is sufficient proof of his guilt. The issue is no longer whether the catastrophes that turned his life upside down indicated that he must have sinned, but rather that his tone of voice indicates that he has lost perspective. Job has forgotten "what sages have told," and what "their ancestors have not hidden" (Job 15:18), which is that God punishes the wicked, even though they seem to think otherwise.

Job retorts, but it turns out that there is no communication any longer between them. "Miserable comforters are you all," he tells them (Job 16:2), bearing witness to the fact that he finds himself where he was before they came: alone with his God, who had turned against him and relentlessly continued to do so. In utter desolation, describing what he is going through, Job uses the imagery of a ferocious warrior coming after him:

> I was at ease, and he broke me in two; he seized me by the neck and dashed me to pieces; he set me up as his target; his archers surround me. He slashes open my kidneys, and shows no mercy; he pours out my gall

on the ground. He bursts upon me again and again; he rushes at me like a warrior. (Job 16:12-14)

Job faces utter despair now that he is without friends to offer him consolation. He has an unrelenting desire to be reunited with God, but not by giving up his own integrity with a false plea of "guilty as charged," just to appease him. So there is no one to turn to but God, and that is what he does, in one of the most moving passages of the entire story:

O earth, do not cover my blood; let my outcry find no resting place. Even now, in fact, my witness is in heaven, and he that vouches for me is on high. My friends scorn me; my eye pours out tears to God, that he would maintain the right of a mortal with God. (Job 16:18-21)

Incredible testimony, is it not? "My eye pours out tears to God, that he would maintain the right of a mortal with God." One could not find a stronger witness for the claim that "man is not alone," as the Jewish sage Abraham Joshua Heschel would have it.[26] Job has lost his fortune, lost his children, and then lost his health, and because of all of these things, he lost the love of his wife, only to find himself in the dreadful position of having lost his friends too—but nonetheless he refuses to accept the conclusion that he is alone.

"I Know That My Redeemer Lives"

Job appeals to God that he maintains the right of a mortal against God, who is accusing him unjustly. As the narrative develops further, it turns out that this claim remains unsurpassed in the remaining exchange between Job and his interlocutors, who now have become his opponents. Beyond this point, nothing is added, theologically speaking, that we did not already hear before. Job now even goes so far as to appeal to God for a warrant against his friends:

My spirit is broken, my days are extinct, the grave is ready for me. Surely there are mockers around me, and my eye dwells on their provocation. Lay down a pledge for me with yourself; who is there that will give surety for me? Since you have closed their minds to understanding, therefore you will not let them triumph. Those who denounce friends for reward—the eyes of their children will fail. (Job 17:1-5)

Job denounces his opponents as traitors, who seek to please God by betraying Job for reward. From here on, things get nasty, because his opponents are very angry about his arrogance: "Why are we counted as cattle? Why are we stupid in your sight?" Bildad retorts (Job 18:3). He points to Job as a self-absorbed man who tears himself apart in his anger against God: "Shall the earth be forsaken because of you, or the rock be removed out of its place?" (Job 18:4). Bildad reiterates his earlier point about the wicked whose light will be put out, but in doing so, he uses descriptions that are clearly meant to include Job: "by disease their skin is consumed"; "they have no offspring or descendant among their people, and no survivor where they used to live" (Job 18:13, 18:19). What so far only was an unknown possibility is now brought out in the open: Job is an ungodly man.

In his response Job apparently does not seek further escalation of their hostility, which leads him—quite unexpectedly—to consider admitting his fault:

> Even if it is true that I have erred, my error remains with me. If indeed you magnify yourselves against me, and make my humiliation an argument against me, know then that God has put me in the wrong, and closed his net around me. (Job 19:2-6)

In his agony Job even turns to his friends to ask for their mercy: "Have pity on me, have pity on me, oh you my friends, for the hand of God has touched upon me! Why do you, like God, pursue me, never satisfied with my flesh?" (Job 19:21-22). He cries out that his words are written down in a book "that with an iron pen and with lead they were engraved on a rock forever!" (Job 19:24). Then Job exalts in what has become known as his most reverent confession:

> For I know that my redeemer lives, and that at last he will stand upon the earth; and after my skin has been thus destroyed, then in my flesh I shall see God, whom I shall see on my side. (Job 19:25-27)

One would expect that his friends would be consoled by this unmitigated confession, but apparently too much has happened between them. They fail to be impressed, and continue to question Job's faith in divine justice. A number of earlier moves return. Bildad asserts that no man can be righteous before God, which Job rejects as a terribly merciless view, given the fact that so many wicked people go unpunished. He is not prepared to let go the difference between innocence and guilt: "I hold fast my righteousness and will not let it go; my heart does not reproach me for any of my days" (Job 27:6). Consequently he challenges the Almighty, by acknowledging the justice of punishing transgression, while holding on to his plea: "not guilty." May God punish him, if fault can be found.

Elihu the Younger

Then Elihu, the son of Barachel the Buzite, comes along. He has kept quiet thus far, he says, because the others are his seniors, so it would not be appropriate for him to speak. But now he can no longer hold his tongue, listening to their weak arguments: "See, I waited for your words, I listened to your wise sayings, while you searched out what to say. I gave you my attention, but there was in fact no one that confuted Job" (Job 32:11-12). Elihu's main contention is that his seniors did not speak in the spirit of God. It is only, he says, "the breath of the Almighty that makes for understanding" (Job 32:8). Only then one can speak truth, which is why he now addresses Job: "The spirit of God has made me, and the breath of the Almighty gives me life" (Job 33:4).

The importance of Elihu's contribution turns out to be highly contested among biblical scholars. In the older commentaries, the received opinion seems to be that what this audacious youngster has to say adds nothing significant to what his seniors had said before him.[27] In contrast, however, others have argued that Elihu's arguments for divine providence trump those made by Job and his friends.[28]

In this last stage of the dispute between Job and his former friends, Elihu is the only one doing the talking. Job does not respond anymore. Apparently, the narrative as it is construed does not depend on his response in order to arrive at a conclusion. Immediately after Elihu is finished, God answers Job from the whirlwind: "Who is this, that darkens counsel by words without knowledge?" (Job 38:2). In talking about "conceit," Elihu apparently had Job in mind, without recognizing that his own words may qualify as well.

God's Wager with Satan

In reconstructing the narrative in the book of Job, I have chosen deliberately to present it from the perspective of human experience—Job's experience, to be precise. It is from this perspective that all the vexed questions arise that Job is struggling with. Why is he suffering when he is innocent? Why does God not respond? Without answers to these questions, what does it mean to praise God's providential care? Where is his righteousness? From Job's perspective his affliction is entirely beyond the scope of human understanding. Why this? Why Job?

In truth, however, the narrative unfolds quite differently, in that its readers have been informed, right at the beginning, about what is *really* going on. It is something that Job and his friends are unaware of. In the first three chapters of the book of Job, prior to being introduced to the contingencies of Job's fate, we learned what happened in the heavenly courtroom.[29] Far from it being the case that God did not take an interest in Job's suffering, or did not care, something quite different turns out to be true. Job's misery is caused by Satan, but not without God's permission. Satan has been allowed by God to make Job suffer as part of a heavenly contest about Job's character. Actually, God starts this whole affair by "bragging" about his servant Job:

> Have you considered my servant Job? There is no one like him on earth,
> a blameless and upright man, who fears God and turns away from evil.
> (Job 1:8)

Satan challenges God on this by saying that Job only worships God because of self-interest. He does not really care about God, but chooses to obey him out of fear: "Stretch out your hand now, and touch all that he has, and he will curse you to your face" (Job 1:11). Satan predicts that Job will forsake God as soon as his blessings are taken away from him. God accepts the challenge. Job will prove to be truly his servant, come what may, and not only because he and his family are healthy and prosperous.

The conversation reminds us of Cathy Crimmins' story, notwithstanding the absence of a religious motive, where she tells about Alan Forman's obscure remarks on his "creation business."[30] Recall the scene in which Al has a question for his visitors: "The defective Alan Forman versus the second Alan Forman that we could create, what do you think?" Of course, they do not know what to say. He continues: "I'm talking about a second Alan Forman, who could just hang out in the universe. What do you think? And what do you think about the defective Alan Forman? Should he really have a right to exist?" Even without explicit religious motive, it seems that from the perspective of "the universe," the TBI survivor has lost his right to existence, given his imperfection. At least that is the question on Al's mind: "Do I have a right to exist, now that I am no longer who I was made to be?"

For entirely different reasons, Job has similar questions on his mind. But, unlike Alan Forman, he does not have access to a Mr. Finkelman. The problem for Job is that the one who is in charge of his life is silent. The only thing he can do is sit down with his friends and try to understand the meaning of what is happening to him. So they do what human beings do to bridge the gap between the "before" and "after"—namely, construct a story, as we have seen in the stories about disability experience.[31]

In the meantime God's wager with Satan proceeds. Having allowed Satan to attack Job by taking all his possessions as well as his children, God claims victory: Job has not fallen. Satan remains unconvinced, however, and challenges God to raise the stakes: attack Job in his bone and flesh, and he will fall. God accepts and tells Satan to go ahead, but without taking Job's life (Job 1:12).

Again, this intrigue is entirely unknown to Job and his friends. In trying to understand how divine providence works, they proceed from a theology of proportionate retribution. As biblical scholarship has shown, this is the key doctrine in most of Near Eastern religion, including the religion of Israel's tribe.[32] God rewards according to the measure of virtue and punishes according to the measure of sin. As their dialogue evolves, however, Job finds that reading his misfortune in this light does not help. It only leads to angry disagreement. Job holds on to his claim against God, which initially is not disputed by his friends: he has suffered beyond measure, while neither he nor his friends understand how he has sinned.

Then a different conception of divine justice emerges through their dialogue. This is a conception that does not pertain to human obedience of God's law and therefore does not correspond to transgression and sinfulness. Instead it correlates with God's unsearchable majesty, in the light of which his creatures cannot but appear as imperfect. The issue of Job's sinfulness now seems to change: his sin is not in his disobedience of the law, but in his lack of reverence for his Creator, whom he holds accountable for indifference to unjust suffering. So his friends chastise him for his impudence, but Job holds his ground by insisting that God's justice cannot be equal to the work of chance and fortune. The dialogue breaks down, and he is on his own again.

In utter despair, Job then calls upon God against God. He prays to the God he knows to represent him in the heavenly court before the God he does not know: the God who is near to him, who granted him "life and steadfast love," and whose care preserved Job's spirit—as opposed to the incomprehensible God, whose majesty is inscrutable, and whose justice, on any human understanding, cannot be distinguished from arbitrariness.

What we have before us, then, are two alternative readings of how divine justice works. Interestingly, in view of these two readings, the intrigue of the heavenly court does not return in the finale, when God at last answers Job (Job 38–42). God does not reveal the true story that he was never abandoned at all, but that in fact he was put to trial because God was certain that his faithfulness would prevail. As a matter of fact, Job is not answered at all in terms of the God in whom he has vested his hope. On the contrary, Job is answered entirely in terms of the incomprehensible God.

Answer out of the Whirlwind

When God finally answers Job, he does not seem to have forgotten the biting sarcasm that Job hurled at him, for now Job gets his share:

> Where were you when I laid the foundation of the earth? Tell me, if you have understanding. Who determined its measurements—surely you know! Or stretched the line upon it? On what were its bases sunk, or who laid its cornerstone when the morning stars sang together and all the heavenly beings shouted for joy? Or who shut in the sea with doors when it burst out from the womb?—when I made the clouds its garment, and thick darkness its swaddling band, and prescribed bounds for it, and set bars and doors, and said, "Thus far shall you come, and no farther, and here shall your proud waves be stopped"? (Job 38:4-11)

God represents himself as the architect of the universe, the one who constructed the earth and set limits to the sea, and the one who lays claim to its creation as *kosmos* instead of *chaos*—contrary to what Job's lamentations have been implying. But this is only the beginning of an elaborate exposition in which different parts and elements of creation are visited with only one purpose: reminding Job of its grandeur, and of the majesty of its Maker. Each time, the logic implied in God's speech is the same: Whose doing was this? Yours? Where were you when I did these things? Regarding the celestial firmament, for example, God says:

> Can you bind the chains of the Pleiades, or loose the cords of Orion? Can you lead forth the Mazzaroth in their season, or can you guide the Bear with its children? Do you know the ordinances of the heavens? Can you establish their rule on earth? (Job 38:31-33)

Apparently Job has offended God deeply with his demand that justice be done and that he be acquitted because of his innocence. Particularly, his insistence—that in the heavenly court there could be no fair trial, because there is no judge "who might lay his hand on us both"—implied that Job speaks to God on an equal footing. With this presumption Job has offended God's majesty by ignoring the unfathomable difference between creatures and their Creator. The tone of voice in which God teaches him this lesson makes Job look silly:

> Where is the way to the dwelling of light, and where the place of darkness, that you may take it to its territory and that you may discern the paths to its home? Surely you know, for you were born then, and the number of your days is great! (Job 38:19-21)

Having visited the elements from which God molded the earth, the sea, and the sky, God then turns to the animal world. Did Job teach the lion to hunt for its prey? Did he set the time when the deer give birth? Ostrich, horse, mountain sheep, wild ox, or hawk: for each of these animals, God ordered its ways so as to fulfill its purpose. Job did not have anything to do with all this, and yet he wants to summon his Creator to justice? Thus God concludes his answer to Job: "Shall a faultfinder contend with the Almighty? Anyone who argues with God must respond" (Job 40:2).

Job bows his head, saying that he has understood the message: "See, I am of small account; what can I answer you? I lay my hand on my mouth. I have spoken once, and I will not answer; twice, but will proceed no further" (Job 40:4-5). Presumably this retreat is too easy to pacify the Almighty, because he is not done yet:

> Will you even put me in the wrong? Will you condemn me that you may be justified? Have you an arm like God, and can you thunder with a voice like his? Deck yourself with majesty and dignity; clothe yourself with glory and splendor. Pour out the overflowings of your anger, and look on all who are proud, and bring them low; tread down the wicked where they stand. Hide them all in the dust together; bind their faces in the world below. Then I will acknowledge to you that your own right hand can give you victory. (Job 40:8-14)

In case Job fails to be sufficiently impressed, the worst is yet to come. The account of God's majestic works now turns to its most frightening part: the defeat of the Leviathan, the Monster of the Sea, the creature without fear that "on earth has no equal" (Job 41:33). Again God's sarcasm shows that he is really angered by Job's presumptuousness:

> Can you draw out Leviathan with a fishhook, or press down its tongue with a cord? Can you put a rope in its nose, or pierce its jaw with a hook? Will it make many supplications to you? Will it speak soft words to you? Will it make a covenant with you to be taken as your servant forever? Or will you put it on leash for your girls? (Job 41:1-5)

God's mission is accomplished when Job confesses the rashness and lack of reverence in his earlier ways of addressing God. He knows that God can do all that he has described and that no purpose of his can be thwarted: "I have uttered what I did not understand, things too wonderful for me, which I did not know" (Job 42:3). So he pleads guilty and declares himself prepared to repent: "I had heard of you by the hearing of the ear, but now with my eyes I see you; therefore I despise myself, and repent in dust and ashes" (Job 42:5-6).

The narrative then closes with the final scene, in which God has restored his servant Job in his former glory, and has given him back his fortune. His brothers and sisters come to visit him, as do all who had known him before. Together they have a meal in his house, and "they showed him sympathy and comforted him for all the evil that the Lord had brought upon him" (Job 42:11).

In Conclusion

In this chapter we have traced two readings of how divine justice works, one of which proceeds from Job's claim to innocence. In this reading, God's justice does not fail to work in accordance with his law, such that wickedness, not innocence, will be punished. On the other hand, there is the reading of Job's misfortune as governed by an almighty God whose justice is inscrutable and beyond human understanding. People get swept off their feet by whatever contingencies they have to put up with in their lives, even to the point where divine justice becomes incomprehensible.

The book of Job construes a narrative to show what it is that Job had to learn. His wounded soul wanders in every possible and impossible direction to come to terms with a divine justice that he does not understand. There is one thing he knows for sure, however, which is that the theology of direct retribution—"cheap theology," in my terminology—is a sham. It is thoroughly discredited by his own experience, such that it cannot do the pastoral work that it is supposed to do.

In this respect, it should be noticed that many classical theologians have adopted the view that the experience of innocent suffering thoroughly discredits any belief in the doctrine of divine retribution.[33] But Job's story shows that this doctrine is to be rejected for another reason as well. Direct retribution curtails God's freedom to do as he pleases. The reason why this is important, however, is *not* to safeguard a theological space for God's arbitrary will. Instead, the reason lies in the thought that upsets Eliphaz. Direct retribution implies a scheme of retributive justice that enables God's creatures to lay a claim on how they ought to be dealt with, which elevates them into the position of God's equals.[34]

This explains the theological argument that is played out so well in this story. God's justice is the justice of the law that he has given his people, but it is also much more than this. It is the justice of his majesty in ruling the universe, often in ways that are beyond human understanding. At least it was so from the perspective of Job's experience. The God who can be as near as a caring Father, can also be as far away as an ice cold distant emperor, whose looting troops bring terror upon his subjects.

It is important to observe, in this connection, that the initial conception of providence, to which Job adhered in the days before his affliction, is not all that different from the view that Satan attributed to him in his wager with God. "Take your rewards away," Satan said to God, "and Job will abandon you." In other words, the ulterior motive of Job's piety, Satan predicts, is the balance between his obedience and God's rewards. Job will prove to be a law-abiding believer because and insofar as God rewards him for doing so.[35] Indeed, Job does come close to fulfilling this prediction when he curses God for abandoning him. But instead of turning away from God, Job does not intend to give up. His bewilderment changes into wild accusation and fury, but—during the debate with his friends—his posture of defiance changes, and finally turns to hope, when he calls upon God against God. Job's life as God's servant is cruelly disrupted, then, but at the brink of giving up, he manages to hang on, against all odds.

If the book of Job teaches us anything about divine providence, it must be that in view of life's contingencies, there may be no answer to the "why?" question. Accordingly, there is no escape from accepting that there are many things happening in our lives that are beyond human understanding. In this regard it is quite significant that Job is *not* reconciled with God because the "why?" question is finally answered. In fact he receives no substantial answer at all, other than to be reminded that the Creator of the universe cannot be held accountable by the Creator's creatures. This is what Job is finally willing to confess.

In comparing the book of Job with our previous stories, it is important to see what his friends do to evade the conclusion that there is simply nothing to say. There must be an explanation, so one after another finds reason to reconsider Job's past. Maybe Job was not as righteous as he appeared to be. Even Eliphaz arrives at this point, not because he assumes that Job's misfortune indicates a dubious past, but because of Job's revolting speech against the Almighty God.

In their own distinctive ways, the other stories we have been reading also seek to escape the conclusion that there is nothing left to say. Whether mediated by the Bunraku puppeteers, Oliver the mythmaker, or Mr. Finkelman, each of these figures provides the escape to a world where things may have a different meaning and are different from their horrific appearance right now.

Seen in this light, Job's rebellion is a remarkable feat of his story indeed. It rejects all explanatory attempts that seek to escape from divine incomprehensibility. The one thing that breaks his heart is that God does not answer him, regardless of what God would have to say if he did. Finally God speaks from the whirlwind, and Job bows his head, not because he is humiliated, but because he is vindicated in his belief that his redeemer lives!

Where does this conclusion leave us, in view of the confrontation with disability experience that we are trying to understand? One thing is clear. The chasm it causes in people's lives cannot be bridged with pious responses seeking to explain why what happens, happens. Such responses inevitably appear as disingenuous. When the story of one's life breaks down, there is no way of plugging the hole with superficial answers. But it does not follow that silence is all that is left. Job's lament is infused with rage, not so much because of his misfortune, but rather because God refuses to respond.

Apparently, Job's prayer teaches us a theology of providence that implies not losing faith in view of life's contingencies, incomprehensible as they are. Whether the broken cord of our life story will be mended is only to be discovered in hindsight. Job's rage is redeemed when he finds peace with God, in spite of the fact that he still does not understand. "I have uttered what I did not understand," he confesses. "I had heard of you by the hearing of the ear, but now with my eye I see you." This confession is not very different from the one made by Martha Beck at the end of her book. Like so many prospective parents, she heard all the bad stuff about Down syndrome, and even though all of it became true—and more— once she was able to see Adam as he truly was, she could only be utterly grateful for her "stupid little boy."

Perhaps the notion of a "wager" is not inappropriate in the end, then, to express what faith in divine providence is all about. Not unlike the wager of God with Satan, in which God was made dependent on Job's resilience, our "wager" with divine providence appears to be similarly structured. Human beings can only learn to live with life's contingencies, without despair or resignation, if they make themselves dependent upon God's resilience to prove God worthy of their trust. Bridging the gap is not something to be commanded at will.

6

FONS OMNIUM BONORUM

*The true goal of theological inquiry is not the resolution of theological prob-
lems but the discernment of what the mystery of faith is.*

—T. G. Weinandy

Introduction

It will come as a surprise to most readers to suggest that the skeptical view
on providence we encountered in the forgoing chapter reflects a great deal
of the sentiment of John Calvin's thought on the matter. This must sound
unfamiliar: Calvin? The Reformer whose searching intellect presumably
had no secret left when it came to understanding God? Indeed, John Calvin. Trying to figure out the contingencies in our lives, Calvin says, we
cannot but conclude that from our human perspective it is all chance and
fortune.[1] This claim is far from what people frequently have understood
the Calvinist attitude toward providence to be, but—as I hope to show—
there is clearly this aspect of *skepsis* in Calvin's thoughts on the subject.

In previous chapters we have been reading real-life stories of disability experience, but in the theological analysis we are about to enter now,
the particularity of such stories vanishes and the concreteness of disability experience is replaced by a much more general experience of adversity and misfortune. The "why" question does not necessarily differentiate

between kinds of adversity, but neither does a theological response. The essential question is why bad things happen to good people. In reflecting upon this question, the issue is not what the specifics of these bad things are—disability, illness, accident, and death—but how their occurrence in the lives of "law-abiding" people is to be understood.

The Christian tradition has responded to this question in terms of divine providence, but then this notion was frequently explained in terms of God's inscrutable ways of controlling the universe, as expressed in the last chapters of the book of Job, which meant that the explanatory force of this response has been close to zero. The alternatives to choose from have been "retribution" or "incomprehensibility." In view of the overwhelming evidence against it, intellectually responsible theology rejects the former, so that what it is left with is the latter, which means there is no explanation at all.

As a matter of fact, the story of Job sets the stage for this reading of providence in a way that very much reflects the baseline of Calvin's theology. As far as Job can tell from his own experience, there is no God that provides for him. There is only misery and calamity, and it befalls him at random. If this is indeed God's doing, then it does not seem to have much to do with justice. Very surprisingly Calvin confirms this perspective to a large extent. In his view, Job's experience is the experience of faithful people. They do not see why God allows the things that are happening to them.

But then the narrative of Job allows the reader a peek into the heavenly courtroom in order to learn what is *really* going on. This is the other perspective, then, hidden from human eyes. It shows that things might look very different from the point of view of God's purpose. In the present case, God has not abandoned Job, but instead allows Satan to attack Job, because he is convinced of Job's truthfulness!

This other side of the narrative is reflected in Calvin's theology too. God provides according to a secret plan that humans cannot possibly know. If they could—as in Job we are allowed to see—then we would be able to see that God works for the purpose of the good. But now that it remains hidden from human eyes we do not understand. Since this "hiddenness" is very much part of his doctrine of providence, Calvin has not earned himself much credit with it. The problem is essentially similar to the one we encountered in the dialogue between Job and his friends.

When an account of God's justice is cast in terms of "hiddenness," then we will feel the need to ask what the difference is between God's "hidden justice" and arbitrariness. After all divine arbitrariness is not all that different from chance, to mention just one thing.

This inevitable question has certainly not contributed to the popularity of the doctrine of providence in recent times, to which the Calvinist tradition might have contributed significantly, at least in the Protestant world. I therefore propose to take the bull by the horns and see what Calvin's theology of providence is about.

Apart from his interest in the book of Job, the reason for looking at Calvin's theology is a particular point of interest that will be proven very significant in the last chapter of this book. Calvin's exposition of the doctrine of providence is shot through constantly with remarks on epistemology. How can people arrive at true knowledge of God's providence? Calvin's answer points to the human heart. Knowledge of providence can only be obtained as "knowledge of the heart."

I will start with an observation regarding the secondary literature. Calvin is in the process of being brought back to life from behind the popular images of dryness, intellectualism, and a repulsive harshness of his views, particularly his views on predestination and providence. The historian William Bouwsma, for example, has presented Calvin as an emotional man full with anxiety about his own life and that of his family,[2] which must be quite surprising for those who believe Calvin's theology to be the epitome of closed-minded dogmatism. In a similar vein, and of particular interest for our present subject, scholars like Brian Gerrish, Susan Schreiner, and Derek Thomas have emphasized Calvin's struggle with the incomprehensibility of divine providence, for which Schreiner and Thomas also have concentrated on Calvin's sermons on Job. It is on their work in particular that I will draw in this chapter.[3]

My constructive aim in this chapter is to show that Calvin has much to say as a pastoral theologian. This will be shown by doing the same with his text that we did with our first-person narratives—namely, close-reading. With respect to Calvin's text, this means that we follow the argument step-by-step, without interrupting Calvin with lengthy debates, in order to see where his argument takes him. The conclusion I will arrive at has two sides. I will argue that as a pastoral account, Calvin's theology of providence is much more convincing than as a systematic account. Unfortunately, the latter gets the upper hand in his reasoning especially when it is inspired by the many polemical debates Calvin was entangled in.

"A Grim Creed Which Made Strong Men"

I will set the stage of the discussion by starting with Gerrish's work. Gerrish is neither the only one nor the first to redirect the research on Calvin's theology, of course, but in the early 1970s, he published a seminal essay on the hiddenness of God—in the Protestant world traditionally taken to be Martin Luther's topic—in relation to Calvin's thought, which contributed much to a new perspective on Calvin's theological epistemology.[4] Gerrish's work is important because of his critique of the widespread misreading of Calvin's God as the ruler who rules the universe as a tyrant, a misreading that according to Gerrish many Calvinists themselves have assisted to become received opinion. To prove his point he quotes for example from the British theologian W. B. Selbie, a Congregationalist within the Calvinist tradition.[5] Selbie claims:

> The Calvinist system is built on the idea of God's greatness and remoteness from man. He is an absolute sovereign whose arbitrary will governs all things.[6]

The characteristics that stand out in this quote are, first, the Calvinist leaning toward systematizing religious beliefs—"the Calvinist system"—and, second, its conception of a deity whose prime qualities are absolute sovereignty and arbitrariness. According to Gerrish, both of these points have contributed to neutralizing Calvin's emphasis on grace and gracefulness. In the work of authors like Selbie, these notions tend to disappear behind absolute divine authority, an observation that is aptly summarized in his comment that Calvinism is "a grim creed which made strong men."[7]

This picture of Calvinism has been very influential indeed, both among theologians and lay people. With regard to the topic of this inquiry, the theology of providence, the nineteenth century British Calvinist Charles Hodge wrote:

> Providence includes not only preservation, but also government. The latter includes the ideas of design and control. It supposes an end to attain, and the disposition and direction of means for its accomplishment. When God governs the universe He has some great end, including

an indefinite number of subordinate ends, towards which it is directed, and He must control the sequence of all events, so as to render certain the accomplishment of all his purposes.[8]

This kind of statement, though only partially reflecting Calvin's thinking (as we will see), can be carried away in different directions, including the direction of theological determinism, which for many interpreters has been the inevitable outcome. In view of such statements, it can hardly be surprising that the general picture of Calvinist theology has not been very favorable at this point, as is testified in Karl Barth's book on Calvin:

> Calvin is not what we usually imagine an apostle of love and peace to be. If what he represents is love and peace, then these things must be very different from what we think they are. What we find is a hard and prickly skin. . . . An iron cage has come that called for iron believers.[9]

In rejecting such verdicts, Gerrish intends to redress what he considers to be gross misrepresentations of at least Calvin's, if not of Calvinist, theology. To prove his point, Gerrish starts with a quote from the beginning of the *Institutes*, where he finds Calvin's fundamental image of God— the Deity is *fons omnium bonorum*, the fountain of all that is good:

> It is not suffice simply to hold that there is One whom all ought to honor and adore, unless we are also persuaded that he is the fountain of every good, and that we must seek nothing elsewhere than in him. This I take to mean that not only does he sustain this universe (as he once founded it) by his boundless might, regulate it by his wisdom, preserve it by his goodness, and in especially rule mankind by his righteousness and judgment, bear with it in his mercy, watch over it by his protection; but also that no drop will be found either of wisdom and light, or of righteousness or power or rectitude, or of genuine truth, which does not flow from him, and of which he is not the cause.[10]

To this image of the fountain of good, Gerrish adds a second image, which is that of "fatherly care"—*paterna cura*—indicating that the father-child relationship is indeed crucial for the explanation of Calvin's theology. Nowhere does one find a more loving disposition—*amoris affectus*—than in a father.[11]

In connection with the subject of this chapter, it is relevant to consider how Gerrish explains the misrepresentation of Calvin's theology. To find "arbitrariness" at the heart of Calvin's doctrine of God, Gerrish says, requires a remarkable exercise of arbitrariness in using the textual sources. He says:

> Such plausibility as the results appear to have is borrowed partly from our image of later Calvinism, and partly from the attempt of modern scholarship to link Calvin's theology with the voluntarist strand in late medieval thought. There is no need to deny real lines of continuity between Calvin and Calvinism, or to reject out of hand the possibility that his language about God may very well have been shaped by Scotist and Nominalist patterns of thinking. But to claim that the notion of an arbitrary despotic will is key to his doctrine of God does scant justice to Calvin's own explicit statements about where the primacy lies.[12]

Gerrish attributes the fact that images like the *fons omnium bonorum* and *paterna cura* have been removed from the center of Calvin's theology due to the scholarly focus on nominalist and voluntarist patterns in late medieval thought. Since he does not deny that there has been this influence on Calvin, however, this is a critical issue indeed. In explaining what it means that God is the fountain of all that is good, Calvin certainly raises suspicions when he speaks of God ruling the universe "by his boundless might."[13] If we take "boundless might" as a theologically crafted phrase, then it will immediately remind the informed reader of the late medieval debate about God's absolute power—*potestas absoluta*—and the role it played in the rise of nominalism and voluntarism.

This preliminary comment is sufficient, I hope, to indicate what we need to investigate. The question is this: What is the relation between Calvin's images of God as the loving father who is the fountain of all that is good, and his understanding of how God rules the universe? In the same connection, how does Calvin's understanding of divine power operate in his understanding of providence? As we will see, Calvin is struggling to combine the notions of God as a loving Father and of God's "boundless might," the final outcome of which attempt is that he accepts divine incomprehensibility. But this is not something we can blame God for, because it resides in our "carnal sense," which for Calvin refers to the intellect that follows its own desires.

Before we start, I would like to make a brief remark on the use of primary sources. Since Calvin's final word on providence has been spoken in the last edition of the *Institutes*, which is considered the *locus classicus* on the subject,[14] this will be our primary source for the following account of his thought. Recent work has shown the importance of Calvin's sermons and commentaries, in this connection, which explains why I will draw on some of these sources too, particularly his sermons on the book of Job.[15]

The Errors of Ancient Poets and Philosophers

Following Calvin's own procedure, we may begin our account of his doctrine of providence by describing the position that he rejects. This is a position that in Calvin's view separates the creation of the universe from its continued governance by the divine will. God is not merely a momentary creator who once and for all started and finished his work, as he is regarded by "profane men," because the presence of divine power shines as much "in the continuing state of the universe as in its inception."[16] Poets and philosophers from antiquity have looked up to the stars in heaven and arrived at the reverence for divine creativity, but they have understood this activity only as the initiating power that sets nature in motion.[17] When they speak of divine creativity, they regard it as a divine energy that was bestowed on all things from the beginning.[18] To understand creation without God's continuing governance, however, is not to understand what it means to confess "God is Creator." Not only did God once create nature by giving it its own patterns of motion, but he also continues to sustain and care for everything he has made.

From these opening remarks, it appears that Calvin rejects the kind of philosophical naturalism according to which all changes in the world can be fully understood in terms of nature's own laws. Interestingly, however, he considers that to be a religious conception, and as such he rejects it.[19] The reason he rejects it is both a doxological and a pastoral one. With regard to the first, Calvin argues that by neglecting divine sovereignty in all things happening in the universe, the profane mind deprives God of glory, and it deprives also itself from a most "profitable doctrine."[20] With regard to the second, he indicates that in believing that God allows "all things a free course according to a universal law of nature,"[21] people are left in the miserable position of believing that they are exposed to whatever natural events bring them. Referring to the book of Psalms, where it says that God "does whatever he wills," Calvin explains that it would not make sense to interpret these words the way philosophers do, which is to say that God is the first agent because he is the beginning and cause of all motion. Instead believers find comfort in times of adversity in confessing that they suffer nothing except by God's command, "for they are under his hand."[22]

The pastoral motive in Calvin's exposition speaks through his use of the language of "benevolence," indicating the practical relevance of the doctrine of providence. It is a guide in keeping one's faith amidst adversity.[23] Those who praise God's providential wisdom benefit from their faith because they know that they may safely rest in his protection, or else bear their sufferings patiently.[24]

As Calvin has explained earlier in book 1 of the *Institutes*, the notion that nature determines the universe in virtue of its own laws is fraudulent: it claims for creation what belongs to the Creator.[25] It deprives God of the praise that is his due. No human being can be excused for not giving praise to God, because all have abundant testimony of the many wonderful ways he works: "This skillful ordering of the universe is for us a sort of mirror in which we can contemplate God who is otherwise invisible."[26] The evidence that God sustains the world is clearly there for everyone to see. We have more than the evidence of heaven and earth, Calvin argues. God's governance is found not only in the gaze "outside" (to the stars, or "nature" in general) but also by going into the inner self as well.[27] Testimony of God's presence is found in the activities of the human soul.

However, while Calvin accepts that there are signs of divinity in the activities of the soul, he rejects the view of ancient poets like Virgil and Lucretius who attribute this divinity to the "inner spirit" of nature itself. By substituting the deity with "nature," they inevitably fail to thank God for the wonderful gifts they praise. What reason could there be, Calvin asks rhetorically, to believe that humankind is divine and not to recognize humanity's Creator, if it is not to defraud God of the gratitude we owe God? That is why we must insist that the human soul only properly regards itself by pointing away to its Creator, rather than seeing itself as a spontaneous manifestation of nature's spirit.

This reversal of the order of Creator and creation is ultimately the failure of the profane mind, according to Calvin. Instead of being led to praise God by the wonders of the natural world, including the world within us, poets such as Vergil and Lucretius set he aside and put nature in his place. They attribute to nature the divine spirit that animates all things.[28] While there is a grain of truth in this, Calvin responds, the thought is nonetheless improper when taken on its own account. Nature is not grounded in itself, and is therefore not divine, because nature is not God; rather, it is "the order prescribed by God."[29] Consequently, human beings can surmount their fear of the natural world only by putting their faith in the recognition that God, not "nature," rules the universe. The belief that God rules with absolute power implies that nature and its forces have no intrinsic power to harm us. "There is no erratic power, or action, or motion in creatures," Calvin claims. God governs all creatures so that nothing happens "except what is knowingly and willingly decreed by him."[30]

While received opinion has it that Calvin's Deity is a harsh ruler who does not have much sympathy for the his creatures, we will find reason for doubting this opinion when we look at Calvin's motive for insisting on God's absolute power. It is not that God and nature are alternative causes for the same effects. God rules over nature, but he does not rule in the same way as nature does. God's motive, the motive of divine providence, is to comfort those who know him as graceful and merciful. If we want to find the cause that once led God to create all things and that now moves him to preserve them, Calvin claims, "We shall find that it is his goodness alone," and this being the sole cause, he adds, "It ought still to be more than sufficient to draw us to his love."[31] For Calvin, the doctrine of providence is taken to address a pastoral concern.[32]

In Calvin's view, this concern marks the distinction from the views of the poets and philosophers that he rejects. Even when they recognize they have their life in God, "they are far from that feeling of grace, because they do not taste that special care by which alone his fatherly favor is known."[33] What we need to understand, apparently, is what it means that God's absolute power is attributed to the Father.

Two Conceptions of Providence
Special and General

To avoid any confusion of creature and Creator, Calvin insists, creation is only properly understood in connection with providence. But this is not easily achieved, he concedes, even when it is testified by "the whole workmanship of the universe."[34] Even though no one can plead the excuse of ignorance, people will not arrive at proper understanding on their own.[35] The reason is what he coins as "carnal sense."[36] Carnal sense will at best see the preserving activity of God in the background of all motion. But this is as far as their insight goes. To explain why this is so, Calvin repeatedly refers his readers to the Letter to the Hebrews 11:3: "Only by faith we understand that the universe was created by the word of God."[37] Faith has its own way of assigning credit to the Creator, even though the impious may look at the stars and rise up to the Creator too.

These opening sections of his exposition indicate that Calvin's principal motive in discussing providence is the proper knowledge of God.[38] The profane mind—"carnal sense"—does not see any further than the idea that all things are from the beginning sustained by a divinely bestowed energy. But faith will see deeper, according to Calvin. God does not only dictate the heavenly bodies to universal motion, because God also sustains and cares for all creatures, even to the tiniest sparrow (Matt 10:29).[39]

Apparently, there is a distinction to be made between two different predications of God. As Creator, he has set into motion the order of nature and its objects according to a universal law, and as Governor and Preserver, he directs all that is happening in the world. Whatever the distinction is meant to convey, which is a question we will turn to in a moment, at this point Calvin only indicates why he needs it. Whereas human beings always have admired the order of creation, and therefore worshiped their Creator; God's work as Governor and Preserver, in contrast, is generally met by unbelief. People in general are of the opinion that all things come about through chance. What Christians ought to believe concerning providence, according to Calvin, is completely lost.[40]

Apparently, what we ought to believe about divine providence is almost generally neglected; people believe in fortune rather than in God's governance.[41] When someone has an accident, is struck by lightning, is shipwrecked but miraculously saved from being swallowed by the sea, is unexpectedly cured from an incurable illness, or is killed by a falling tree, in all such cases people are prone to ascribe the events to fortune or misfortune, according to Calvin.[42] In contrast to this widespread unbelief, however, Scripture teaches that God's providence is opposed to fortune and fortuitous events. This pertains both to human concerns—for which Calvin points to the Gospel of Matthew 10:30, where Jesus assures his followers that all the hairs on their heads are numbered—and also to "inanimate objects." Calvin writes, "Each one by nature has been endowed with its own property, yet it does not exercise its own power except in so far as it is directed by God's ever-present hand."[43] There are no natural objects, therefore, that are not an instrument in the hand of God. Calvin urges his readers not to neglect the connection between objects being moved by their own nature and those being moved by God's hands. God's rule entails his omnipotence. This does not mean, however, that omnipotence is a general principle of "confused motion," as if God commands a river to flow through its once-appointed channel; instead, it is omnipotence that directs "individual and particular motions."[44]

Furthermore, Calvin also argues against a theological conception that limits divine providence to foreknowledge. God's governance does not only pertain to God's eyes but also to God's hands. It involves not only foreknowledge of a future event, but also God's will to care for matters unknown to us. When Abraham said to his son "God will provide" (Gen 22:8), he meant not only to assert God's foreknowledge of a future event. He also intended to say that God will show a way out of perplexed and confusing situations, which indicates that divine providence is manifest in divine action, and not only in divine foreknowledge.[45]

To correct the view of providence as a principle of motion directing the universe without specifically directing the actions of individual creatures, Calvin deploys the distinction between a *providentia generalis* and a *providentia specialis*.[46] This he uses to argue that God directs all things according to his end, but does so in different ways.[47] With regard to this distinction between general and special providence, there seem to be several possible misunderstandings that may arise out of how Calvin explains its point.

One way to read what he says is to assume that God exercises governance of the world in both a *direct* and an *indirect* manner. Upon this reading there would be two modes of divine providential agency. It is true, Calvin concedes, "that several kinds of things are moved by a secret impulse of nature, as if they obey God's eternal command, and that what God has once determined flows on by itself."[48] This explanation may lead us to conclude that his distinction between "special" and "general" marks a division of labor. Some things in the world move according to their laws that God once installed; other things are moved directly by his ever-present hand.

Secondly, his explanation may be taken to mark the distinction between how God presides over *the order of nature*, which he does with his general providence, and how God presides over *human action*, which he does with his special providence. Thus the distinction between "general" and "special" may be taken to regard different "objects" of God's providence. This suggestion is supported by the fact that Calvin distinguishes God's rule, with regard to human affairs, by saying that they are outside the ordinary course of nature, which seems to imply that God rules the natural world differently from how he rules the human world.

Finally, one might also take Calvin's distinction to point to different kinds of divine activity: *foreseeing*, as distinct from *intervening*. Since he criticizes the view that restricts providence to divine foreknowledge, and supplements it with God's intervening action in individual events, this suggests the distinction between general and special providence to be concerned with different powers that God uses in his providential action.[49]

To show why *each* of these three readings misinterprets Calvin's distinction between "general" and "special" providence, it is sufficient to quote only one example, which is taken from a passage where he speaks about the sun. Obviously, if there is one natural "object" that appears to move entirely according to its own nature, it must be the sun, for it "has a force more wondrous or glorious" than that of any other creature.[50] While it nourishes and quickens all things, which makes all creatures dependent upon its brightness, it does not itself seem to depend upon anything but its own nature. Calvin rejects this view, however. God intervenes in the course of the sun directly, Calvin asserts, adducing an argument from Scripture. He starts with the book of Genesis where we read that before God created the sun in order that the earth may be lighted and heated so that it can be filled with greens and fruits. This indicates that also the sun is not a "principal necessity" but merely an instrument of the Creator that is handled by God through his own action.[51]

To lend this claim credibility, Calvin goes on to recite the events of direct divine intervention in the course of the sun in the days of Joshua (Josh 10:13) and King Hezekiah (1 Kgs 20:11): God commanded the sun to stop to turn the tides in Israel's wars, and therefore disrupted the fixed pattern of solar motion.[52] The sun does not rise and set daily because of its own motion, Calvin argues, it does so because God's "fatherly favor" governs its course,[53] after which he continues with the observation that even though there seems to be a fixed pattern of seasonal change from winter to spring, to summer and fall, there is nonetheless much diversity in it, which shows that each year, month, and day the amount of sunlight is governed by "a new, *a special*, providence of God."[54] Thus the example of the sun rebuts all three misunderstandings listed above by showing that 1) the sun is an object that is *directly* governed by God's will, and that 2) it is treated similarly as other creatures including *human beings*, and that 3) it is the object of God's *intervening action*.

Regardless of what one makes of the force of this example, it clearly indicates that the point of Calvin's distinction between general and special providence must be found elsewhere, namely in its *theological* motive. The notion of special providence brings about a crucial element that the traditional philosophical view—the general conception of providence—cannot convey, which is that God rules the world according to his deliberate will and that his governance is *for the good* of his creatures. With his special providence, God shows *paterna cura*, fatherly care.[55]

This is particularly evident when we pay attention to the fact that Calvin more than once quotes from the letter to the Hebrews: "Only by faith we know that the universe was created by the word of God."[56] The motive guiding this quotation is his understanding of God's special providence as *Christ is working with the Father*. To make the point explicit, he quotes Christ's saying that he had worked together with the Father from the beginning (John 5:17). He also quotes from Hebrews 1:3, where it says that all things are sustained by Christ's command.

The distinction between *providentia specialis* and *providentia generalis*, then, is best understood as a distinction of different perspectives on providence, rather than a distinction between different ways of divine rule.[57] The special conception is essential to the Christian understanding of God because it underlines Christ working together with the Father.[58] In contrast, the "general" conception of providence refers to what by the light of human reason is discerned of the natural order that God laid out in creation. Calvin opposes the view that limits divine providence to the latter, because no natural object moves independently from the Father's deliberate will, not even the sun.[59] This holds for the motion of individual human beings as well.[60]

Knowledge of the Heart

As indicated before, the reluctance in accepting a robust doctrine of providence in modern times seems to have much to do with Calvin's version of it. His argument about the sun suggests why this may be so. The determination of all things has become unacceptable because of the modern aspiration to human freedom. Calvin's theology of providence has attracted much negative response in this respect. Many of his readers have been taken aback by its tendency toward theological determinism.[61]

The most prominent objections have been (1) that making God the primary cause of all that happens in the world leads to theological determinism; (2) that this necessarily leads to eliminating human freedom, wherefore human beings cannot be culpable for evil deeds; and (3) that since human action is also carried out according to God's plan, it follows that God must be responsible for the evil we do.[62]

Before we will look at these points in the next chapter, there is reason to pay attention to the epistemological condition that Calvin places on the discussion of these matters. Unless the mind proceeds in a particular way, it cannot but produce false results. As indicated already, his notion of "carnal sense" is meant to emphasize, among other things, a limited capacity for proper understanding, such that from the perspective of our human experience, there is nothing self-evident about divine providence.[63] Even though Calvin believes that what Scripture teaches about God's "secret providence" has never failed to at least kindle some sparks in people's hearts, so that it is "always glowing in the darkness,"[64] it does not sound like a great deal of confidence in human understanding. Nonetheless Calvin has acquired a reputation for being overly intellectualist in the pursuit of rational answers in a domain of impenetrable questions.[65] In view of this reputation, it is striking to see how Calvin again and again insists upon the "sluggishness" of the human mind as well as upon the flaws of our mental capacities. It is important to pay attention to these epistemic qualifications, because they will help us to understand more adequately what Calvin has to say on contested issues such as human freedom and responsibility.

Following classical voices like Augustine and Basil the Great, Calvin insists that Christians cannot accept the notion of fortune or chance. He recalls a passage in Augustine's *Retractationes* where Augustine lamented that he once used the notion of fortune where he should have talked about God's will. The interesting point about his reference is that Calvin quotes Augustine's explanation of why he might have used these terms interchangeably: "Perhaps what is commonly called 'fortune' is also ruled by a secret order, and we call 'change occurrence' only that of which the reason and the cause are secret."[66] There is clearly a difference between fortune and the will of God, but in a sense there is a similarity too. The goddess of fortune is blind and distributes good or bad to people for no apparent reason. From the perspective of human experience, Calvin maintains more than once, this must be admitted for God's providence as well: God governs and preserves the world according to a secret plan, which—given our limited understanding—makes the things happening to us look fortuitous. Therefore he proposes a distinction:

> Since the sluggishness of our mind lies far beneath the height of God's providence, we must employ a distinction to lift it up. Therefore I shall put it in this way: however all things may be ordained by God's plan, according to a sure dispensation, for us they are fortuitous. Not that we think that fortune rules the world and men, tumbling all things at random up and down, for it is fitting that this folly be absent from the Christian's breast! But since the order, reason, end, and necessity of those things which happen for the most part lie hidden in God's purpose, and are not apprehended by human opinion, those things, which it is certain take place by God's will, are in a sense fortuitous. For they bear on the face of them no other appearance, whether they be considered in their own nature or weighed according to our own knowledge and judgment.[67]

This passage needs some unpacking in order to see how Calvin proceeds. Apparently there are two different descriptions of events in the world. An event happens before our eyes as a chance occurrence. This means that there is an element of contingency in it: as far as we can tell, it also could not have happened, or it could have happened differently, or at another time. In the second description, there is nothing left of this contingency. The event had to be exactly what it was—where, and when, and how—since it was ordained within the larger scheme of God's providential plan.

Let us look at these descriptions as two different perspectives on one and the same event. So, from the perspective of our knowledge and judgment, a random event does appear as fortuitous; but from the perspective of the divine will, it is determined by God's purpose. According to Calvin, these descriptions can be true at the same time. But how can this be?

Take as an example a young man wandering in the field who is struck by lightning. Considered for what it is—"in its own nature"—and for all we can tell, this is a chance occurrence that would be adequately reported by newspapers as an unfortunate accident.[68] Since, for the Christian, presumably no such thing as fortune exists, the description of what *really* happened must be different.[69] Since God, and not fortune, rules the universe, this includes natural phenomena like thunder and lightning as well. Even so, it would be quite reckless for a Christian reporter to write that a young man has been killed by the wrath of God. It is not that this description could not be true, but the problem for the Christian reporter would be that if this event were to be reported as factually accurate, then it should be explained how this can be known to be true.

Calvin does not rule out the possibility that God has a hand in such accidents, but he is nonetheless very reluctant to make a great deal out of it. For the most part, the order of things within which the event took place—the reason why it happened, the end for which it happened, or why it had to happen—are "hidden in God's purpose."[70] So, it cannot surprise us that most people would call this an accident. But what will a Christian think at this point?

> Just this: whatever happened in a death of this sort, will be regarded as fortuitous by nature, as it is; yet he will not doubt that God's providence exercised authority over fortune in directing its end.[71]

From the perspective of human understanding, then, contingency is an inevitable aspect of our experience. That is why Calvin suggests a double perspective on the causation of natural events: the first regards what the human mind can "see"; the second regards what it "will not doubt."[72] What God has determined must take place, even when the event itself is neither unconditional nor necessary as far as its own nature is concerned. In the case of the accident described before, this may be taken to mean that there were other causal conditions,[73] or that it was coincidental that lightning struck him.[74] In other words, there is nothing *in the event itself* pointing directly to God's will. This is why in our daily experience events usually do not wear their providential nature on their sleeves. This is also why Calvin claims that divine providence can only be distinguished from the perspective of faith, and that what from the perspective of human experience appears as contingency, is recognized by faith to have been a "secret impulse" from God.[75]

It should be noticed that Calvin is not making a point here about what Christians know. He is not saying that because of their faith Christians have a more accurate understanding of where, and when, and how divine providence works. "Faith" in this connection regards a disposition of the heart. Without appropriate disposition we can hardly avoid entangling ourselves in "inscrutable difficulties," Calvin warns his readers.[76] Figuring out divine providence is not a mind game for clever people. Instead it is about responding faithfully, with a reverent heart that is to say, to adversity and uncertainty.

Curiously, when it comes to the prerogative of believers, Calvin's argument moves in just the opposite direction. Particularly, believers run the risk of taking the stand against God, he says, because they will be inclined to think that God owes them a good turn. Whenever the thought creeps in that we are tossed and turned by blind fortune, "the flesh incites us to contradiction, as if God were making sport of men by throwing them about like balls." If only we had "quiet and composed minds, ready to learn," we would see that God always has the best reason for his plan.[77] At this point of his exposition, Calvin's thought clearly reminds us of his sermons on the book of Job,[78] for this self-righteous response to God is precisely what he blames Job for. Job is lacking in humility before his Maker.

In Calvin's vocabulary, the notion of the "flesh inciting us to contradiction" introduces the suspect part of our human nature, of course. As revolting human beings, we are always ready to ask God to account for his miserable way of ruling the universe, or at least the part of it that affects our own lives. "But we must so cherish moderation that we do not try to make God render account to us, but so reverence his secret judgments as to consider his will the truly just cause of all things," Calvin claims.[79] Those who are pure at heart will not doubt God's justice, and will exercise patience rather than obstinacy.

Therefore the providential nature of apparently fortuitous events is accessible only to reverent eyes. When the sky darkens and a violent tempest lashes out and our senses are benumbed by fear, we should remind ourselves "the disturbances in the world deprive us of judgment." In doing so we risk calling God to account and passing a sentence on things we do not understand.

Calvin finds a strange discrepancy in how we respond to other human beings compared to how we tend to respond to God. When it comes to sentencing other human beings for harming us through their actions, we exercise moderation in our judgments in case we have no indication of malevolent intentions—how absurd, then, says Calvin, that we do not hesitate to "haughtily revile the hidden judgments of God that we ought to hold in reverence."[80] As a matter of civility, well-educated people usually do not conclude there is malicious intent when someone hurts them by accident. When God is concerned, however, people do not seem to be so reverential, as to treat God in the same "civil" way.

With these caveats in mind, it is clear that Calvin's claim about "faith" recognizes "a secret impulse from God" to work for the good of God's creatures, where "carnal sense" only perceives fortune and chance, which indicates the link in Calvin's theology between providence and grace.

In Conclusion

In pondering whether there will be a future for him unlocked from his "locked-in" syndrome, Jean-Dominique Bauby raises the question, "Does the cosmos have keys?" Calvin's answer to this question is both clear and complicated. Yes, the cosmos does have keys insofar as everything that happens is part of God's plan, but it is also clear that human understanding is too limited to be able to know what this plan entails. More important still is the fact that thwarted expectations of what life has to offer make people turn against God and hold him accountable. Calvin commends providence as a most fruitful doctrine in that it can save people from believing that their lives are subject to the whims of fortune and chance, but this is only true for those who will humble themselves before God with a reverent heart. At the same time, however, Calvin argues that as far as their human experience can tell, people will only see chance and fortune at work in their lives. In view of both of these claims, the question arises of how to recognize God's hand as the hand of the one who is the fountain of all that is good.

We have seen that in answering this question, Calvin insists upon epistemic virtue. Thinking appropriately about providence should be undertaken with a reverent heart that will abstain from any attempt at prying into God's secret plan. The notion of a "secret plan," however, raises more questions than it can answer, for it makes discerning the difference between divine justice and arbitrariness, with respect to God's intervening action, very hard indeed. It raises questions about theological determinism as well as about human freedom.

These concluding remarks indicate that in the next chapter we need to pursue the relation between, on the one hand, Calvin's image of God as the loving Father and the fountain of all that is good, and, on the other hand, his image of God as the majestic but incomprehensible Ruler of the universe. More specifically, the question is what difference does it make for his doctrine of providence that it is developed in the context of *Christian* theology? How is Calvin's doctrine of providence the expression of God's *paterna cura*, the work of the loving Father that we have come to see in the light of the Son?

7

PROVIDENCE IN CHRIST

The true goal of theological inquiry is not the resolution of theological problems but the discernment of what the mystery of faith is.

—T. G. Weinandy

"Another Hidden Will"

In discussing the story of Job, we already saw that Calvin's assessment reflects two sides of how Job responds to his misfortune. On the one hand, he believes that Job in rejecting divine retribution defends "a good cause," but on the other hand, Job handles his case badly because he is lacking in reverence.[1] This is where Job goes wrong. The way he addresses God with biting sarcasm is way out of line. God's inscrutable majesty forbids that his creatures be so pretentious as to bring him to justice, which is according to Calvin what Job is attempting to do.

As we have also seen, however, Calvin's line of reasoning here has dire consequences, for it forces him to accept the notion of a second justice that goes beyond God's justice as revealed in his law.[2] It is not that there is anything wrong with retributive justice, but the concept does not work for how God deals with human beings. God is not bound to respond to their actions according to what they deserve. This is not to say that God is unjust, but that his justice is beyond human understanding. The obvious

145

question is whether this second justice can override the justice that is revealed, thereby making God's creatures subject to an arbitrary will. As we will see, this second justice operates within the sphere of divine incomprehensibility, which makes it hard to explain the difference from arbitrariness.

We left off with Calvin's argument that we should pay God at least the courtesy that we pay to our follow humans when, in judging their actions, we are uncertain of their intentions. Forgetting our place, we are ready to hold God accountable, in spite of the fact that we do not know his plan. Following this line of argument, Calvin cannot but defend God's incomprehensibility, to which we will now turn.

The argument begins with a number of biblical passages to prove this point. Against those who reject the notion of divine incomprehensibility, Calvin cites Psalm 36:6: "Thy justice is like mighty mountains, thy judgments are like the deep sea." And from the Letter to the Romans, he adds: "What fathomless wealth lies in the wisdom and knowledge of God! How inscrutable his judgments! How mysterious his methods!" (Rom 11:33-34). Many more texts from both the Old and the New Testament could have been added, but now Calvin makes an unexpected move. Instead of quoting more texts to support his case for incomprehensibility, he refers to a passage in the book of Deuteronomy that seems to point in the opposite direction. It says:

> This command which I am enjoining upon you today is not beyond your power, it is not beyond your reach; it is not up in heaven, that you should say "Who will go up for us and bring it down to us and let us hear it, that we may do it?"—nor is it over the sea, that you should say "Who will cross the sea for us and bring it to us and let us hear it, that we may do it?" No, the word is very near you, it is on your lips and in your mind, to be obeyed. (Deut 30:11-14)[3]

How are these two positions to be reconciled? How can God's judgments be inscrutable, his methods be mysterious, and at the same time his words be on our lips and in our minds? Calvin answers the question through an inference: Since Moses proclaims that the will of God is not far from his people, because it has been given in the law, it must follow that God has another *hidden* will.[4] Given how Calvin staged this inference, and particularly his Latin phrasing of it—*aliam voluntatem absconditam*—he evokes the imagery about the darker side of God.[5] This does not seem to be Calvin's intention, however, because he immediately redresses it by saying that there is no deep abyss to be afraid of here, because "God illumines the minds of his own with the spirit of discernment."[6] God's will is given in his commandments as they are written in his law. That is all we need to know. Calvin continues to argue that Moses has expressed both ideas in these words (quoting from Deuteronomy): "The secret things belong to the Lord our God, but the revealed things belong to us and to our children forever, to observe all the words of this law" (Deut 29:29). There is wisdom that is known to God alone, and there is "a portion of wisdom prescribed for men." The aim of the distinction is no other than to "humble our minds." Since God keeps for himself the right to rule the universe, which humans do not possess; it is an obligation of "soberness and moderation" to assent to God's supreme authority, so that God's will may be for all of us "the sole rule of righteousness, and the truly just cause of all things."[7]

To avoid all misunderstandings at this point, Calvin distances himself from the idea that there is a hidden will in God that is *separated* from his revealed will. Would there be two separate wills, *then* one of them could not be in accordance with his revealed justice, otherwise it would not be separate.

In this connection Calvin mentions the Scholastics—the *Sophistae*—to whom he attributes the view he is rejecting. God's will as the sole rule of righteousness is not "that absolute will of which the Sophists babble," with which they are "separating his justice from his power."[8] Calvin refers here to a theory about divine power that is commonly ascribed to Scotist and Occamistic circles in late medieval philosophical theology.[9] The theory, as Calvin understands it, invents a notion of absolute divine power—*potestas absoluta*—that is not necessarily informed by divine justice, and, in that sense, is separated from God's power that works in created order—*potestas ordinata*. This distinction Calvin regards as unbiblical and heretic. In the treatise *De Aeterna Dei Praedestinatione*, he scorns the same view by saying that it is easier to take the sun's light from its heat, or its heat from its fire, than to separate God's power from his justice.[10]

These observations again indicate how in Calvin's theology of providence a pastoral motive is continuously in control of his thinking. Even the slightest glimmer of light between God's will and God's justice would

cause his entire argument to fall apart. One cannot hope to reassure people who experience horrible events in their lives by telling them that what
from their perspective appears as a stroke of blind fortune will prove to
be in accordance with God's secret plan—not, at any rate, if one does not
clarify, at the same time, that this secret plan is not the manifestation of
an arbitrary will. For indeed, *without identifying* God's secret plan with his
eternal justice, it is necessarily true that his rule cannot be distinguished
from blind fortune. Distributing "good" and "bad" among people, without
any reference to justice, is exactly what blind fortune does. In other words,
allowing at this point the distinction ascribed to the "Sophists" would
mean that the doctrine of providence as Calvin understands it loses its
point. No one could find any solace in it and go on with their lives without
despair. Rather than questioning God's justice, therefore, we should "with
becoming humility" submit ourselves to God's unknown plans and not
inquire into things beyond our judgment.[11] God's providence can therefore only be understood properly and profitably by those who accept God
as the Creator and Governor of the universe, and "with becoming humility" submit themselves "to fear and reverence."[12]

However, if the doctrine of providence is to have any practical meaning at all, more must be said, because, as Calvin has pointed out, "God
illumines the minds of his own with the spirit of discernment."[13] Without
some kind of understanding, they again would have no ground to know
providence from fortune, which is exactly what Calvin wants to deny at
all costs, because then they could find no comfort in it either. Before we
arrive at this "sprit of discernment," however, Calvin first wants to deal
with a few objections that are leveled against his theology at this point—
the most important of which is the objection of theological determinism.

Theological Determinism

Since there is nothing in the universe that happens without God willing it,
Calvin denies that some things happen according to the divine will while
others are the result of fortune. There is no division of labor between different kinds of causes—God's will being one of them.

Nonetheless Calvin retains some space for the notion of the fortuitous, as we saw, but only on the level of epistemology, not on the level
of metaphysics. Events in the world often are *seen* as fortuitous, which is
not to say that they *are* fortuitous.[14] That is to say, there is nothing that

happens in the world that does not have God's will as its primary cause. It is at this point, however, that the objection of determinism comes in.

If it is true, as Calvin's biblical reflections point out, that God's will is decisive in all motions and events, does it really matter then what human beings think or do? Suppose that you are accused of killing someone. When you are charged with manslaughter, your defense is to say that God instigated this killing, because would he not have willed it, he would have restrained you, and the killing would not have happened. The example is ludicrous, of course, but its lack of subtlety seems to reflect Calvin's massive judgment. If God's will determines everything, including human action, how is it that people can be held responsible for their actions?

This question invokes the next step in Calvin's investigation. To believe that God's will decides what happens in the world does not mean that it does not matter what people do. Calvin decries claims to that effect as "abominations."[15] The result of such abominations is that people may begin to think they can evade responsibility for their own actions: "All crimes, because subject to God's ordinance, they call virtues."[16] Having their action ordained by God's will does not cancel human responsibility, however, neither with regard to things in the past nor with regard to things in the future.

To defend this view, Calvin starts with a text from the book of Proverbs: "The human mind plans the way, but the Lord directs the steps" (Prov. 16:9). This text does not imply two separate aspects of our action, he says, as if humans do one thing (planning their ways), while God does the other (directing their steps). We have already noticed that Calvin denies any division of labor in this respect. What he means with quoting this verse is that there are two ways of looking at the same action that are simultaneously valid. In planning our ways, "we are not at all hindered by God's eternal decrees," by which he is directing our steps.[17] The reason is, Calvin explains, that whatever the means for taking care of our affairs, they also will be given by God.

We should not think of divine providence, therefore, as if the world is a stage on which human beings act as puppets under the control of the Great Puppeteer.[18] Divine providence is not to be mistaken in this manner, as if God were both the owner and the director of a theater of marionettes. To explain what he means, Calvin adds that God's providence does not meet us "in its naked form," but that "God clothes it with the means employed." Those who think they can put the blame for their crimes on God are mistaken in attributing "the happenings of past time to the naked providence of God."[19]

With the notion of "providence in its naked form," Calvin addresses the logic of causation. In the present context, "providence in its naked form" would mean that God's will is causing people to act without mediating causes. The closest analogy to this notion of providence would be indeed a puppeteer having puppets on a string. In formal language, "providence in its naked form" refers to actions that have God's will as both their necessary and sufficient cause. This is another way of saying that such actions have no other cause than that God wills them.

According to Calvin the notion of providence "in its naked form" is mistaken, however, at least with regard to human action.[20] From the fact that God's will is the *determining* cause of human action, it does not follow that it is the *only* cause. When a man is killed, it cannot plausibly be argued that this killing was due *only* to God's will, as if nobody else was involved. "God clothes it [the act of killing] with the means employed," Calvin reminds us, which is to say that there are other causal conditions involved. Even if it were true that the killing was caused by God's will—which for Calvin must be an open question—this does not mean that the deed was *not* the killer's doing. Divine causation does not cancel the causality of human action. The killer's act is just that: the *killer's* act.

Insofar as human responsibility is concerned, the metaphor of the puppet theater is mistaken, then, because the difference with marionettes is that humans do not act without intention. For Calvin, human intention can go in two directions. It aims either at serving the will of God, or it aims at obeying the agent's desire. In obeying God's will, the agent is striving toward the goal to which the agent is called by that same will. Actions with this intention are performed in accordance with God's law as revealed in Scripture. Killing a man may be a lawful act, in this sense, when it is striving toward a goal that is justified by that same law. The other possibility, however, is that the agent is pursuing the agent's own desires and, in doing so, acts against God's commandment. In that case the agent disobeys God's will.[21] Either way, Calvin intends to say, human beings remain at all times responsible for their own actions because they act on their own intentions. The eradicable cause of human responsibility, therefore, is intention.

Human Freedom and Responsibility

With this argument Calvin intends to show how human beings can be instruments of divine providence without losing their responsibility for what they do. Many of Calvin's readers have maintained their doubts at this point, however.[22] They want to know what it means exactly to say that human actions are *instruments* of divine providence. If God's will caused them, how can they be the agent's *own* action? Or does Calvin's argument about intention imply that humans are free in choosing the intention on which they act?[23]

The latter possibility certainly would have saved Calvin a great deal of apologetic trouble. It could then be said that human action is free in effectuating its own intention, which still allows that it follows God's will in the sense that he foresees its consequences. This claim should not be very problematic. Every so often the result of human action does not even come close to what it was intended to be, and not many of Calvin's readers would have doubted that God's wisdom is infinitely greater than human foresight.

Unfortunately, Calvin's view on the matter forecloses this semi-Pelagian evasion. Human intention is not to be left out as a safe haven of human freedom, because *it is also determined by God's will*. At least this is what Calvin maintains. Interestingly, the reason is explained, again, in reference to Augustine. He points to Augustine's attempt to avoid a conception of providence that makes God responsible for our evil actions. When even an act of unjust killing is caused by his will, how could God not contract some defilement from it?

To avoid this implication, Augustine proposes a solution: God does not cause people's wrongdoings; he merely permits them and then decides to put them to service for his own plan. Calvin's comment is as clear as it is chilling. He argues that the wish for a moderate view that overcomes "the appearance of absurdity" would be excusable, lest it tries "to clear God's justice of every sinister mark by upholding a falsehood." It surely must seem absurd to punish a human being who fails to see when it is blinded at God's will and command. Hence the solution of attributing its defect to God's permission instead of his will, but Calvin disagrees because God, "openly declaring that he is the doer," declines this evasion.[24]

God has openly declared "that he is the doer." In Calvin's view Scripture does not leave a shadow of a doubt about this. Reiterating his quote from the book of Psalms 115:3 saying that God does whatever he wills, Calvin gives a number of examples, each of which intends to show that God deliberately willed evil things to happen for reasons only known to himself.[25]

Some of his more powerful examples in this connection are taken from the book of Acts, where Peter more than once asserts that delivering Christ in the hands of his enemies was "the hand and plan" of God.[26] One has only to be moderately versed in Scripture, according to Calvin, to know that "permission" is not acceptable as a solution. Not only are there many testimonies in the Bible to the contrary, but "permission" also betrays a mistaken understanding of providence. It suggests a picture of God sitting in a watchtower, awaiting the chance to use human acts for his own purposes. This is totally unacceptable to Calvin because it means that the execution of the divine plan is made dependent upon human will.[27]

No doubt his kind of reasoning at this point has earned his doctrine of providence the reputation of harshness, for example, in view of the claim above that one cannot "clear God's justice of every sinister mark by upholding a falsehood." Surely the skeptical mind will want to ask just how many sinister marks divine justice can bear before it ceases to be justice? And what is one to make of his quotation from Psalm 115 that God does whatever he wills? Can this text prove the absolute sovereignty of God's will— "his boundless might"[28]—without implying that divine power operates irrespective of divine justice (which implication brings Calvin very close to the view he vehemently criticized in the *Sophistae*)?

But if "permission" is ruled out, then how does one answer the question about human freedom? If God does not merely permit what people do, but actually governs their inclinations and intentions, how could there possibly be any space left for human freedom to make up their minds independently from God's will? Calvin responds immediately, following upon his rejection of "permission," and of course he answers again in terms of his scriptural sources.

Referring to a remark in the book of Proverbs about how God turns around the heart of a king (Prov 21:1), Calvin adds that this could have been said about any human being. There is no doubt that God works "inwardly in men's mind," as when it is said, for example, that he causes the blindness of our minds or the hardening of our hearts. In Calvin's eyes, all the evidence suggests that God decrees not only our actions, but also our intentions. Surprisingly, however, he claims the same condition for human intention that he has upheld for human action: while God acts upon the human will, it is at the same time the human agent who wills the act.

Primary and Secondary Causation

To explain how this concurrent agency is to be understood, Calvin takes recourse from an old idea that originates from Plato. It regards the distinction between "primary" and "secondary" causation. He argues that "A godly man will not overlook the secondary causes."[29] He will not fail to acknowledge with gratitude the benefits received from other human agents just because he believes that God is the primary cause of their actions. Thus he will praise the Lord as "the principal author" of these beneficial acts without failing to honor the human agents administering them. But this act of gratitude itself is again rooted in God's will as its primary cause. "It is by God's will that he is beholden to those through whose hand God willed to be beneficent."[30]

So when someone gives you a break and does you an undeserved favor, you will express your gratitude toward this person as a "godly man" would do, and also thank God for his kindness, because you know that God's will caused your benefactor's action. The expression of gratitude makes sense only because you assumed that the agent deliberately intended to do you a favor, which in Calvin's view proves the point.

He also argues for the reversed case. When a "godly man" suffers a loss because of his own negligence or imprudence, he will know that this occurred because of God's will, but not without accepting his own responsibility for being negligent or imprudent. Providence, as Calvin has already declared, does not meet us "in its naked form," because God "clothes it with the means employed."[31] There is not only *primary* causation in the form of God's will; there is also *secondary* causation in the form of all kinds of causes that God uses as instruments. Therefore a "godly man" will not conclude directly from a given action or event that God's will is its sole cause and overlook human intention as a secondary cause.

Here the logic of causation begins to create problems, however, which becomes apparent as soon as we press the question as to what the distinction between primary and secondary exactly entails. How can God's will be a cause similar to other causes in terms of its causality, but dissimilar from other causes in terms of its primacy? Does it mean that God's will is a cause similar to natural causes? If so, is it subject to the laws of nature? If not, because of the difference according to its primacy, in what sense can it then be identified as a cause? Once one really starts to think about God's will as a cause, Calvin's reasoning becomes more and more obscure.

At this point it may be helpful to look back at Martha Beck's struggle with what she named her "rationalist credibility."[32] She could not in her right mind believe in "signs" and "voices" from another world as causes in the real world, because there was no way to prove that they were actually effective in some sense. The problem with Calvin's account of God's will as the primary cause of human intention is that it pushes in the same direction. It places God's will as a supernatural cause in the same box with natural causes. Unlike the modern mind, Calvin's thought was not troubled by an empiricist mold, of course, but the question that his theology of providence faces is ultimately not dissimilar. What does it mean to say that God's determining will and human impulse are causes with similar kinds of effects in the natural world? It is not accidental that Martha Beck realizes that accepting her supernatural aids as "friends" brings her very close to what the Mormon people back in Utah believed with regard to the miraculous deliverances from their deity. In their view, when it comes to causal efficacy, the divine will is indistinguishable from being struck by lightning, or winning the national lottery, or being miraculously saved in a car crash. Calvin's logic of causation allows for precisely this possibility. God's will acts as primary cause amidst other causes of the same kind, though they can only be secondary. The question for Calvin's theology, then, is this: if there is an unfathomable difference between Creator and creation (which is the vortex of Calvin's thought), how could their operating principles be causative and effective on the same plane?

Looking at Calvin's account for an explanation, one will find that there is none. While Calvin's scriptural sources lead him to believe that there is nothing in the universe that God's will does not control, including our mental states, it is impossible for human reason to explain this. That is to say, a person of faith will gladly accept *that* God's will operates upon human intentions, but *how* it operates and for what purpose are questions passing human understanding.

There is only one way out of this deadlock, which Calvin clings to when he wants to remind his readers that providence can only be fully appreciated from the perspective of faith. Losing this perspective, one falls into the kind of logical conundrums that "carnal sense" demands us to resolve. Calvin does not have much patience for the presumably independent mind that demands answers before it submits itself to the testimony of Scripture. In this regard, there is no third way in Calvin's faith. You are either considering God's doing in the world as you have learned from Scripture, never forgetting that it is your Creator that you are dealing with, or else you hold him accountable from your own point of view for actions attributed to God by his believers. In view of these alternatives, trying to account for the divine will is a "calumny" that Calvin will not undertake. Instead he proceeds with how the Christian heart will receive its "best and sweetest fruit."[33] Since it has been thoroughly persuaded that all things happen by God's plan, and that nothing takes place by chance, the Christian heart will never fail praising God as the principal cause of things. But at the same time it will pay attention to the secondary causes in their proper place. It will not doubt that God's providence preserves it, and that it will never suffer anything but "what may turn to its good and salvation." Accordingly the Christian heart will know that the plans, wills, efforts, and abilities of human beings are under God's hand, and "that it is within his choice to bend them whither he pleases and to constrain them whenever he pleases."[34]

Here we find Calvin again use the distinction between primary and secondary causes in an attempt to explain concurrent causality, but the question remains whether his comment explains anything at all. When secondary causes are "means employed" by God's will, how can they be causes at the same time? In a recent study, Terry G. Wright has argued that Calvin's distinction of primary and secondary causation tends to reduce every creaturely action or event to mere instrumentality.[35] To explain this, Wright looks extensively at how the two causalities appear in Calvin's work. In this connection, the statement quoted before—"God's providence does not always meet us in its naked form, but God clothes it with the means employed"—is pertinent. It indicates precisely the question raised above: if events in the world are "means employed" by God's will, how can they be seen as genuine causes?[36]

Putting the focus on the analysis of simultaneous causation, Wright suggests that a secondary cause cannot be efficacious *qua cause* if at the same time God's will is the primary cause that determines it. The real question, however, is not whether or not secondary causes can be efficacious, but whether the concept of causation *as such* can be helpful at all.[37] Calvin, at any rate, saw himself compelled to acknowledge that he could not explain how God's will as primary cause works.[38]

More important for our purposes, however, is that Calvin's attempt has not brought him one inch closer to the question he set out to answer—namely, what does it mean to say that "God illumines the minds of his own with the spirit of discernment"?[39] Since this illumination is the condition that enables "God's own" to see the difference between providence and fortune or chance, the failure to answer the question is not inconsequential. It is hard to see how believers could find comfort in the one if there is no way to distinguish it from the other. If all that can be said is that from our human experience there does not seem to be a difference, then the conclusion must be that the difference sought after is wanting.

It is at this point that Wright's critique of Calvin's reliance on the distinction of primary and secondary causation is most poignant. The presupposition that God's sovereignty must be equivalent to "pancausality" fails to recognize that God's action in the world has a specific purpose that is revealed by the work of Christ.[40] Thus it appears that in using the distinction between the two kinds of causality, Calvin is left with a doctrine of divine providence that fails to do what he wanted it to do, which was to explain it as distinctively *theological*.

A Trinitarian Approach

Having presented his critical argument, Wright opens a different perspective on providence by pursuing a Trinitarian approach. It is insufficient to portray divine providence predominantly in terms of God's will to act, he says, because "the Trinitarian focus is lost and the particularity of God's action in Christ is diluted."[41] Wright observes, rightly in my view, that once we lose sight of God's specific action in Christ, it is inevitable to talk about divine action in general terms, which is what the language of primary causation reflects.[42] It regards the sovereign power of God's will over all of creation, but the God to whom this power is attributed only answers to the philosophical description of what an all-powerful deity must be:

absolutely omniscient, omnipotent, and so on. It does nothing to explain, at any rate, what a conception of divine providence might be like when it takes into account the redemptive work of Christ.

In this respect, many of the Protestant classics on providence show a remarkable resemblance, as has been observed by Karl Barth: "The Lutheran and Reformed teachers are all at one in teaching the divine lordship over all occurrence both as a whole and in detail without attempting to say what is the meaning and purpose of this lordship." This observation led Barth to speak of their teaching as an "empty shell": it nowhere addresses the Triune God in whom Christians claim to believe—namely, as God the Father, the Son, and the Holy Spirit.[43] As Wright points out, this is all the more strange when we remind ourselves of the fact that in the New Testament it is abundantly testified that God works in the world through Christ, and in Christ, so that conceptualizing the mediation of God's will in terms of a general causality is far removed from the specificity that the New Testament points to:

> If we wish to understand God's providential activity within creation, we ought to follow the New Testament's lead and grasp the particularity of Christ as the only one through whom this activity is mediated. In the life of Christ, we see God's providence made flesh.[44]

In other words, in order to succeed in what Calvin is aiming at, a Christian doctrine of providence should be able to show how God's providential will is mediated by the Son and the Spirit—in other words, not *that* God is ruling the universe, but *how God does so* is what distinguishes a Christian doctrine of providence.

Let me at this point return to the task of rethinking providence in view of the firsthand accounts of disability experience that we canvassed in chapter 2. Being confronted by disability, we have heard, people find their lives falling apart. They are looking into an abyss and have no clue as to how the gap between the "before" and "after" can be bridged. In order to find comfort and regain trust that their lives will have a future, people need to find a connection to regain the sense of purpose in their lives.

Looking back at what we have learned so far from Calvin's classical doctrine of providence, we see that it is unlikely that they have found what they were looking for. In the words of Karl Barth, there is no meaning and purpose to be found there, because meaning and purpose remain hidden in God's secret plan; there is only the determination of all that occurs. Whenever the "why" question was raised, Calvin's response indeed was that we do not know. In a sense this is quite strange, because at many places in the New Testament it is made perfectly clear what God's plan and purpose is about:

> He is the image of the invisible God, the firstborn of all creation: for in him all things in heaven and on earth were created, things visible and invisible, whether thrones or dominions or rulers or powers—all things have been created through him and for him. He himself is before all things, and in him all things hold together. (Col 1:15-17)

This is Paul's account of God's plan, as he sees it realized in Christ, the true image of God. What is more, this account follows an introduction in which he refers to his prayers, for the people in Colossus, since the day he has been informed about their faith:

> Since the day we heard it, we have not ceased praying for you and asking that you may be filled with the knowledge of God's will in all spiritual wisdom and understanding, so that you will lead lives worthy of the Lord, fully pleasing to him, as you bear fruit in every good work and as you grow in the knowledge of God. (Col 1:9-11)

When people's lives are shipwrecked by disaster, and they turn to God for their consolation, this is what he promises them: in Christ "all things hold together." This means that there is a place to go when trying to bridge the gap between the "before" and "after." If it is true that *all* things are *in* Christ and *for* him, then it must also be true that learning to live with life's contingencies is mediated by his presence in the world. As the gospel abundantly testifies, in Christ all human suffering is acknowledged, not as what alienates people from God, but as that which places them right in his sacred heart.

Although there is certainly a great mystery in this, it is far from the "hiddenness" that Calvin has been talking about, as if God were concerned with a secret that he wants to keep for himself. No, there is "knowledge of God" that people, according to Paul, can grow into. As a matter of fact, this was recognized by Calvin when he said that "God illumines the minds of his own with the spirit of discernment."[45] This is the remaining question, then—namely, how to acquire this spirit of discernment that will teach people to see the difference between God's purpose, and fortune and chance.

The Spirit of Discernment

When the "why" question arises from people's lips—we learned in an earlier stage of this inquiry—they do not ask for a cause; they ask for a purpose. They want to understand meaning. "What does my disability mean?" "What did I do wrong?" When they are religious people, they want to know why God made this happen, or at least allowed it to happen. These are questions that people ask in lamenting the calamities that befall them. Therefore we should take them seriously.

Again, the reason is not that disability is a tragedy or a disaster, as I have explained before, but the experience of being confronted by it certainly is, at least initially, as the literature abundantly testifies. The experience turns people's lives upside down, and nobody in their right mind will at that point begin to explain to them that they are mistaken. Of course they can be mistaken about what to expect, but, even so, this is something they have not found out yet at the time of their experience. They do not know that in many ways people with disabilities live reasonably happy lives, more or less like other people. As I said before, the experience of disability as tragedy is real because it is prior to discovering the grounds on which that experience can be contested.

As I hope to show, however, redirecting the theology of providence in Wright's sense may also help to redirect the "why" question and draw it away from the language of tragedy and calamity.[46] Characteristically, the "why" question is a backward-looking question. It can be restated as "What happened before, so that this occurred later?" Whatever the experience of disability is, it is supposedly seen as a consequence of some preceding condition that can explain it. In this connection, "explanation" may not be all that helpful, as was considered in the opening chapter. Even if a satisfactory explanation could be given, it would probably not silence the question. Lament is about agony and pain, as I said following John Swinton, but "explanation" does not take the pain away. Surely there is a true need for understanding, but understanding does not necessarily take the form of *explanation*; it might also take the form of *discovery*. Instead of asking why God allowed this to happen, we can also ask, "Where is God present in all of this, and how?" In many ways, Scripture testifies that God will not forsake "the work that his hand has begun,"[47] so why not ask what it means, in this connection, that he remains faithful to his creation?

If we take this as our lead, then Calvin's claim that God will illuminate the minds of his own with the spirit of discernment falls right in place. Discernment is then directed toward discovering God's active presence in the midst of their affliction. Discernment is the ability to see, so that the spirit of discernment must be their guide in finding out what there is to see. In rethinking providence as mediated through the work of Christ, the spirit of discernment can only be the Spirit that God the Father communicates with God the Son, and through the Son with God's creatures. The leading question then becomes how God's Spirit may guide their understanding and toward what it will direct their eyes to see.

To unpack the various elements entailed in this proposal, the first thing to consider is that the providence of God is about effectuating a promise, the promise that God made in view of his creation (Gen 1:28),[48] and renewed in his calling of Abraham in whom all the families of the earth will be blessed (Gen 12:3). God does not abandon the work of his hands. The Hebrew Bible testifies how God keeps this promise, first by his covenant with Israel mediated through the law that Moses received, then by being present in the tabernacle, and later in the temple in Jerusalem. As Israel's prophets signal time and again, however, God's people fail to keep their part in the covenant he made with them. They do not carry his law in their hearts, so God seeks to renew his promise. To this purpose, God sends Jesus into the world as his Son, according to the Christian tradition. The central message of the New Testament becomes John 3:16: "For God so loved the world that he gave his only Son, so that everyone who believes in him may not perish but may have eternal life."

There can be no doubt, according to this testimony, that God has not withdrawn his promise to sustain his creatures and bless their lives. Consequently, this fundamental belief warrants the question of how God's promise is at hand in people's lives.

The first thing to consider in this connection is that it is not only a promise about some future state of affairs, although it is also that. God's promise is mediated into the present. To put it differently, God's promise is his presence. As Wright puts it, "God promises that the world in its entirety shall be the place of his presence," which is what Wright calls "the eschatological foundation of providence."[49] To be open to this promise is particularly hard in the midst of the contingencies that govern our lives. More often than not, they suggest God's absence rather than God's presence, especially when we are afflicted by calamities. Nonetheless, in the Christian view, divine promise is not only a *futurum*, but also a presence, which is testified by the name the Gospel of Matthew gives to God's incarnate Son: *Immanuel*, "God with us" (Matt 1:23).

Secondly, there is the question of mediation. It may be true *that* God promises to be present in the midst of our afflictions, but *how* is he present? Here the answer can only be one thing: through the Spirit that unites God with the Son. Jesus' journey as the Son of God begins with his baptism in the river Jordan, where the Spirit descends upon him (Matt 3:16; Luke 2:21). Throughout his mission the Spirit sustains him, particularly when he is tempted to forsake it, or when he has doubts about its fulfillment: "When the Son was tempted to turn away from the Father's will, the Spirit was with him to enlighten his mind, to clarify the issues, to urge him towards the right choice, but not to make that choice for him."[50] In the Gospel of John, finally, Jesus promises the gift of his Spirit to his friends: "I have said these things to you while I am still with you. But the Advocate, the Holy Spirit, whom the Father will send in my name, will teach you everything, and remind you of all that I have said to you" (John 14:25-26). According to the testimony of Acts 2, this promise is delivered when God sends his Spirit upon the assembled followers of Jesus in Jerusalem. God's promise for those that seek him in the midst of their affliction is the gift of his Spirit, the *Paraclete*, who will be with them to comfort them and guide them.

Thirdly, how will the Spirit guide them in their practice of discernment? How will it teach them to see? There is a long tradition in the teaching of the prophets that when God's Spirit touches human beings, this will result in a change of hearts. For example, in Ezekiel we read: "A new heart I will give you, and a new spirit I will put within you, and I will remove from your body the heart of stone. I will put my spirit within you and make you follow my statutes and be careful to observe my ordinances" (Ezek 36:26-27). Similarly, in Jeremiah we read about a new covenant that God wants to install, which is also directed at changing people's hearts: "This is the new covenant I will make with the house of Israel after those days, says the Lord: I will put my law within them, and I will write it on their hearts; and I will be their God, and they will be my people" (Jer 31:33). The same thought occurs in the introduction of Paul's Second Letter to the Corinthians:

> Surely we do not need, as some do, letters of recommendations to you or from you, do we? You yourselves are our letter, written on our hearts, to be read and known by all; and you show that you are a letter of Christ, prepared by us, written not in ink but in the Spirit of the Living God, not on tablets of stone but on tablets of human hearts. (2 Cor 3:1-3)

Discovering the presence of God in the midst of affliction, it appears, depends on a particular kind of disposition, which I named an epistemic virtue when elucidating Calvin's claim that knowledge of providence is "knowledge of the heart."[51] Discerning God's presence is not primarily a matter of the mind, then. People benumbed by calamity feel that their lives are falling apart. When they manage to open up to a new situation, they notice they will change. This is how the Spirit of God works in them: their response to what is inevitably a new reality begins to change. To paraphrase Calvin's dictum, God illuminates the minds of his own by changing their hearts. That is how his Spirit guides them in practicing discernment. The spirit of discernment, in other words, is about transformation.

Finally, what are they changed from, and what are they changed to? When the apostle Paul speaks of what the Spirit does, he consistently speaks of love, *agape*. That is how one recognizes the gift that the Spirit is. It communicates God's love to human beings so that they will love one another. Therefore, Paul can reassure his fellow Christians in Rome that no one can separate them from the love that has come to them from the Father through the Son (Rom 8:35, 8:39). This is why he can say that love is the greatest good: "If I have prophetic powers, and understand all mysteries and all knowledge, and if I have all the faith, so as to remove mountains, but do not have love, I am nothing" (1 Cor 13:2). This love has been poured into their heart through the Holy Spirit. The gift of love enables "God's own" to endure suffering, Paul argues, knowing that suffering produces endurance, and endurance produces character, and character produces hope, and hope does not disappoint us because God's love has been poured into our hearts through the Holy Spirit that has been given us. (Rom 5:5)

People are changed from the benumbing fear that befalls them when they are hit by calamities, when life as they know it seems to be falling apart. Their hearts are changed and opened to see the love that is present in their lives and kindles their hope again.

In this respect, there are clear differences between the stories we read in the first part of this inquiry. A powerful image in this connection is created by Martha Beck's language of "opening up" and "remaining closed." Her own example shows how she is opened up once she begins to see the gift that her son Adam is. Everything about his existence with Down syndrome turned out as troublesome as it was predicted to be, and more, but she discovered the gift of love that this little boy was. The spirit of discernment taught Martha Beck what there was to see, even though it took her some time to recognize it.

Jean-Dominique Bauby's story is more complicated. The true miracle is that even he began to see a glimmer of hope when he was pondering the fact that his true friends had been there for him; they had been there from the beginning and stayed. So, even here, the spirit of discernment did not fail to do its work. But at the time he was opening up, despite his locked-in syndrome, death closed his eyes, for good.

Finally, Cathy Crimmins' story is, in a sense, the saddest story of these three. Cathy had a hard time adjusting to her new life, notwithstanding the fact that her husband, Al, and their daughter, Kelly, were reunited and found each other after a very hard time, especially for Kelly. Then there is also the fact that, according to Cathy, Al was in some ways a happier man than he was before his accident. But she is stuck with the memory of the "old" Al, the man who sang "Wild Thing" for her at their wedding. If she had only been able to reset the clock and make Al step five minutes later into his sailing boat, the teenager's speedboat would have missed him, and their lives would have remained the same. Even though Cathy had an acute awareness of the sheer contingency of what happened to them, she held on to what in her own mind their life together was about. Consequently, despite Al's significant recovery, their new life could in her eyes only be a "reasonable facsimile" of what it once had been.

Her story indicates a final point that needs to be recognized. The spirit of discernment was not absent from her new life, but somehow it failed to convince her. What this reminds us of is that this spirit is a promise, and as such it is a gift; it is not a determination. People are free to accept it, or not, because God wants to be loved in freedom, not because he has ordained their love.

The spirit of discernment, then, promises to lead people to see what there is to see: the Spirit of Christ, in which all things were created and which holds all things together, has not faded from their lives. The fountain of all that is good has not dried up; it only requires new eyes to see this. In the moment of fear, when people face the chasm between the "before" and "after," the presence of God in all of creation is gone. Reality has imposed itself upon them in the most unmerciful way, so the only thing they know for sure is the absence of God. That is when the "why" question arises from their lips. It is the question of why God has forsaken them, even though he promised not to hand over their lives into *chaos*. Faith in divine providence, then, is faith in his active presence in creation to remain faithful to the promise that his creatures will not be abandoned.[52]

Calvin's Ambivalence

To do full justice to John Calvin, we ought to admit that his theology allowed him to have said all this, and in many ways he did say it, and much better. Not only did he emphasize that providence is about the "very many and very clear *promises*" that God watches over the well-being of his flock.[53] He also reminded his readers of Christ's promise that not even a tiny sparrow will fall from the roof without the Father's will, let alone that things would happen to people without his will, since they are surely closer to him than the sparrow (Matt 10:29-31). Moreover, he also reminded them of the many "singular proofs" of God's fatherly care.[54] Whenever they experience that things are going their way, the "servants of God" will attribute such things wholly to him. In regaining confidence and opening up themselves for the love of others, they will say to themselves, "Surely it is the lord who has inclined their hearts to me, who has bound them to me that they should become instruments of his kindness towards me."[55]

In view of Barth's criticism that Calvin's doctrine of providence does not say anything about purpose,[56] it is striking that Calvin did emphasize the participation of the Spirit. Not only is the beauty of the world and its preservation owed to the powers of the Spirit, but the Spirit "everywhere diffused, sustains all things, causes them to grow, and quickens them in heaven and earth."[57] These quotations lead Wright to conclude that, in Calvin's theology,

> providence . . . has an explicitly pneumatological component: the life of the world is a gift of God, imparted to it by the Spirit. Importantly, the Spirit does not act independently; he effects that which the Father plans by conforming it to the pattern established by the Son, in whom alone is found "the ordered disposition of all things."[58]

Evidently, there is a clear conception of purpose, after all, in Calvin's doctrine of providence, which leaves us with the question of how it relates to his assertions about the hiddenness and secrecy of the plan of an incomprehensible God.

Wright explains this apparent tension in terms of Calvin's remaining ambivalence in this respect. His deep-seated conviction of the unfathomable difference between Creator and creation caused him to hold a distinctive pessimism with regard to human beings. Human beings are nothing compared to God, according to Calvin, so even if there would have been no fall, there *still* would be the need for a mediator to relate God's divinity with our humanity.[59] This unfathomable difference has only been aggravated by the fall. There is no way to be at peace with God other than through his mercy. Human sinfulness is total depravity, which means that true knowledge of God's providential will is lost because of original sin. Accordingly, Calvin says, "After the common sense of the flesh we regard as fortuitous whatever happens either way, whether good or evil, and so are neither aroused by God's benefits to worship him, nor stimulated by lashes to repentance."[60]

Calvin's ambivalence constantly seems to draw him toward the darker side of human existence. The benefits of divine providence are not depicted in the wondrous gifts of the Spirit, as they could have been, but are in Calvin's mind apparently more manifest in the dangers that people face daily: "Mount a horse, if one foot slips, your life is imperiled. Go through the city streets, you are subject to as many dangers as there are tiles on a roof. If there is a weapon in your hand or a friend's hand, harm awaits."[61] And so on. Given the many uncertainties that besiege human life, the thought of being subjected to the power of blind fortune is what makes our lives, in Calvin's eyes, truly miserable. It will drive God's servants "to put off rashness and overconfidence, and will impel us continually to call upon God." He will reward them with "good hope," he assures, so that they may face whatever the dangers that are surrounding them.[62]

Hence, there is "the immeasurable felicity of the godly man" who knows there is no such thing as blind fortune.[63] It is obvious for Calvin that ignorance of providence is the ultimate source of all miseries: the highest blessedness lies in the knowledge of it. While such statements were meant to reassure his flock, they could hardly fail to leave them with many questions too. For if the world appears "to be aimlessly tumbled about," while at the same time "the Lord is everywhere at work,"[64] the query as to how these statements are related will be difficult to forestall. Yet this is what we see Calvin constantly doing: human depravity blocks understanding; therefore, do not ask what you are bound to misjudge. This drift toward the incomprehensibility of divine providence has left strong marks on Calvinist thought, despite its reputation of intellectualism.[65] There is a lingering tendency toward skepticism that subtly shows itself precisely at the point where Calvin answers the skeptical mind: "Let them inquire and learn from Scripture what is pleasing to God so that they may strive toward this under the Spirit's guidance . . . being ready to follow God wherever he calls."[66]

8

STORIES WE LIVE BY

Contingencies require narrative for their explanation.

—*Stephen Jay Gould*

Introduction

Following the lead in the works of Kenneth Surin and John Swinton, we found that responding to the "why" question is a practical rather than a theoretical task. When in the midst of people's afflictions the "why" question arises, it testifies failing confidence and trust. Bridging the gap in their lives is a matter of beginning to see things differently. Rethinking providence in a Trinitarian way, we began to see how the promise of God to sustain his creation is involved. Following Wright, I explored the thought that providence can be understood as God's presence. God is present in the world with the Spirit in which all things were created, and which holds all things together. The fountain of all that is good has not dried up. It only requires new eyes to see.

When life's contingencies hit them in the most unmerciful way, however, this is not what people experience; what they do experience is the absence of God rather than his presence.

As we have seen, this is ultimately the cause of Job's devastation. Calamity he can handle, up to the point where even the death of his children does not make him turn away from God—nor does the fact that he does not understand why these things are happening. What he cannot accept, however, is that God apparently has abandoned Job and that he does not answer. Job's is the question of why God has forsaken him.

The turning point comes when God responds from the whirlwind and answers Job about his absence. God's response comes with sarcasm similar to that which Job hurled at him before ("Where were you?"). God wants to know, "Where were you when I laid the foundation of the earth? Tell me, if you have understanding. Who determined its measurements—surely you know!" (Job 38:4-5). Then Job comes around and admits that he was led astray by judging things he did not understand. He confesses, "But now I see you with my eyes" (Job 42:5). This is the crucial point. People recover from devastation once a change of heart has opened their eyes to see differently, which is another way of saying that it requires transformation.

In this final chapter, I want to explore this "transformation" by looking once more at a first-person account of disability experience. It is again a story where the birth of a child with a disability looms large upon its parents. From that story we will learn how the spirit of discernment guides the parents to see the gift of love in which all things were created, and which holds all things together, including life with a disabled child. As we will see, the perception of their experience is slowly but gradually changing. It changes from a story of catastrophe into a story of hope. But it certainly required a transformation of their hearts to be able to see this. Bridging the gap, in other words, is the task of rereading one's experience of the past, in a different light, such that a new story emerges. This story will be a story of transformation.

A question of particular concern in this connection is how this transformation is to be God's action. Providence, in whatever understanding, must be rendered as something that God does. God provides. To explain what this means is what the doctrine of providence is supposed to do. If God's providential action is explained as the presence of God's Spirit, then the question must be how this is responsible for the transformation of the human heart that apparently is involved in overcoming the confrontation with disability.

The Story of Joseph

To indicate how these connections are supposed to work, I propose to look at one of the most powerful biblical examples, which is found in the story of Joseph (Gen 37–45). In a nutshell, Joseph finds himself betrayed by his brothers, who hate him for elevating himself above them as the future leader of Jacob's clan. When his sons are out in the field with his herd, Jacob asks Joseph, their younger brother, to see how they are doing. Joseph finds them in Dothan, where they seize him and throw him in the dungeon, left to die. His life is saved, however, by Judah, one of his brothers. Judah convinces the others that a dead brother will not bring them any profit. So he persuades his brothers to sell Joseph to Egyptian merchants and make some money out of this sale, and in this way succeeds in saving his brother's life. At the end of the story, Joseph, elevated to the position of viceroy of Egypt, reminds them of this episode. The brothers are very distressed hearing their history of crime rehearsed, and fear his revenge. But then Joseph speaks:

> I am your brother, Joseph, whom you sold into Egypt. And now do not be distressed, or angry with yourselves, because you sold me there; for God sent me before you to preserve life. For the famine has been in the land these two years; and there are five more years in which there will be neither plowing nor harvest. God sent me before you to preserve for you a remnant on earth, and to keep alive for you many survivors. So it was not you who sent me here but God. (Gen 45:4-7)

There are apparently two readings of the story of Joseph's betrayal by his brothers, then: one from the point of view of human experience (in this case the experience of both Joseph and his brothers), and the other from the point of view of divine providence. On one level, it is the story of jealousy and betrayal by Jacob's sons, who absolutely hate their father's favoritism regarding their younger brother. On another level, it is a story of how God protects Joseph, against all odds, not necessarily for his own sake, but in order to provide Jacob's clan with a savior: "Even though you intended to do harm to me, God intended it for good, in order to preserve a numerous people, as he is doing today" (Gen 50:20).

The logic of this comment indicates how, in Joseph's understanding, his brothers at one time disposed of their father's favorite son, but how *in hindsight* what really happened was something quite different. Their evil deed of selling their brother to Egypt opened up a totally unexpected possibility of a new future, a future that would save Israel's tribe. In other words, the logic explains how a transforming future may arise out of a different account of the past.

This pattern, however, requires that there are alternative readings at hand. One possibility is that such alternative readings are *invented*. As I have read them, both Jean-Dominique Bauby's and Cathy Crimmins' stories show how this might work. Bauby invents "substitute destinies" in order to keep alive the belief that the locked-in syndrome will not become the defining episode in the story of his life. Crimmins' husband invents Mr. Finkelman to create the "second" Alan Forman, who is to replace the "defective" Alan Forman. Both stories provide examples to contrive a future that is different from what the current situation predicts.

In another way, the alternative reading of her story also presents itself in Martha Beck's book. It is initiated by the birth of her son, Adam. Learning to live with this kid with Down syndrome, and particularly the part that Adam himself plays in it, marks the inception of a transforming process in which Martha is "reborn," as the subtitle of her book indicates.

The question that ultimately matters, in all these stories, is this: what is the reading of what has happened to us in which we will place our confidence? What is the story that will enable us to continue living, rather than dying? The very fact that there are alternative readings already implies that some kind of transformation will be involved. People's lives have been disrupted dramatically, and the question is how they adjust themselves to this reality. The fear for this reality stems from the fact that it replaces a known "before" with a largely unknown "after." Alternative stories indicate the ways in which people are struggling to redefine their old selves in the light of their new reality. The question, in other words, is a question of transformation in the process of discovering a new self.

If people do turn to religion, and therefore to God in order to find answers, their questions will be framed accordingly, but not with more certainty. Joseph found his true story *in hindsight*. In the midst of the experience of devastation, hindsight is typically not available. Therefore, when people turn to God in this situation, what may come to their mind is a line from the Lord's Prayer: "Your will be done on earth, as it is in heaven." Then their heart cries out: *But what are you teaching me?*

A Good and Perfect Gift

The story I will read in this connection is Amy Julia Becker's book *A Good and Perfect Gift*, which is about sharing the life of Beckers' family with their daughter Penny. There are many connections with Martha Beck's book, but the difference is that the Beckers did not know a child with Down syndrome was coming their way, so their story starts in the delivery room right after Penny is born. It starts at the moment the doctors indicate that there may be something "wrong" with her. Furthermore, Amy Julia Becker makes explicit what in Martha Beck's book remains implicit— namely, that she tries to understand what is happening to her in terms of divine providence.

Being from the East Coast, Becker has cultural surroundings that also differ from that of the Becks (from Utah). But not unlike the Becks, Amy Julia Becker and her husband are also intellectuals—not necessarily "Harvardized" intellectuals, but intellectuals all the same. One day, when Amy Julia is taking Penny out for a walk, together with Amy Julia's mother, she asks what her mother is reading these days:

> I could feel my throat tightening. I wondered why I had even asked the question. It was one of the things I couldn't stop thinking about, that Penny wouldn't share my love for books, for words, for reading and writing. That I'd never be able to give this part of myself to my daughter.[1]

Her mother responds wisely by saying that Amy Julia is the only one out of four daughters who talks with her about books. This is an attempt to open up the possibility that books might just not be the only way to have a rewarding life. That Penny will not share her mother's life of the mind does not mean that she will not come alive, it only means that she will come alive in a different way.[2]

When they return from their walk outside, Amy Julia goes to her room to have some time for herself, while her mother takes care of Penny. She ponders how words that describe intelligence are related to light, words like bright, and brilliant. Then she thinks of words describing the opposite: dull, or drab. Somehow the opposition does not work because Penny's eyes are full of light and her face and body full of life.[3] It is a moment of the beginning awareness that her daughter's way of having a fulfilling life might be very different from her own, but for the moment this is a discovery that her soul is as yet not able to embrace: "I knew my love for Penny was shattering idols and overturning prejudices and teaching me to value so much more beyond the life of the mind."[4] But right now her sorrow is greater than her hope, and she is grieving the thought that there is a part of her that her daughter will never know.

Amy Julia Becker realizes that to be able to fully accept her daughter Penny, she not only has to adjust to all the hazards that may come with Down syndrome (How is Penny's cardiac condition? What are additional health problems? Will their health insurance cover what needs covering? and so on). The real adjustment goes much deeper than this in that she will have to let go of seeing herself as the intellectual mother who loves chatting with her daughter over the books they read. There are many possible descriptions of herself as a mother that Amy Julia can imagine, but "I am the mother of a child with Down syndrome" is not among them. Not yet. She faces the hard task of letting go of the old self—the image of the mother having conversations, about the life of the mind, with her daughter—and the discovery of a new self, as argued before. This new self is as yet unknown, but it will have, as one of its defining characteristics, her being the mother of a child with Down syndrome.

Fear

As soon as the young mother is informed about her daughter's diagnosis, her response is to be overwhelmed by fear. After some preliminary tests, Penny is brought back to them in the recovery room, where she is handed down to her father, Amy Julia's husband, Peter. He holds her in his arms, rocks her, and strokes her cheek. When she is watching them, Amy Julia finds her mind flooded with questions that block her from seeing the sweetness of Peter become a father. *"How could this happen? What does it mean for her? Will I be able to be proud of her? Will I be able to love her?"*[5]

That very first night, Amy Julia goes through the same plethora of emotions that we have heard about from other parents. It is all about "why?" and "what did we do wrong?" and "how I had come to be this person, this mother."[6] It is as if describing her daughter as a child with Down syndrome turns Amy Julia into a stranger to herself, into "this person."

The time for transformation has not yet come. First there are questions that need answers.

Rereading the notes in her diary from which this episode in her book is composed, Becker is reminded of her expectations during her pregnancy. The ways she describes them perfectly illustrate the supposition of a moral geometry governing her life. She could not imagine that words like "mental retardation" or "birth defect" would be spoken in connection with a child of hers. "It was as if having kids had become an equation: youth plus devotion to God plus education equaled a healthy and normal baby, . . . As if I were entitled to exactly the baby I had imagined, a little version of myself."[7] There was no way that they had deserved this, she told herself, which indicates how Penny was perceived, initially. She was less than expected; she did not fit into the equation.

Of course, the fears spill over to questions regarding their families— "*What if our families don't love her?*"[8]—and others in their environment. Even though husband Peter is a much more a "hands on" kind of person than Amy Julia is, he also has his fears. When Penny is handed down to him for the first time, he welcomes her into his world with a smile: "Hello beautiful." When his wife tells him he is going to be a wonderful father, he shakes his head and responds that he too is afraid. So the young couple is drowning in the questions they are facing: "*What do we do with a child that is mentally retarded? What if people think this is our fault? What if they pity us? What will it take for us to be able to care for her?*"[9]

Having read other people's accounts, Amy Julia knows that at some point these questions receive answers, but, in the moment that these questions arise, the answers are further away than ever. She still has to convince herself that Penny is indeed the daughter she wants. The way she sets the stage for this question is loaded with thoughts about providence. Going back to the early days of her pregnancy, she reminds herself that she was thinking that if she had waited a little longer she could have finished school, and Peter would have had three months free from teaching. But then a different thought hits her, a thought so powerful it was more like hearing than thinking: "*But if you had waited, then you wouldn't have had this child.*"[10]

At the time she actually had these thoughts, Amy Julia did not have a clue about Penny's Down syndrome, and she was sure the child she was carrying was the child she wanted. But now she realizes in hindsight: What if we had waited? We would not have had Penny. Should I have waited, therefore, now that I know her condition?

"Hindsight" is a peculiar phenomenon. It raises a hypothetical question: *had I known then what I know now, would I have willed what was about to happen?* Here I recall how Cathy Crimmins' thoughts go back in time in a similar way. She wanted to turn back the clock, make their little boat leave the dock a few minutes later or earlier and miss the reckless teenager's speedboat. Since she perceives what happened to them only as the loss of "old" Al, her response to the hypothetical question is a resounding "No!" She would at all costs have tried to prevent what was about to happen when her husband left with his little boat. Cathy Crimmins has never shown an interest in rereading their past; she wanted to see her story continued as she knew it before the accident.

In the story of Martha Beck, the opposite is true. When she realizes that all her fears for her family's future with Adam actually came true, and more, her only comment is, "Thank God." The difference between the two stories indicates how hindsight works. Hindsight makes a difference only once one has discovered that one is no longer the same.

Whoever Receives This Child

Should Amy Julia Becker have waited to have a child, now that she knows her daughter's condition? The answer to this question comes not through self-reflection, but from a friend. At the time Penny is born, this friend is gone for a wedding in her family. Back home she finds a message, from Amy Julia, on her phone, in which Amy Julia informs her about Penny's Down syndrome. The next day, they get together on the phone, and soon Amy Julia finds herself comforting her friend, rather than the other way around. At some point in their conversation, her friend, fumbling her words, confesses that she was very upset when she heard about Penny's Down syndrome. But then she was reminded of a few words Jesus said: "Whoever receives this child, receives me." "I looked it up," her friend said. "It is in Mark. I think I was supposed to tell you that."[11]

Amy Julia immediately recalls the second thoughts about her pregnancy at the time when she had said to herself, "Then you wouldn't have had this child." Had they waited, they would not have had Penny. What if her friend was right in reminding her of Jesus' saying?

From here on, a new perspective begins to unfold in Becker's narrative, slowly but gradually, in which this line from the Gospel of Mark returns several times. What if for some reason, not yet known to her, she was meant to have this child. Later that same night, she is going back to the months of her pregnancy, and the tests and the ultrasounds and the delivery itself, and she keeps asking herself what she could have done differently. The countering thought that Penny's life, the extra chromosome and all, may be purposeful is just too much.[12]

As this reflection admirably testifies, discovering a new perspective is not a task to be mastered, because it is not something the person involved has under control. Her friend indicated a different perspective (you may have received a gift), and so did her mother (not all people thrive on books; some people thrive on other things), but Amy Julia is not yet there to make these thoughts her own.

A few weeks later, her husband, Peter, is away with a sports team of the school where he teaches. He calls his wife to say hello and tells her that he met a woman in the street, struggling to get through too many inches of snow while attempting to cross over. "I told the team to go ahead," he said, "and went back to help her." He had not really been looking at her, and when she turned to him, he noticed she had Down syndrome. "I just hope there will be someone who goes out of their way to help our daughter cross the street," Peter says.[13]

"Help" is a word that one normally would not relate to the Beckers, Amy Julia realizes. They are everything that people usually appreciate: well educated, good looking, in shape, well-to-do, and so on. They are people very much in control of their own lives—that is, until Penny comes along. She recalls having a conversation with Peter, before they were married, about not having children. Each of them had asked themselves this same question, and both had answered with a resounding "Yes": no children at all was definitely an option. The reason was they did not like limitation. They were people used to doing what they wanted, enjoying lots of work and lots of freedom:

> And here we were, with a child who would limit us more than we ever imagined. Penny would walk later than other kids and with less stability. Her body was more prone to infection. She would have troubles solving problems. She might never live on her own.[14]

When Peter comes back from the sports trip, his wife is almost lost in the many questions that are on her mind, but there is one that she fires away as soon as he is home: "If you could take away the extra chromosome," she asks, "would you?"[15] The question makes perfect sense. Only a few months earlier, she would not even have noticed reading in the newspaper about the seemingly hopeless diagnosis of "mental retardation." Nor would she have frowned upon her hairdresser's advice to have her children before the age of thirty-five, "so they won't be screwed up." In other words, before Penny came along, Amy Julia accepted all the unreflective common sense judgments about children like hers, and she is still not over them—hence the question about the extra chromosome. Her husband answers, "Yes, if I could take it away, I would." Amy Julia responds she would do so too.[16]

Haunted by these words, she realizes how strong her love for her baby has grown in such a short time, but part of her also says that Penny's Down syndrome is a gift she does not appreciate. This is a troublesome thought. It triggers memories from the days she received the gifts that made her very grateful, and very aware, of God's provision in her life—not this time, however.

Yet she is ready to admit that there are beacons of light. For example, there is the Down syndrome support group that is a great help in the first six months; it is a group of five or six young couples, in the same situation, to share stories with. It fills her with gratitude: "I had been given this group of people, even though part of me wanted to resist the gift."[17]

On another occasion Becker then reminds herself of a Bible class in church and what they had been studying there: Jesus telling his disciples, time and again, that their calling is to receive him, that their life with him would be a life of abundance, but that it would take them nonetheless where they would *not* want to go. That is very much like how she feels right now. Their newborn daughter will bring them a life not of their choosing. But then she also recognizes her growing love for Penny and begins to understand the process that she is going through:

> Every time I recognized the purity of my love for Penny, I was dying to an old part of myself, an old part that thought that the only ones worth loving were the ones who could be productive and articulate and considered attractive and successful.[18]

Here we find the beginning of the same kind of transformation that we found in Martha Beck's book. From what both of these mothers tell us, we understand that it does not come easy, not at all, but coming it is: slowly and irresistibly, but with a lot of agony and birth pain. There is the old self, the self that harbors all the prejudices about disability, particularly when framed as "mental retardation." But this old self now has to find a way to get renewed. Phrased in this way, the question accurately indicates the complex relationship of activity and passivity in these stories. Like Martha Beck, Amy Julia will be renewed, but she nonetheless has to find her way to let this happen.

How? Amy Julia does not have a clue, but realizes that at the time Jesus was telling his disciples this message, they had no clue either. The only thing they knew was what Jesus told them: "No false piety, no stoicism. Just a statement of reality: The road ahead would be hard, but this is the road where I will be with you."[19] One thing about her own road ahead is absolutely certain: Penny will have Down syndrome, no matter what! *Whoever receives this child receives me.* The remaining question is how to receive the gift.

"Just Penny"

Remembering how her mother had pointed out to Amy Julia that Penny would come alive, even if not through her intellect, but she was grieving the fact that she would not share reading books with her daughter, a thought stuck in her mind. What was there to be sad about? Really? Failing IQ scores? Less than average physical strength? She always assumed it to be very sad to have a child with an intellectual disability or to be a person with such a disability. But why? Of course, in a Nietzschean universe Penny's existence was a tragedy, an abnormality, biology gone wrong. "But in a God-created universe, what was good and not good in her? And was it different from that which was good and not good in the rest of us?"[20]

The answer to this question comes in an unexpected way. Asking herself again and again how her daughter would have been without the extra chromosome, Amy Julia begins to see what is wrong with wondering what the "real" Penny is like, the one that is hidden behind her diagnosis. She wants to be able to change her daughter instead of receiving change herself.[21] The thought indicates the beginning awareness that a change of self will be involved in accepting Penny as she is.

In the meantime the machinery of medical tests and examinations is turning full speed, with Amy Julia running around like crazy between hospitals and clinics and sharing results with the parents of the Down syndrome support group. Even though none of Penny's test results is particularly alarming, these visits are loaded with statements from doctors and therapists about Penny's delayed development, about how she compares to other kids with Down syndrome, and about what she might or might not be able to do or learn.

Amy Julia strongly resents these messages, well intended as they are. After their visit to the geneticist, she complains to her husband about being fed up with information: "I want to hear this kid with Down syndrome loves the tuba, and this other one loves playing golf with his dad, and this one has a hard time spelling but loves to dance."[22] No more statistics! No more predictions of who Penny will never be. Amy Julia wants just stories:

> It was still hard for me to believe that she wouldn't solve math problems or read literature. And yet it was easy to believe that she would rush to a friend, or even a stranger, in need. Easy to believe that she would continue to bring light and life. And it was getting easier to believe that, as time went on, she would tell me the stories that I needed to hear.[23]

What are the stories, then, that Amy Julia is missing? Actually, they are stories that are all around her, and have been for some time, if only she will learn to take notice. Here is one of them. She and Penny are visited by a few high school girls whom Amy Julia has assisted with their Bible studies. Being at home in Amy Julia's house, one of the girls picks up a birth announcement with a picture of Penny on it. "It's perfect," she says, as if nothing else matters. She shows it to the other girls. They agree. Perfect.

Amy Julia is stunned. She has a perfect life? Her life is as imperfect as it has ever been! She reviews her daily hassles of getting everything done, the questions, and the tears, but she does not tell the girls, of course. Then, on top of it all, there is Penny's Down syndrome. What is so perfect about that? Does not the language surrounding Down syndrome persistently suggest a special state of imperfection—abnormal, birth defect, cell division gone wrong?[24]

After the girls have left, she is alone with her daughter, giving her a massage to stimulate her muscle tone. A word from the Gospel comes to her mind: "Be perfect as your heavenly father is perfect." She interrupts her massage, and retrieves her Greek dictionary. The root of the word perfect, she finds out is *telos*. It can be translated as "perfect," but it can also be translated as "the end for which you were created."[25]

Now there is a thought! Penny created for a purpose? A perfect family they would never be, Amy Julia knows that for sure. But maybe her daughter would bring them closer to becoming the family *they were created to be*. "A seed had been planted in that fallow ground, through a comment from a high school student." Elated by this discovery, Amy Julia lays down on the floor next to her daughter, and is happy: "A shaft of sunshine warmed my shoulder and bathed her face in light. She grabbed hold of my index finger and I whispered, 'Hello, beautiful girl. And thank you.'"[26]

The things that are happening in our lives can be read in any number of ways, I said earlier in this book. So your firstborn turns out to be a child with Down syndrome. How are you going to read that? A tragedy? What is the story you think this tragedy is going to be part of? Just a matter of tough luck? A bad straw in the genetic lottery? "Biology gone wrong," as Amy Julia likes to phrase it herself? Are there different stories to be told, and if so, what are they?

Her desire for a different story indicates that Amy Julia Becker is done with reading her life with her daughter in ways that mainly tell her how to deal with "deficit." The whole variety of "who sinned?" stories no longer work for her, which also holds for the ones with a more contemporary spin, such as "whose genes are screwed up?"[27] In the end they only keep one from seeing what there is to see:

> And as much as I wanted order and reasons—as much as I wanted answers, even if those answers included judgment—instead I received this truth: Penny is neither a rebuke nor a reward. She is a child. Not a product of sin, nor a biological happenstance, nor any lesson we needed to learn. No, this happened that the glory of God might be revealed.[28]

With that thought Amy Julia feels her anger dissolve, she says. When she wakes up the next morning it is not the birds she hears. "It was the babbling sounds of my daughter, awakening me to the day."[29]

The stories that Amy Julia Becker needed to hear, it appears, were the ones that enable her to find her new self. The thought that Penny was born so that the glory of God might be revealed sticks in her mind. It means that there is nothing in her daughter that keeps her mother from saying that she is perfect. There is nothing wrong with Penny; she *is* the end of her creation.

This very message is brought home to Amy Julia, sometime later, by one of the high school girls mentioned before. She walks into their house to find Penny sitting on the floor, clapping, bouncing, waving, and doing her newest cute trick: taking her face between her two hands with a lovely smile.[30] Amy Julia is shaking her head with unbelief. "I could never have imagined that my daughter with Down syndrome would be like this," Amy Julia says. The girl shakes her head, waits a moment, and then responds, "She is not your daughter with Down syndrome. She's just Penny."[31]

Recalling the many stages of disappointment and grief that the Beckers—like most families—have been going through, one cannot but feel how totally redeeming that remark must have been. At any rate, that is what Amy Julia feels:

> I felt a wave of recognition wash over me, as if my heart had been waiting to hear the truth of her statement. It had taken us nearly a year, but we finally figured it out. Penny was not a mistake. She wasn't a Down syndrome baby. To us, she was even no longer our-daughter-with-Down-syndrome. She was just Penny.[32]

A New Self

Providence, to cut a long story short, is about how the love that God sends into our lives guides us in discovering a new self, the self that finds itself at the other side of the chasm and, in that sense, is transformed to receive a new future. This is the provision God makes through the presence of the Spirit.

In the previous paragraphs, we have received a glimpse of how this works. Amy Julia is gradually changing in her views and perceptions of her daughter. When this happens it is mostly by instigation of people surrounding her, commenting upon how she views their experience, in ways that make her see differently. The "why" question is losing its grip on her, in the sense that it is unmasked as a question that derogates their daughter Penny as the true gift of life. The presence of the Spirit is embodied, in other words, by those who raise questions that succeed in opening up Amy

Julia's soul in her capacity of being Penny's mother. Yes, she is the mother of a child with Down syndrome, and it is good.

Understanding providence, therefore, is not about trying to figure out why God sends these events upon you rather than others. There is no way of answering the "why" question in those terms with any degree of confidence, because from the perspective of human experience, it all appears a matter of fortune and chance: being in the wrong place at the wrong time, a stupid accident, cell division run amok, biology gone wrong, and so on. More importantly, even, in trying to answer the "why" question one is likely to miss the most important point, which is to ask not why God is "the doer"—to quote Calvin—but how he is present in the midst of people's affliction. To answer this question, one needs to learn to see with different eyes.

In the meantime, however, the events that caused the crisis remain what they are. Realizing this is very important. The fact that Amy Julia Becker learned to see differently does not eradicate the distress that Penny has to endure—for example, from all the necessary visits to doctors and clinics. Put more generally, the belief in divine providence is extremely harmful when it is taken to mean that all is well that ends well. The wrong inference would be to assume that *because* past events are seen in a different light, the meaning originally ascribed to them was mistaken.

Why that conclusion would be a false one is again indicated by Joseph's story. When Joseph tells his brothers that God saved him, he does not mean to cover their crime. He seeks to comfort his brothers by showing them what *really* happened, but he does not spare them the truth about what they did to him: "I am your brother, Joseph, *whom you sold into Egypt. And now do not be distressed, or angry with yourselves, because you sold me there.*" Similarly, later in the text, he says, "Even though *you intended to do harm to me,* God intended it for the good." God's redemptive action is *only* real because the experience that he is redeeming was real.[33]

Consequently, what has changed in the course of Becker's story is not Penny's disability, but Amy Julia's ability to see. Penny is going to have an extra chromosome in every cell of her body no matter what. She is, and never will be other than, a person with Down syndrome. Whatever causes people with Down syndrome to suffer in their lives will be part of Penny's life too, one way or another. To accept this, and at the same time accept that life is good as it is, is hard work, and it will remain so.

Discovering a new self, then, is far from being an act of joy. It hurts and can be very, very painful, as our stories testify. "Hallelujah" is hindsight, if it comes at all. Perhaps "self-denial" is a word that comes to mind, but to regard it as such would be a mistake too. Self-denial signifies a willful decision, not to speak of strategy. But the old self is not given up as a deliberate act of self-denial. It dies, but this death is not of one's choosing. It is dying spiritually. It is the self losing itself.

Here we see the beginning of an answer to the question I raised in the introduction to this final chapter—how is being transformed to be God's action? The answer comes as a negative: at any rate, this process is beyond our control. It is not a deliberate act of a believer who understands it must die spiritually. Far from it. It is an unsolicited task, about the last thing one would choose to do: accepting "death" of oneself at a moment when it is far from clear that there will be a new self and far from clear how one will be "reborn," if at all. Nothing in this process is under control. Each and every one of the stories we have been reading in these chapters tells us about people who are lost in their world. The new self is not a project; it is not something one can *find* in an active sense, insofar as "finding" presupposes knowing what one is looking for. One does not know.

Nor is it something one discovers on one's own account. This is where the positive part of the answer to the above question starts kicking in. It is usually other people—friends and relatives, occasionally professional people—who hint at different ways of looking at things, not so much by way of advice—"you may try looking at it differently"—but by way of demonstration, like the high school girl in Becker's story, or the old farmer selling shrubs at the supermarket's parking lot in Martha Beck's story.

Whatever the particularities of these stories, they testify when and how people's understanding of their pasts can change. This is seen clearly in the stories of Martha and Amy Julia. They discover aspects of themselves in the past that they now regard as questionable. In their stories this plays out in the unreflective "common sense" kind of prejudice about people with intellectual disabilities—"mental retardation"—that they initially shared with their surrounding culture. Learning to see differently led them to conclude that old selves can be pretty much blinded from seeing what there is to see.

In this respect, the fact they have been guided by others marks another important point. The people that succeed in opening up Martha and Amy

Julia do not preach; they do not admonish, let alone rebuke. They simply demonstrate a way of looking differently: "I don't think your daughter is a child with Down syndrome. She's just Penny." Or: "Things aren't always what they seem, are they?"

These are true moments of wonder. These are moments of redeeming consolation, in which we recognize the *Paraclete*—that is, the Spirit of Christ. "I felt a wave of recognition wash over me" is Amy Julia's response to the girl making the remark about her daughter being just Penny. "As if my heart had been waiting to hear the truth." These are moments of confirmation that there will be ways to bridge the gap. But much of this takes time. Believing providence takes time. *Knowing* that God has not abandoned you is knowing *in hindsight*. But not only does it take time; it needs reconfirmation too, from time to time, because the disability experience is not going away.

Finally, the presence of others, in whose words and deeds the Spirit of Christ receives practical embodiment, turns out to be redeeming. It sustains people existentially and spiritually in their experience with disability. An attempt of rethinking providence in terms of God's presence, rather than his judgment, may inspire us to find ways of being present in this redeeming sense.

"Honesty"

Finding a connection between the "before" and "after" that can bridge the gap does not always follow the same pattern. Sometimes the loss is permanent, and there is not much of a life coming back, as is the case with Jean-Dominique Bauby. But even there we saw the beginning of a new day, when he realizes the presence of reliable friends who have been with him from his very first day in the hospital. Would it be too much to say that the spirit of discernment would regard the presence of these friends as a reason to thank God for the fact that Bauby in his loneliness was not left behind?

For Cathy Crimmins the outcome remains ambivalent. Cathy cannot leave behind the man who sang "Wild Thing" at their wedding party. Or is it perhaps more adequate to say that she cannot leave the woman behind who was addressed with that song? Even though Cathy admits that after his recovery Alan Forman is a happier man than he used to be, she nonetheless would give anything to get back the man who married her.

Trying to understand the experience of TBI survivors appears to be more complex, therefore. Someone like Alan Forman certainly had to discover his new self after the accident, and the sense in which he is said to be "happier" afterward may indicate the extent to which the old self is left behind. The situation for close relatives might to be different, however, insofar as they may be inclined to stick to the memories of a past they treasure. When they do, the challenge of affirming a new life will be much harder. For Cathy Crimmins the past has not changed; she has just lost it. She therefore faces the difficult task of living a new life with an old self.

Is her story the sadder one, as I suggested before? In a sense, I would say, it is. She is looking up to the "Other Cathy," the one that Al creates when he is trying to figure out how a new life for his family is going to be possible. She takes this figment of his imagination as rebuke, because she thinks she is lousy at taking care of people. She has pushed herself in the corner of Al's room, so to speak, as "not the caring type." This is sad, because page after page testifies to her doing exactly that, caring for her husband and daughter. But as her conversation with Al's case manager indicates, she wants herself to be regarded as an independent woman, with a life of her own. The case manager offers her consolation by telling her that she is mourning for their lost life together. But Cathy does not want her life to be lost; she wants it back. Even a holiday trip to the coast, that she thinks was "heaven," cannot prevent her from answering the neighbor's question, about being restored to their former life, by saying that it is a "reasonable facsimile."

What follows from this story, then, theologically speaking? Was there no presence of the Spirit in this case? I do not see the reason to deny that there was. Friends that accompanied her every day to visit Al, the people from the hospital, and particularly the people from the rehab center. They all indicate that her family had not been abandoned. The Christian faith says that God does not abandon people, not even when he has to die for it.

In Cathy Crimmins' story, "dying" seems to be the issue, however. God offers his presence in the Spirit of Christ, but he does not force the gift upon people, as I said before. God wants to be received in freedom. What we have learned, however, is that knowing how to receive the gift seems to involve parting from one's old self. When he is asked whether the kingdom is coming, Jesus responds that the kingdom is not coming with things one can see. So he tells his audience not to go and look for it somewhere, because it is already among them. But to see this requires a transformation: "Those who try to make their life secure will lose it, but those who lose their life will keep it" (Luke 17:33).

There is a caveat regarding these comments, however. In the attempt to arrive at some level of understanding, it is easy to be carried away by "happy ending" stories, such as are told by Becker and Beck, since they demonstrate a human heart transformed in the process of overcoming catastrophe. But this does not mean that, in the not-so-happy-ending stories, the notion of a transformation is entirely absent. It may be working by default. For some people the not-so-happy-ending stories seem to indicate that all this transformation business is fine, but that it does not work for them. In their view, there is something disingenuous about this language of "being transformed" by the experience of disability, given the horrors it entails. For example, a striking aspect of some of the book reviews of Cathy Crimmins' story is the frequent laudation of its "honesty," indicating the presumption that the more it depicts disability experience as "horrific," the more "honest" the story must be. Consequently, since there is no hint of transformation to a new Cathy, the story must be true, or so it seems for these reviewers.

Remember, however, that Martha Beck assured her readers that everything she feared about living with Adam's Down syndrome came true, and some of it was even worse than she had anticipated. The difference between "happy ending" and "not-so-happy-ending" stories, therefore, may not be the degree of "horror," or "tragedy," or even pain. Nor may it lie in the level of "honesty" with which their narrators describe their experience. The difference may well reside in the question of what they have learned to see.

While honesty has everything to do with it, this does not mean that the only honesty that counts is a raw description of the facts. The honesty involved in transformation is the willingness of letting go and discovering why, in certain respects, the self that one is leaving behind is indeed "old."

Within the Christian tradition, the language of a "new self" is not innocent, of course, because it is fraught with eschatological meaning. Whoever has received a new self is a witness to the coming of the kingdom, according to Paul, because becoming this new self is what it means to participate in the life of God. This is at any rate what Paul means when he is speaking of those who have received a life in the Spirit as "first fruits" (Rom 8:22). That is why the words of Amy Julia Becker's friend—"Whoever

receives this child, receives me"—were so heavily charged with eschatological meaning. They opened up the question of whether Penny is not just
the person she is created *to be*.

In the meantime, however, we have to understand that "receiving this
child" is not just an equivalent of "giving birth to." As Amy Julia Becker's
story demonstrates so well, "receiving" is an act of an undivided heart.
Once this is understood, nothing could be more evident than what this
friend is telling her. If you know how to receive Penny as part of God's creation, then, surely, you will receive Christ, because in him all things were
created, and in him all things hold together.

Providence Revisited

The stories in which we find our lives evolving can be read in any number
of ways. The occurring events are not fixed entities but derive their specific meaning from the light in which they are seen. Usually the dominant
light comes from our own purposes, the things we want, and the things we
expect to get out of our lives. In case life's contingencies hit us, and hit us
hard, the "why" question arises from our souls. The question signifies the
lack of coherence, of life stories falling apart. Bringing the notion of God's
providence to bear on these experiences is tricky, because it easily falls
into the trap of ending up as "cheap theology." But there may be a point
in the attempt, because it may make a difference—not to silence people's
lament, but to change the light by which they are trying to move on. There
may be a different way of looking at things.

With this suggestion the stage is set for revisiting the doctrine of providence, which we will do in this final section, as a summary of the main
argument of this book. By and large the Christian tradition is in agreement
that divine providence is about the question of how God works in creation,
but there is much less agreement as to how his action, in this respect, is to
be understood. Disputed in particular is the doctrine of God's "special"
providence, by which is meant his direct intervention in human affairs for
the good of his creatures, a doctrine that has stirred much debate, at least
within the Protestant tradition. This we have discussed in looking at Calvin's theology.

There we have seen that it is perceived as "deterministic" because of its
tendency to undermine human responsibility and freedom. And indeed, it
is not difficult to find passages in Calvin's work to support this perception,

passages that make one understand why his doctrine came to be characterized as a grim creed for strong men.[34] I only recall his response to Augustine's attempt to forestall the idea that God should be responsible for the
evil done by his creatures, which made Calvin insist that God does not
merely permit evil deeds but actually *wills* them. God openly declares "that
he is the doer," according to Calvin.[35] In the same connection, he criticized Augustine's position for trying "to clear God's justice of every sinister
mark," which left us with the question of just how sinister God's justice may
appear to be, before it ceases to be recognizable as justice.

For Calvin such a question would be entirely inappropriate. It suggests that human beings are in a position to hold God accountable for
what he does or does not do. It betrays the arrogance of people who have
forgotten that it is their Maker that they are questioning. This explains
why Calvin did not like Job. In view of his "arrogance," Calvin insisted
on the unfathomable difference between the Creator and creation. Even
when human beings had not fallen into sin, they still would not be able to
understand providence—hence the recurring emphasis on the incomprehensibility and hiddenness of God's will.

For two reasons this emphasis caused Calvin great difficulty in
explaining with a sufficient degree of confidence how God's providence
works. The greater the emphasis on the hiddenness and incomprehensibility of God, the lesser the reassurance that the belief in his providence
might bring. Since this pastoral concern was Calvin's most important aim,
this was a serious difficulty. The second reason is that it was not at all easy
to understand how a hidden will could produce effects in the world.

Calvin's solution was to rely on the classical distinction between
primary and secondary causation in order to explain how God's providence works, and in doing so he constantly reminded his readers of the
limitations of human understanding. Providence, he argued, can only be
understood with a reverent heart and with "becoming humility." But thus
arguing, he in fact *presupposed* the kind of reassurance that his doctrine
was aimed to install.

The main problem of this classical distinction, as we have seen, is in
explaining God's will within the conceptual frame of causality. It will turn
out very difficult not to explain the divine will as the equivalent of a natural
cause. Calvin was aware of this problem, of course, and insisted that God
only uses things in this world—historical events, human actions, nature's

works—as instruments for his own purposes, while remaining transcendent from the world of secondary causes. It is hard to see, however, how something that is not itself a natural cause can have the same effects as natural causes. The question led me to conclude that the distinction between primary and secondary causation does not explain anything at all.

More importantly still is the conclusion that in using this distinction, Calvin failed to say anything substantial about purpose, with regard to God's providential action. If everything in the world can be used as an instrument of his will because hie is in control of it all, then the only thing we have learned is that God is the greatest imaginable superpower in the universe. This is particularly true when all our queries about purpose are answered in terms of God's secret plan, as Calvin was wont to do.

It is at this point that we switched to the question of whether the work of Christ should not give a Christian theology of providence its particular direction. Here we followed the inspiration from Karl Barth's theology to ask how understanding providence will turn out when we realize that it is the Triune God we are thinking about. We took as our lead Calvin's claim that God will illuminate the minds of his own with the gift of the spirit that enables us to discern the true nature of his providence.

Thinking about this claim led to this question as to what it means to speak of the spirit of discernment as a gift. This question was answered by reference to the witness of the apostle Paul, where he is saying that the spirit of discernment is the Spirit that God has sent into the world through God's Son. Paul's confession of Christ's mediating role in creation in Colossians 1:16-17 provided the key. All things have been created through him and for him. He himself is before all things, and in him all things hold together. One could say that from a Christian perspective this is the answer to Jean-Dominique Bauby's question, "Does the cosmos have keys?" The answer is this: it does. The key is that all things are created and hold together in Christ.

Does this answer mean that, in the end, this inquiry is failing in its intention to honor lament and not silence the "why" question? I hope not.

There are two reasons for believing that it does not silence people. The first is that the argument does not in any way seek to answer the "why" question; it only seeks to understand theologically what happened in our stories that made the question go away as part of an old self. The second reason is that in this attempt we discovered the crucial role of consoling friends who with their presence help others to regain confidence that life can be good again. Their presence is redeeming, as I said before, but it is so only because what needs redeeming is *real*. The experience of redemption is to see differently in looking back. It is hindsight. Understanding providence in this manner is honoring lament, therefore, in that it takes full measure of people's affliction, without allowing it to have the last word. The redeeming presence of loving kindness and friendship has the last word.

From here the question as to the purpose of God's providence is substantiated as well. If providence is the activity with which God sustains creation, it follows that the purpose of this activity is identified in Christ's name: Immanuel, "God with us." God is with us as the Christ who is present in the gift of the Spirit that God the Father sent upon him, and that he has promised to his friends. God's provision for those who are open to receive his gift is the gift of the Spirit, the *Paraclete*, who will be with them to comfort them and guide them. Those who have received the gift of the Spirit will find themselves changed. They have received being changed, as Amy Julia Becker put it.

Guided by the light of this Spirit they learn to see differently, because it is the spirit of self-giving love. That is what the Holy Spirit does. It communicates the love of Christ to human beings so that they will love one another. The Spirit has poured this love into their hearts. These things are inseparable, as Paul says to his fellow Christians in Rome.

Finally we asked about the practical meaning of this gift. If people find themselves changed, what are they changed from, and what are they changed to? This question took us back to the immediate concern of this inquiry: people's response when they are all of a sudden confronted by disability. The first-person accounts that we have been reading indicate the response of a benumbing fear because people feel that their lives are falling apart and that their expectations and hopes for the future are gone. What they are changed from is hopelessness.

What they are changed to is something we have also read in their stories, as it was particularly well articulated by the story we read in this chapter. They are changed into a new self that enables them to negotiate the gap between the "before" and "after" by trusting the reality of friendship and love. The fountain of all that is good has not dried up; it continues to pour out friendship and love to those who are open to it. These are people who have learned how to die as an old self, which they managed to do because they found new eyes to see. Only to the extent that they are transformed into a new self, people succeed in moving beyond the initial experience of disability as a tragedy. Providence is the active presence of God, mediated by the Spirit, to guide us in learning to see the new life that is around us, and is there to be seen.

The stories people live by are full of contingencies, the experience of which needs to be negotiated and dealt with, otherwise it cannot become part of their stories. Again, this is not to deny that disrupted lives are lives lived in pain and agony. Sometimes the disruption is very, very hard, and there is not much one can do about it. Many people experience the confrontation with disability in this way.

It does not need to have the last word, however. The stories we have read in these chapters suggest that there is a possible response, even when this experience is very painful. This response is to allow oneself to be guided by the reality of friendship and love in facing the daunting task ahead. Whenever this happens, when friendship and love have revived their hearts, it is not unusual for people to say, "We have been blessed."

NOTES

Foreword

1 Karl Barth, *Church Dogmatics*, ed. G. W. Bromiley and T. F. Torrance (Edinburgh: T&T Clark, 1957–1975), III.3 §48 The Doctrine of Providence, Its Basis and Form, 18.

2 Barth, *Church Dogmatics*, III.3, §48, 18.

Chapter 1

1 This chapter expands on material taken from Hans Reinders, "Is There Meaning in Disability? Or Is It the Wrong Question?" *Journal of Religion, Disability & Health* 15, no. 1 (2011): 57–71.

2 BBC Disability Ministry, www.webjam.com/bbc_disability_ministry.

3 Gregory Fraser, "Ars Poetica," in *Strange Pièta* (Lubbock, Tex.: Texas Tech University Press, 2003), 3. I am indebted to Susannah B. Mintz' paper "Ordinary Vessels: Disability Narrative and Representations of Faith," *Disability Studies Quarterly* 26, no. 3 (2006), accessed July 29, 2011, http://www.dsq-sds.org/issue/view/34. I will return to the paper later in this chapter.

4 Thomas E. Reynolds, *Vulnerable Communion: A Theology of Disability and Hospitality* (Grand Rapids: Brazos, 2008), 37.

5 Examples are found in William C. Gaventa Jr. and David L. Coulter, eds., *Spirituality and Intellectual Disability: International Perspectives on the Effect of Culture and Religion on Healing Body, Mind, and Soul* (New York: Haworth, 2001), but these examples are not particular for monotheistic religions. For references to indigenous religious

views, see, e.g., Samuel Kabue, Esther Momba, Joseph Galgalo, and C. B. Peter, eds., *Disability, Society, and Theology: Voices from Africa* (Limuru, Kenya: Zapf Chancery, 2011).

6 Amy Julia Becker, "Raising Children with Disabilities in an Age of Achievement," presentation for The Summer Institute on Theology and Disability, Catholic Theological Union, Chicago, July 18, 2012 (unpublished).

7 In the next section, I will return to this point.

8 Reynolds, *Vulnerable Communion*.

9 Reinders, "Is There Meaning in Disability?" 62.

10 Nancy Eiesland, "Liberation, Inclusion, and Justice: A Faith Response to Persons with Disabilities," in *Impact: Feature Issue on Faith Communities and Persons with Developmental Disabilities* 14, no. 3 (2001/2002): 2–3, published in Minneapolis by the University of Minnesota's Institute on Community Integration and edited by A. N. Amado, B. Gaventa, V. Gaylord, R. Norman-McNaney, and S. R. Simon.

11 Arne Fritzson, "Disability and Meaning," in Arne Fritzson and Samuel Kabue, *A Church of All for All: An Interim Statement*, WCC document, released September 2, 2003 (Geneva: World Council of Churches, 2003), 1–23.

12 World Council of Churches, *A Church of All and for All*, 3.

13 World Council of Churches, *A Church of All and for All*, 3.

14 Eiesland, "Liberation, Inclusion, and Justice," 2.

15 Nancy L. Eiesland, *The Disabled God: Toward a Liberatory Theology of Disability* (Nashville: Abingdon, 1994), 24.

16 Eiesland, *The Disabled God*, 25–26.

17 Eiesland, "Liberation, Inclusion, and Justice," 2.

18 Eiesland, "Liberation, Inclusion, and Justice," 2.

19 Eiesland, "Liberation, Inclusion, and Justice," 2.

20 Eiesland, "Liberation, Inclusion, and Justice," 3.

21 An impressive example for the field of psychology is provided by Chris F. Goodey's masterful work *A History of Intelligence and of Intellectual Disability: The Shaping of Psychology in Early Modern Europe* (Burlington, Vt.: Ashgate, 2011).

22 This task is not particular to Christian theology, because one finds exactly the same argument in Judaism and Islam. See Hans S. Reinders, "Theology and Disability: What is the Question?" in *Searching for Dignity: Conversations on Human Dignity, Theology, and Disability*, ed. Julie M. Claassens, Leslie Swartz, and Len Hansen (Stellenbosch, South Africa: Sun Media, 2013), 31–42.

23 I am referring to the Gospel of John 9:2.

24 See above, ch. 1 n. 20; see also Eiesland, "Liberation, Inclusion, and Justice," 6–7.

25 See, among others, Harold H. Wilke, *Creating the Caring Congregation: Guidelines for Ministering with the Handicapped* (Nashville: Abingdon, 1980); Stewart D. Govig, *Strong at the Broken Places: Persons with Disabilities and the Church* (Louisville, Ky.: Westminster John Knox, 1989); Deborah Creamer, "Finding God in Our Bodies: Theology from the Perspective of People with Disabilities," *Journal of Religion in Disability & Rehabilitation* 2, no. 1 (1995): 27–42; Kathy Black, *A Healing Homiletic:*

Preaching and Disability (Nashville: Abingdon, 1996). See also Eiesland, *The Disabled God*; Reynolds, *Vulnerable Communion*. I will return to these negative responses in the next section.

26   Reynolds, *Vulnerable Communion*, 11–13. The same experience is had by students in institutions for higher education in theology who are refused because they are deemed unfit, either for church ministry or for theological research. Robert C. Anderson, ed., *Graduate Theological Education and the Human Experience of Disability* (Binghamton, N.Y.: Haworth, 2003).

27   Reynolds, *Vulnerable Communion*, 16.

28   Criticizing this dichotomy, disability studies scholars have coined the phrase of the "temporarily able bodied" to indicate that "disability," in some form or other, is part of the human condition. It does not contradict the human condition, as the dichotomizing distinctions suggest.

29   "They have pronounced us sacraments of grace, without listening to our fierce passion to be participants not sacraments." Eiesland, "Liberation, Inclusion, and Justice," 35.

30   See Hans S. Reinders, *Receiving the Gift of Friendship: Profound Disability, Theological Anthropology and Ethics* (Grand Rapids: Eerdmans, 2008), 43–44.

31   See Larry J. Waters, "Reflections on Suffering from the Book of Job," *Bibliotheca Sacra* 154 (1997): 436–51.

32   As we will see later in chapters 6 and 7, this is the problem that caused John Calvin much trouble in his doctrine of providence.

33   "The Psalter is remarkably unified as a reflection on the path from lostness into God's story, incorporating us in God's not-yet completed journey." Brian Brock, *Singing the Ethos of God: On the Place of Christian Ethics in Scripture* (Grand Rapids: Eerdmans, 2007), xvii–xviii.

34   When these lines were written, the world was in shock about the shooting of seventy teenagers in a youth camp in Norway on Friday, July 22, 2011. Imagine yourself in the position of their families, and you will realize that punishment and reward have very little to do with it. Numerous other examples could be added that would suggest the same.

35   In an interesting study on incomprehensibility, Martin Hailer points effectively to this correlation. He says that the classical theological conception that posited the absolute divine attributes as its starting point (like omnipotence, eternity, etc.) could not but use the doctrine of providence as an aid to explain why the experience of adversity and suffering does not contradict divine absoluteness. This resulted in the view that people can only be comforted by the belief they do not suffer because of fate or chance, but because of the hand of their God. Consequently, according to Hailer, the will of a loving God to which adversity and suffering are attributed cannot but appear as incomprehensible. Martin Hailer, *Die Unbegreiflichkeit des Reiches Gottes* (Neukirchen-Vluyn: Neukrichner Verlag, 2004), 36. As we will see much later in this study, Hailer's insight is vindicated entirely in Calvin's doctrine of providence.

36   In his book on providence, the Dutch Calvinist Gerrit Berkouwer opens his chapter on the subject with the claim that "theodicy is a justification of God's providential rule,"

thus tying the two issues closely together. Gerrit C. Berkouwer, *The Providence of God* (Grand Rapids: Eerdmans, 1952), 232. In the course of his exposition, it appears that Berkouwer regards the "why" question as its central concern that needs to be taken seriously, but that he rejects the theodicy in the usual sense of justifying God in view of evil (246–48, 249–50). In his otherwise impressive study *Theology and Disability: Reimagining Disability in Late Modernity* (Waco, Tex.: Baylor University Press, 2007), Amos Yong also discusses the doctrine of providence by linking it immediately to the theodicy question, which he names—with a term borrowed from Christian Link—the "unresolved problem" of the doctrine of providence (160). Yong's primary concern is to dislodge the connection between the occurrence of disability and the notion of the fall. In the traditional view, the fall is responsible for evil, both moral and natural, such that disability, when viewed as evil, must be its consequence, and, therefore, must be attributed to original sin. Yong leaves this traditional view behind by finding support for his disability perspective in new developments both in theology and the sciences that leads him to argue that disability cannot be attributed directly to the will of God since it is quite frequently caused by contingencies such as genetic mutation (162–96). However, Yong never returns to the question of providence that remains *independent* from the question of theodicy. Even when it is accepted that the occurrence of disability very often is a matter of contingent events, these events nonetheless cause human suffering—hence the ubiquity of the "why" question, which from a theological perspective raises the question of God's providence.

37   John Swinton, *Raging with Compassion: Pastoral Responses to the Problem of Evil* (Grand Rapids: Eerdmans, 2007).

38   Swinton, *Raging with Compassion*, 10. Emphasis in original.

39   In actual fact Swinton reports, "The agonizing flow of his unrelenting anguish silenced me. I often wonder if I could have said more. . . . I had nothing to say because there was nothing to say that would make sense or create logic in the midst of such apparent unreason." Swinton, *Raging with Compassion*, 10.

40   See Berkouwer, *The Providence of God*, 245 ("There remains, however, after the most profound attempts to construct a theodicy, a feeling of uncertainty, a suspicion withal that the bruising reality of life cannot thus be justified").

41   Of course John Swinton, *who actually is a very good friend*, would be the first to say so.

42   Swinton, *Raging with Compassion*, 10.

43   Swinton, *Raging with Compassion*, 14.

44   "Many apparently logical theodicies make little sense when they encounter the reality of evil and suffering as people experience them in 'real time.'" Swinton, *Raging with Compassion*, 17.

45   Swinton, *Raging with Compassion*, 79–80.

46   David Hume, "Enquiry Concerning Human Understanding," in *Dialogues Concerning Natural Religion*, ed. Norman Kemp Smith (London: Thomas Nelson, 1947), 66.

47   Berkouwer, *The Providence of God*, 247.

48   For a general critique of treating the theodicy question independently from any historical and social context, see Walter Brueggemann, *The Message of the Psalms: A Theological Commentary* (Minneapolis: Augsburg, 1984), 169.

49   This point has been made convincingly by several authors in recent times, so I do not think it necessary to rehearse all the arguments. See Kenneth Surin, *Theology and the Problem of Evil* (Oxford: Blackwell, 1986); Douglas J. Hall, *God and Human Suffering: An Exercise in the Theology of the Cross* (Minneapolis: Augsburg, 1986). For an extended—concurring—comment on both, see Stanley M. Hauerwas, *Naming the Silences: God, Medicine, and the Problem of Suffering* (Grand Rapids: Eerdmans, 1990).

50   Surin, *Theology and the Problem of Evil*, 13. Emphasis in original.

51   Saint Anselm, who coined this phrase, did not think he could replace faith with understanding. Nor was he interested in doing so. In the first chapter of his *Proslogion*, he writes, "The believer does not seek to understand, that he may believe, but he believes that he may understand: for unless he believed he would not understand." (Anselm, "Proslogion," in *Classical Readings in Christian Apologetics, A.D. 100–1800*, ed. L. Russ Bush [Grand Rapids: Zondervan, 1983], 249). As Thomas Williams argues, "For Anselm faith is more a volitional state than an epistemic state: it is love for God and a drive to act as God wills. . . . So 'faith seeking understanding' means something like an active love of God seeking a deeper knowledge of God." Williams, "Saint Anselm," in *Stanford Encyclopedia of Philosophy* (Spring 2011 Edition), ed. Edward N. Zalta (Stanford: Stanford University, 1995–), article first published May 18, 2000 and substantially revised September 25, 2007, http://plato.stanford.edu/archives/spr2011/entries/anselm/. An apt formulation of what Anselm meant comes from Etienne Gilson: "The very primacy of faith over reason is something which [Anselm] believes before he understands, and believes in order to understand." Gilson, *The Spirit of Medieval Philosophy* (Notre Dame, Ind.: University of Notre Dame Press, 1934), 34. I owe this quote to Gregory Sadler, "Saint Anselm's *Fides Quaerens Intellectum* as a Model for Christian Philosophy," *The Saint Anselm Journal* 4 (2006): 39.

52   See Nicholas Wolterstorff, *Lament for a Son* (Grand Rapids: Eerdmans, 1987), 69.

53   Charles Taylor, *A Secular Age* (Cambridge, Mass.: The Belknap Press of Harvard University Press, 2007).

54   Taylor, *A Secular Age*, 222.

55   This conception is usually named "general providence." A classical source that is often referred to is Cicero's *De natura deorum*. In chapter 6 we will return to the notion of general providence and see how it came to be distinguished in Reformed theology from "special providence."

56   According to Berkouwer, the central concern of deism's providence was "pre-established harmony." Berkouwer, *The Providence of God*, 237. According to Sonderegger, it was the perfection and sufficiency of creation. Katherine Sonderegger, "The Doctrine of Providence," in *The Providence of God*, ed. Francesca A. Murphy and Philip G. Ziegler (Edinburgh: T&T Clark, 2009), 146–47.

57   On the deist conception of providence, see Michael J. Buckley, S.J., *At the Origins of Modern Atheism* (New Haven, Conn.: Yale University Press, 1987).

58   Taylor, *A Secular Age*, 223.

59   Taylor, *A Secular Age*, 223.

60   Taylor, *A Secular Age*, 225.
61   Taylor, *A Secular Age*, 232. Apart from science and modern thought, Berkouwer explains the "crisis" of the doctrine of providence by pointing to the rising pessimism in the course of the twentieth century due to its catastrophic events. Berkouwer, *The Providence of God*, 7–8.
62   What has happened, apparently, is that religious apologetics in the eighteenth century tended to accept the need of defending the Christian religion within the confines of natural science, which explains why until the present day, the theodicy problem is dealt with in an unhistorical and decontextualized manner. Surin, *Theology and the Problem of Evil*, 13.
63   "Providence," eNotes, accessed on February 8, 2011, http://www.enotes.com/science -religion-encyclopedia/providence.
64   See Ted Peters, *Playing God? Genetic Determinism and Human Freedom* (London: Routledge, 1997).
65   Peters, *Playing God?* 1.
66   Francis Collins, foreword to *Playing God? Genetic Determinism and Human Freedom*, by Ted Peters (London: Routledge, 1997), ix.
67   Peters shows how the argument that we should not take control over what God created depends on a similar relation of competition: God as the Creator of natural order, including the human gene pool, is set up against the creations of mankind in science. Peters, *Playing God?* 14–16.

Chapter 2

1   Brett Webb-Mitchell, *God Plays Piano Too: The Spiritual Lives of Disabled Children* (New York: Crossroad, 1993), 2.
2   Synapse, "Why Me? Possible Answers to Tricky Questions," *Bridge* 2 (2011): 27, Magazine of Synapse, Brain Injury Association of Queensland.
3   "Life Is for Living 2005: 25 New Zealanders Living with Disability Tell Their Stories; Miranda—What a Hidden Disability Means for Me," Office for Disability Studies, Ministry of Social Development, accessed August 7, 2011. http://www.odi.govt.nz/ resources/publications/life-is-for-living/miranda.html.
4   Ellen Painter Dollar, *No Easy Choice: A Story of Disability, Parenthood and Faith in an Age of Advanced Reproduction* (Louisville, Ky.: Westminster John Knox, 2012), 23.
5   Zig Ziglar and Julie Ziglar Norman, *Embrace the Struggle: Living Life on Life's Terms* (New York: Howard Books, 2009).
6   Michael Oddy and Michael Walker, *Why Me?* Brain Injury Rehabilitation Trust, www.thedtgroup.org/media/77979/BIRT_Why_me.pdf.
7   This quote is from a blog. www.xojane.com/it-happened-to-me/it-happened-to-me -contest-entry-my-moms-traumatic-brain-injury-was-published-by-sassy-and-not -much-has-changed. Accessed October 27, 2013.
8   Oddy and Walker, *Why Me?*
9   Amy Julia Becker, *A Good and Perfect Gift: Faith, Expectations, and a Little Girl Named Penny* (Minneapolis: Bethany House, 2011), 24–25.

10   Martha Beck, *Expecting Adam: A True Story of Birth, Rebirth, and Everyday Magic* (New York: Berkley Books, 1999), 182. Emphasis in original.

11   Beck, *Expecting Adam*, 184.

12   Hilly Schenkhuizen-Lok, *Een kind als Clary* [*A Child Like Clary*] (Kampen, The Netherlands: Kok, 1983), 46 (my translation).

13   Becker, *A Good and Perfect Gift*, 46–47.

14   Jet Isarin, *De Eigen Ander: Moeders, deskundigen en gehandicapte kinderen* (Amsterdam: Damon, 2002), 28 (my translation).

15   Becker, *A Good and Perfect Gift*, 46.

16   I once asked a young adult with paralyzed legs who had strong Christian convictions whether she believed that she would be able to walk in the kingdom of God. "It would be very good for that person to be able to walk," she said, "but I probably would not recognize her as 'me.'"

17   Emerson Jane Browne, "Move On Already!" *Dancing Upside Down* (blog), July 13, 2011, http://www.dancingupsidedown.com/move-on-already/. Emphasis in original.

18   The GCS was originally published in 1974. Graham Teasdale and Bryan Jennett, "Assessment of Coma and Impaired Consciousness: A Practical Scale," *Lancet* 2 (1974): 81–84.

19   DeAnna Frye and JoAnn M. Ovnic, "Memory Problems after Brain Injury," November 9, 2009, www.lapublishing.com/blog/2009/-memory-brain-injury.

20   Frye and Ovnic, "Memory Problems after Brain Injury."

21   "ADHD Questions," HealthCentral, http://www.healthcentral.com/adhd/c/question/481013/126447/.

22   Dan Windheim, "Living with Traumatic Brain Injury," *ARC Light Magazine* 10, no. 3 (1995).

23   Windheim, "Living with Traumatic Brain Injury".

24   "Traumatic Brain Injury: This is the Story of My Traumatic Brain Injury," http://traumaticbraininjuryhope.blogspot.com. Emphasis in original.

25   See Becker, *A Good and Perfect Gift*; see also Stephanie O. Hubach, *Same Lake, Different Boat: Coming alongside People Touched by Disability* (Phillipsburg, N.J.: P&R Publications, 2006). For a general description, see Hans S. Reinders, *The Future of the Disabled in Liberal Society: An Ethical Analysis* (Notre Dame, Ind.: The University of Notre Dame Press, 2000), 175–92.

26   In her book *Over the Waterfall*, Marilyn Martone includes pictures—of both kinds—of her daughter Michelle who suffered severe traumatic brain injury after being hit by a car. The pictures themselves speak volumes about what happened to this girl. Marilyn Martone, *Over the Waterfall* (CreateSpace Community, 2011).

27   Windheim, "Living with Traumatic Brain Injury."

28   Windheim, "Living with Traumatic Brain Injury."

29   Beck, *Expecting Adam*, 196.

30   For more on the double relationship with God implied in this verse, see chapter 5, pp. 104–6.

31 Michael Dorris, *The Broken Cord* (New York: Harper & Row, 1989), 76.

32 Oddy and Fussey, "Why Me?"

33 Beck, *Expecting Adam*, 194. Martha Beck here indicates a way in which the "why" question never goes away; the child to whose existence it is attached continues to live the life that provokes the question in the first place. Beck continues with this insight: "The hardest lesson I have ever had to learn is that I will never know the meaning of my children's pain, and that I have neither the capacity nor the right to take it away from them" (194).

34 Dorris, *The Broken Cord*, 71.

35 Nancy Mairs, *On Being a Cripple*. http://thelamedame.tumblr.com/post/309384 17648/on-being-a-cripple. Accessed November 1, 2013.

36 Gabri de Wagt, *Mijn zoon en ik: Leven met een gehandicapt kind* (Bloemendaal, The Netherlands: Nelissen, 1994), 16 (my translation).

37 Swinton, *Raging with Compassion*, 21. Swinton argues in particular that Augustine's way of dealing with the problem of evil runs the risk of making suffering persons responsible for their own suffering (21–26).

38 Isaiah Dau, "Facing Human Suffering: A Biblical and Theological Perspective," in *Suffering, Persecution and Martyrdom: Theological Reflections*, ed. Christof Sauer and Richard Howell (Johannesburg: AcadSA, 1995), 109.

39 Stanley M. Hauerwas, *Naming the Silences: God, Medicine, and the Problem of Suffering* (Grand Rapids: Eerdmans, 1990).

40 Hauerwas, *Naming the Silences*, xi.

41 Hauerwas, *Naming the Silences*, 66–67.

42 Paul Ricoeur, "Evil, a Challenge to Philosophy and Theology," *Journal of the American Academy of Religion* 53, no. 4 (1985): 640. I owe this reference to Swinton, *Raging with Compassion*, 25.

43 Beck, *Expecting Adam*, 197.

44 Dorris, *The Broken Cord*, 260.

45 Jean F. Lyotard, *The Inhuman: Reflections on Time*, trans. Geoffrey Bennington and Rachel Bowlby (Cambridge: Polity, 1991).

46 Nicholas Wolterstorff, *Lament for a Son* (Grand Rapids: Eerdmans, 1987), 69.

Chapter 3

1 A note on identification: whenever I mention Martha, or Martha Beck, I intend to identify the person who is one of the main characters of the story; whenever I refer to Beck, I intend to identify the author of the book *Expecting Adam*.

2 Beck, *Expecting Adam*, 9.

3 Beck, *Expecting Adam*, 12. Emphasis in original.

4 Beck, *Expecting Adam*, 16.

5 Beck, *Expecting Adam*, 98.

6 Beck, *Expecting Adam*, 98.

7 Beck, *Expecting Adam*, 96.

8   Beck, *Expecting Adam*, 160–61.

9   Beck, *Expecting Adam*, 161.

10   Beck, *Expecting Adam*, 163.

11   Beck, *Expecting Adam*, 169-170.

12   Beck, *Expecting Adam*, 170. Early in the story Martha states her empiricist conviction in this way: "If something is reliable, real, then it must be testable. That is the single thing that establishes the scientific validity of any hypothesis—if you create the same conditions, any number of times, you will get the same results" (48).

13   There are other manifestations of the mysterious that I have left out of my account of Beck's story, mainly for reasons of space, but which deserve at least to be mentioned. One of these Martha calls the "Seeing Thing." It seems to be a kind of clairvoyance that enables Martha to see John when he is actually thousands of miles away in Asia. It turns out that she sees John doing things in places at the time he was actually doing them, then and there. Beck, *Expecting Adam*, 46–47, 107, 228, 263, 277.

14   Beck, *Expecting Adam*, 164.

15   Beck, *Expecting Adam*, 327.

16   Beck, *Expecting Adam*, 169.

17   It is not by accident that Gerrit Berkouwer's discussion of the classical doctrine of providence entails a full chapter on "Providence and Miracles." Berkouwer, *The Providence of God*, 188–231.

18   Beck, *Expecting Adam*, 207–8.

19   There are many more episodes worth mentioning in Beck's book than I will be capable of doing. For example, left out are all the episodes about families and friends, even though they add significantly to the force of the book, particularly the episodes about people who were there when they were needed, like Martha's friends Sibyl and Deirdre, or John's boss Mark. Their presence fits in the category of unexpected blessings at moments when things appeared very gloomy.

20   Beck, *Expecting Adam*, 285.

21   Beck, *Expecting Adam*, 290. This is about as close as Beck gets to a providential reading of her story.

22   Beck, *Expecting Adam*, 305.

23   Beck, *Expecting Adam*, 310.

24   Beck, *Expecting Adam*, 312.

25   Beck, *Expecting Adam*, 74.

26   Beck, *Expecting Adam*, 74.

27   Beck, *Expecting Adam*, 75.

28   Beck, *Expecting Adam*, 76.

29   Beck, *Expecting Adam*, 71.

30   Beck, *Expecting Adam*, 71.

31   Beck, *Expecting Adam*, 71.

32   Beck, *Expecting Adam*, 189.

33   Beck, *Expecting Adam*, 189.

34   Beck, *Expecting Adam*, 189. Emphasis in original.

35   Beck, *Expecting Adam*, 190.
36   Beck, *Expecting Adam*, 318.
37   Beck, *Expecting Adam*, 270.
38   Beck, *Expecting Adam*, 98.
39   Remember Nancy Eiesland's account of her experience of being confronted by these formulas. See ch. 1, p. 8.

Chapter 4

1   "I knew that our lives would never be the same again," is the first thought of Stephanie Hubach after her own son with Down syndrome is born (Hubach, *Same Lake, Different Boat*, 7).
2   Ziglar and Ziglar Norman, *Embrace the Struggle*, 27.
3   David Cotton, "I Don't Know What to Pray For," in *Brain Injury: When the Call Comes; A Congregational Resource* (New Brunswick, N.J.: The Elizabeth Boggs Center, 2010), 5.
4   Cathy Crimmins, *Where Is the Mango Princess? A Journey Back from Brain Injury* (New York: Vintage Books, 2001), 26.
5   The site www.waiting.com was created by an attorney working in the area of injury law by the name of Gordon S. Johnson Jr.
6   Crimmins, *Mango Princess*, 4.
7   Crimmins, *Mango Princess*, 6.
8   Crimmins, *Mango Princess*, 31.
9   Jean-Dominique Bauby, *The Diving Bell and the Butterfly*, trans. Jeremy Leggatt (New York: Harper Perennial, 2008), 12.
10   Bauby, *Diving Bell*, 16.
11   Bauby, *Diving Bell*, 16.
12   Bauby, *Diving Bell*, 17.
13   See ch. 2, n. 37.
14   Bauby, *Diving Bell*, 24–25.
15   Bauby, *Diving Bell*, 40.
16   Bauby, *Diving Bell*, 39.
17   Bauby, *Diving Bell*, 39.
18   Bauby, *Diving Bell*, 25.
19   Bauby, *Diving Bell*, 33.
20   Bauby, *Diving Bell*, 101.
21   Bauby, *Diving Bell*, 124–25.
22   Bauby, *Diving Bell*, 123.
23   Bauby, *Diving Bell*, 94.
24   Bauby, *Diving Bell*, 94. Emphasis added.
25   Bauby, *Diving Bell*, 77.
26   Bauby, *Diving Bell*, 78.
27   Bauby, *Diving Bell*, 83.

28   Bauby, *Diving Bell*, 120.
29   Bauby, *Diving Bell*, 137.
30   Bauby, *Diving Bell*, 138.
31   Crimmins, *Mango Princess*, 47–48.
32   Crimmins, *Mango Princess*, 47–48.
33   Crimmins, *Mango Princess*, 51–52.
34   Crimmins, *Mango Princess*, 52.
35   Crimmins, *Mango Princess*, 55.
36   Crimmins, *Mango Princess*, 57.
37   Crimmins, *Mango Princess*, 87-88.
38   Interestingly, Bauby's case in this respect is exactly the opposite of Alan Forman's case. Whereas Bauby's mind is intact, but is entirely "locked in" a body that does not do much more than perform its unconscious life preserving functions (breathing, heartbeat, etc.), one could say that Alan Forman's mind is locked out of his body. His brain has lost its mind, which makes Cathy fear that the "real Al" is no longer there.
39   Crimmins, *Mango Princess*, 92–97.
40   Crimmins, *Mango Princess*, 93.
41   Crimmins, *Mango Princess*, 93.
42   Crimmins, *Mango Princess*, 93.
43   I passed by an earlier scene where Cathy is accusing herself of "self-centeredness" because of her impatience for Al becoming his old self again. Crimmins, *Mango Princess*, 58.
44   Crimmins, *Mango Princess*, 94.
45   Crimmins, *Mango Princess*, 95.
46   Crimmins, *Mango Princess*, 95. Emphasis in original.
47   Crimmins, *Mango Princess*, 95.
48   Crimmins, *Mango Princess*, 96.
49   Crimmins, *Mango Princess*, 96.
50   Crimmins, *Mango Princess*, 96.
51   Crimmins, *Mango Princess*, 96. Emphasis in original.
52   Crimmins, *Mango Princess*, 97.
53   Crimmins, *Mango Princess*, 97. Emphasis in original.
54   Crimmins, *Mango Princess*, 103. Emphasis in original.
55   Crimmins, *Mango Princess*, 114.
56   Crimmins, *Mango Princess*, 115.
57   Crimmins, *Mango Princess*, 118.
58   Crimmins, *Mango Princess*, 127.
59   Crimmins, *Mango Princess*, 127.
60   Crimmins, *Mango Princess*, 145.
61   Crimmins, *Mango Princess*, 151.
62   Note the term "demonstrate" here; the claim is not that the authors answer the question. It is that their stories show different ways of dealing with it.

63   Crimmins, *Mango Princess*, 240.

Chapter 5

1   Harold S. Kushner, *When Bad Things Happen to Good People* (New York: Avon, 1981).

2   I found weblogs indicating that the Americans with Disabilities Act recognizes pso-
     riasis (the skin disease commonly attributed to Job) as a disability, but I found no
     official sources to confirm this.

3   Important sources on Calvin's reading of Job are Derek Thomas, *Calvin's Teaching
     on Job: Proclaiming the Incomprehensible God* (Geanies House, Scotland: Christian
     Focus, 2004); Susan E. Schreiner, *Where Shall Wisdom Be Found? Calvin's Exegesis
     of Job from Medieval and Modern Perspectives* (Chicago: University of Chicago Press,
     1994).

4   This is Calvin's comment: "We have further to mark that in all this disputation Job
     maintained a good cause and contrariwise his adversaries maintained an evil one.
     And yet it is true that Job maintaining a good cause did handle it ill, and that the other
     setting forth an unjust matter, did convey it well. To understand this well will be as
     the key to open unto us all this whole book." *Sermons of Maister John Calvin, upon the
     Booke of Job*, trans. Golding (London: Bishop, 1574; repr. Carlisle, Pa.: The Banner of
     Truth Trust, 1933), 1, col. b.32–37.

5   For a very helpful source that covers much of the older scholarly work on the book
     of Job, see "Job Commentaries," accessed July 24, 2012, www.preceptaustin.org/
     job_commentaries.htm.

6   See, e.g., George A. Barton, *Commentary on the Book of Job* (New York: Macmillan,
     1911), 2. Much of the scholarship followed the authority of Wilhelm Martin Leb-
     erecht de Wette (1780–1849), whose view on the issue of the "prologue"—as well as
     the "epilogue"—is particularly enlightening in this connection: "The perfection of
     the work requires their rejection because they solve the problem which is the sub-
     ject of discussion, by the idea of trial and compensation, whereas it was the design of
     the author to solve the question through the idea of entire submission on the part of
     man to the power and wisdom of God." Quoted from Albert Barnes, *Notes, Critical,
     Illustrative, and Practical on the Book of Job with a New Translation*, vol. 1 (New York:
     Leavitt, 1852), xix–xx. The logic is clear: because the text does not present a unified
     position, the dissenting parts must be rejected as a later addition.

7   See Katharine J. Dell, "Job: Sceptics, Philosophers, and Tragedians," in *Das Buch Hiob
     und seine Interpretationen*, ed. Thomas Krueger (Zürich: Theologischer Verlag, 2007),
     1–20. Dell argues that the book of Job presents a range of possible answers to intricate
     and intertwined theological questions, without arriving at firm conclusions. Because
     of its preoccupation with linguistic and theological coherence, this possibility could
     not have satisfied biblical scholarship in the nineteenth century, and led it to argue
     for different sources. With this approach in mind, Dell comments, "The contradic-
     tions of these answers has long caused a problem for interpreters of Job as they seek to
     comprehend the book and, although redactional issues are relevant, seeking to make

sense of the book as a whole (as it must at some point have been conceived) is also of concern. If the author of the dialogue and God's speeches imprinted his personality on the book substantially at this point then other redactions are of minor concern in relation to this 'main' vision." Dell, "Sceptics, Philosophers," 7n26.

8   See, e.g., Francis I. Andersen, *Job: An Introduction and Commentary*, Tyndale Old Testament Commentaries (Downers Grove, Ill.: InterVarsity, 1980), 20–21. Regarding the hypothesis of a different source of the "prologue" and "epilogue," Andersen argues on grounds of text composition for a unified reading.

9   This approach is inspired by Walter Brueggemann, *Theology of the Old Testament: Testimony, Dispute, Advocacy* (Minneapolis: Fortress, 1997). Brueggemann sees an analogy between the times of conflict when Israel's theology was shaped—the claims of which could not be but contested by its cultural environment—and the current situation of cultural contestedness that Christian theology finds itself in. Given that it can no longer depend on the legitimacy of dogmatic orthodoxy, Christianity represents a variety of voices competing with one another and with other voices that are in conflict with it. Christian theology can learn from the disputational and conflicting nature of Old Testament theology, so says Brueggemann, in being pluralist and argumentative in its testimony: "It is my judgment that while the OT can make assumptions about and claims for what is real, it is unable and unwilling to do so by way of silencing countervoices." Brueggemann, *Theology of the Old Testament*, 65.

10   For a similar view, see Nicholas Adams, "The Goodness of Job's Bad Arguments," *The Journal of Scriptural Reasoning* 4, no. 1 (2004), accessed July 25, 2012, http://etext.lib .virginia.edu/journals/ssr/issues/-volume4/number1/ssr04-01-e03.html. See also Katharine J. Dell's reading of the book of Job as a specimen of skeptical literature. Dell, *The Book of Job as Skeptical Literature*, Beihefte Zur Zeitschrift Fur Die Alttestamentliche Wissenschaft 197 (Berlin: de Gruyter, 1991). Dell argues that the text presents different views on various related questions, and that the rich composition of themes indicates a range of possible answers to these questions, without coming to a definite conclusion for or against one side or another.

11   I have not found commentaries relating Job's tragedy to the apparently doubtful behavior of his children, which Job seems to have condoned, given that he seeks to excuse them before God with offerings, just in case.

12   Zigler and Zigler Norman, *Embrace the Struggle*.

13   "[Job's] friends came and sat down beside him. Their theory of suffering was the one which up to that time Job had held. They could not look upon him without deep and genuine sympathy. But it was equally impossible for them not to look upon him without feeling that he must have been a terrible sinner—that his whole life, which appeared so righteous, was after all a horrible sham. Their sympathy was accordingly tempered by cold condemnation. Job felt it through their silence, and it added to his agony." Barton, *Commentary on the Book of Job*, 7–8. Job's friends do not get any credit in most traditional readings of the text. On the opening speech of Eliphaz, e.g., a nineteenth century commentary reads: "There is a conspicuous want of feeling in Eliphaz. . . . He charges Job with the inability to derive from his own principles

that support which he expected them to afford to others, and seems almost to rejoice malevolently that one who had been so great a help to others was now in need of help himself." Stanley Leathes, "Job," in *An Old Testament Commentary for English Readers by Various Authors*, ed. Charles John Ellicot, vol. 4 (London: Cassell, 1884), 11. As I will show, however, there is no reason to read Eliphaz' speech in this way, other than received opinion.

14   See Derek Thomas, "When Counseling Doesn't Help: Job 4–7," First Presbyterian Church of Jackson, Mississippi website, accessed July 24, 2012, www.fpcjackson.org/ resources/sermons/Derek's_SERMONS/job; see also J. R. Dumelow, ed., *Commentary on the Holy Bible by Various Authors Complete in One Volume* (New York: Macmillan, 1909), 296.

15   See, e.g., Henry Morris, "Study Notes on Job," in *The Defender's Study Bible: King James Version* (Emeryville, Calif.: World Publishing, 1996) ("This was an evil spirit—perhaps Satan himself—diabolically implanting an accusation against Job in the mind of Eliphaz, which would be used later with telling effect to try to undermine Job's faith" [on Job 4:15]).

16   Derek Thomas' explanation of Calvin's reading of Job develops the thought that Job might not find fault in himself, according to the justice that humans know, which is justice according to the law, but that there is also another kind of justice, which Calvin sometimes names as "hidden," or "secret." It resides in God's majesty and regards the imperfection of creatures in view of the absolute perfection of the Creator. For a wealth of textual evidence, see Thomas, *Calvin's Teaching on Job*, 105–6; see also Schreiner, *Where Shall Wisdom*, 105. Calvin saw his notion of "double justice" supported by the claim that even God's angels are flawed in view of his majesty as their Maker (Job 4:18). The distinction between "creatureliness" and "sinfulness" as two different states of imperfection suggests the possibility of separating moral imperfection from ontological imperfection. Calvin uses the metaphor of humans gazing at the brightness of the stars, which completely fades away at dawn because of the radiant power of the sun. Such is the difference, according to Calvin, between human creatures, heavenly creatures like angels, and their Creator.

17   Since the effects of the fall do not apply to God's angels, they cannot be charged with sin, but they are charged with "error" nonetheless (Job 4:18). Calvin was not content with the conclusion of a state of "natural"—i.e., nonmoral—imperfection. He maintained that even when, as creatures, we act in conformity with the law, we can still be cursed because of God's secret *justice*—thereby insisting on the nexus between imperfection and morality (*Sermons of Maister John Calvin*, 174, col. a47). The remaining question is whence comes this need to eliminate the distinction that was introduced to explain the difference between the two kinds of divine justice, which was the distinction between moral and ontological perfection. Whence comes the need for retaining the language of "fault" and "guilt" for a condition that simply exists in *being*? See William J. Bouwsma, *John Calvin: A Sixteenth Century Portrait* (Oxford: Oxford University Press, 1988), 42. Derek Thomas finds the answer in the fact that Calvin never was at ease with the preliminary supposition that created the problem in

the first place—namely, the supposition of Job's innocent suffering. Thomas, *Calvin's Teaching on Job*, 106.

18   In contrast, according to Calvin, Job's friends had an evil cause but handled it well. It is an evil cause in that they held on to the simple version of instant divine retribution, which Calvin rejects, but they handled it well because of their reverence for divine majesty. "With becoming humility" is a phrase Calvin uses in the same connection, as we will see later. See ch. 7, p. 148.

19   This is what Calvin names God's hidden or secret justice. Various authors have noted Calvin's interest in this theme of hiddenness. E.g., Harold Dekker observes, "One of the most distinctive features of Calvin's entire pastoral theology is his accent on the hidden in God, and the final mystery of all His dealings with His children. He has no better comfort to offer to troubled spirits than the unrevealed purposes of a God of sovereign grace." Dekker is of the opinion that "the incomprehensibility of God, and the final inscrutability to man of all His doings, constitute the leading thought in Calvin's preaching on Job." Harold Dekker's introduction to John Calvin, *Sermons from Job* by John Calvin, trans. Leroy Nixon (Grand Rapids: Eerdmans, 1979), xxx. See also Potgieter, who points out that Calvin describes Job's suffering in terms of the hiddenness of God. Pieter C. Potgieter, "Perspectives on the Doctrine of Providence in Some of Calvin's Sermons on Job," *HTS Theological Studies* 54, no. 1–2 (1998): 36–49. Susan Schreiner argues that "Calvin's exposition of Job is characterised by a recurring tension between divine revelation and divine hiddenness." Schreiner, *Where Shall Wisdom*, 94. A similar ambivalence on Calvin's views, in this respect, is found in Cornelis van der Kooi, *Als in een spiegel: God kennen volgens Calvijn en Barth* (Kampen, The Netherlands: Kok, 2002), 132–36. For a general account of Calvin's interest in the theme of the hiddenness of God, see Brian A. Gerrish, "To the Unknown God: Luther and Calvin on the Hiddenness of God," in *The Old Protestantism and the New: Essays on the Reformation Heritage* (Chicago: University of Chicago Press, 1982), 131–49.

20   This verse is one of the instances that demonstrate Adams' point about embracing pain as the essence of Job's argument, a point that goes unrecognized when dogmatic coherence is the main concern. Job is suggesting that a merciful God would kill him, which is completely out of sync with a dogmatic point of view, unless one begins to see that Job's love for God is greater than his love for life, or, perhaps better, that there is no point in going on living when one considers oneself to be disconnected from God, *while God does not seem to care.* See Adams, "The Goodness of Job's Bad Arguments."

21   A clear example of what Adams means by "dogmatic coherence" is found in Matthew Henry, "Matthew Henry's Complete Commentary on the Whole Bible: Job 6," StudyLight.org, accessed July 25, 2012, http://www.studylight.org/com/mhc-com/view.cgi?book=job&chapter=006 (where he comments on the passage of Job 6:8-10). Henry ignores Job's desperation about divine justice and offers a psychological explanation for his behavior: "Ungoverned passion often grows more violent when it meets with some rebuke and check. The troubled sea rages most when it dashes against a rock." Nonetheless Job stands convicted: "Job had been courting death, as that would

be the happy end of his miseries. For this Eliphaz had gravely reproved him, but he, instead of unsaying what he had said, says it here again with more vehemence than before; and it is as ill said as almost anything we find in all his discourses, and is recorded for our admonition, not our imitation." According to Adams, what Job says is ill said, unless one considers the argumentative force of *his pain* in being abandoned by the one he is most beholden to, which is what "dogmatic coherence" apparently does not allow.

22   Accordingly, my proposal here is to read this episode in light of Calvin's conception of a "double justice," and then understand Job as making an argument *for* God's justice as he knows it and *against* the notion of God's hidden justice that he refuses to accept. Following this lead, I suggest, we will be well prepared for Job's prayer in chapter 16, which is a crucial passage to understand. There we find Job calling upon God against God!

23   Bildad does point to a possibility, however, that there was something the matter with Job's children—for right at the start, they are introduced as a bunch of rich kids going from one party to the next: "His sons used to go and hold feasts in one another's house in turn; and they would send and invite their three sisters to eat and drink with them" (Job 1:4-5). See also the comment above in n. 11. Job was worried about their way of life, but he did not confront them. Instead he would rise early in the morning to burn offerings for each of them: "It may be that my children have sinned, and cursed God in their hearts." Apparently, Job was less certain of the purity of his children's hearts than he was of his own.

24   See Barton, *Commentary on the Book of Job*, 108.

25   It is one of the stronger indications of the literary genius of this story that Job takes the step to a 'double stage' for his defense that in fact imitates the image of a heavenly court in Job 1–3: what happens on the stage of Job's earthly existence is decided upon at the heavenly stage of the divine court; by analogy: justifying himself in view of his earthly catastrophe will not succeed unless there is someone speaking up for him in heaven. There must be an intercessor to represent the case of mortals in the heavenly courtroom. Without such help, no mortal could ever have any hope to be acquitted from sins not committed. The distance between Creator and creatures would simply forbid any form of defense, unless these creatures are represented by one who sits in God's court and has the right to speak on their behalf.

26   Abraham J. Heschel, *Man Is Not Alone: A Philosophy of Religion* (New York: Farrar, Straus & Giroux, 1951).

27   See, e.g., Barton, *Commentary on the Book of Job*, 24; Barnes, *Notes, Critical*, xxxiv.

28   Larry J. Waters defends this view, for example. See Larry J. Waters, "Elihu's Theology and His View of Suffering," *Bibliotheca Sacra* 156 (1999): 143–59. Although Waters does not mention Calvin, his arguments sound quite familiar from the perspective of Calvin's sermons: "Before Elihu's intervention the debate had been anthropocentric and not theocentric. Elihu rectified that situation and injected a recognition of the divine into the discussion. Another purpose Elihu had in mind was to get Job and the three to understand that God is not limited in the way He deals with the suffering

of humankind. God acts when, where, and how He has sovereignly decreed. This is not to discourage prayer or a humble, submissive, and righteous lifestyle, but rather to encourage a life of faith and trust" (144). For the view that Elihu, not Job, is Calvin's champion when it comes to the theology of providence in the book of Job, see also Adams, "The Goodness of Job's Bad Arguments." While Elihu speaks impeccably about the Almighty, Job makes too many assertions that in fact question God's righteousness, which is absolutely unacceptable to Calvin. According to Adams this explains why Calvin asserts that Elihu is not included in God's denunciation of Job's friends (Job 42). Moreover, it also explains why Calvin does not know what to make of God's endorsement of Job as the one who has spoken rightly (Job 42:7).

29 There is a curious similarity between the story of Job and the stories we have been reading before, which is that each of them, in their own specific way, turn to a device of "double staging," indicating that somehow there is a script that mortals remain unaware of, or at least cannot control. They may have a sense of what is going on, but in truth they do not. Whether in the question of whether the cosmos contains the key for opening up the cocoon of locked-in syndrome, or disguised as the Bunraku puppeteers, or Mr. Finkelman, or an intercessor in the heavenly court, each of our stories presupposes a perspective that what happens in our lives is decided on a different plane.

30 See ch. 4, pp. 88–89.

31 In the story of Martha Beck, the Bunraku puppeteers are similarly posed as the agents of the heavenly court—God and Satan—in making things happen in the "real" world that are beyond human comprehension. The mise-en-scène is the same "double staging" that suggests what happens in the real world is inexplicably controlled by "supernatural" agents. Apart from the similarity, however, the difference between these stories is also very significant. The puppeteers *make human beings move* like puppets—when Martha's pregnancy survives an alarming hemorrhage, she feels their hands supporting her and the soothing warmth emanating from the hands into her body—which is what the agents in heaven do not do. In Job's story he is a pawn rather than a puppet, pushed and shoved around, but only to see how he *responds*.

32 The doctrine has been described as a theology of "direct retribution," as "compensational theology," as "tit for tat" theology, and as "primitive religion," all of which indicate what earlier in this book was named "cheap theology." It has as its basic doctrine the rule of "measure for measure," according to which the exchange of virtue and reward, punishment and sin, is a zero-sum game. Even though Calvin recognizes that this rule does not add up in human experience, this is not the main reason why he rejects it—as have many other classical theologians. The main reason is that it curtails God's freedom and thereby limits divine sovereignty. See Potgieter, "Perspectives on the Doctrine," 36–37. This explains why he is more impressed by Job's friends—particularly Elihu, who bring this point to bear upon Job's lack of humility.

33 Apart from Calvin, this is true for Aquinas, e.g., who argued that providence does not entail that good persons be able to avoid temporal evils. See Matthew Levering, "Aquinas on the Book of Job: Providence and Presumption," in *The Providence of God*,

ed. Francesca A. Murphy and Philip G. Ziegler (Edinburgh: T&T Clark, 2009), 9. In his commentary on Job, according to Levering, Aquinas explains providence in view of the Christian belief in the afterlife, in which full justice will be established. Key to this interpretation, as regards Job, is the text of Job 19:25-27, where Job proclaims that his redeemer lives, and then—according to the Vulgate text that Aquinas had before him—continues: "And on the last day I will rise from the earth. And I will be surrounded by my own hide again and in my flesh I will see God." As Levering explains, modern biblical scholarship does not support this reading, so that the assumption that Job had a strong notion of the resurrection is untenable, but this does not eliminate the importance of what Aquinas had to say on the book of Job—namely, that "it does hold out hope that God will reverse the conditions of existential hopelessness and gloom." Levering, "Aquinas," 22. The book of Job certainly believed that. What is more, however, it also holds that in Job's case this belief was vindicated (note its final chapter), which is another reason not to tie providence too exclusively with eschatology.

34   As we have seen, the point here is to acknowledge the ontological difference between Creator and creature. In this connection it should be noticed, with regard to Beck's "double staging," that her metaphysics did not imply an ontological difference between Martha and her Bunraku puppeteers. That is to say, it is not an ontological difference in the sense that they act similarly to natural causes in producing effects in the "real" world.

35   This observation is pertinent to my earlier remarks on reading the book of Job as a text in which different and conflicting conceptions of divine providence are debated. Both in the "prologue" and "epilogue," the deity takes the position that Job's religion does not have moral geometry as its ulterior motive. Job is not loyal to God because of enlightened self-interest, but because he believes God is his redeemer.

Chapter 6

1   See below in the section "Two Conceptions of Providence: Special and General."
2   Bouwsma, *John Calvin.*
3   Thomas, *Calvin's Teaching on Job*; Susan E. Schreiner, "Exegesis and Double Justice in Calvin's Sermons on Job," *Church History* 58 (1989): 322–38; Susan E. Schreiner, "'Through a Mirror Dimly': Calvin's Sermons on Job," in *Calvinism and Hermeneutics*, ed. Richard C. Gamble (New York: Garland, 1992), 231–49; Schreiner, *Where Shall Wisdom*. For Calvin's exegesis of the book of Job, see in this chapter, pp. 141–42.
4   Brian A. Gerrish, "'To the Unknown God': Luther and Calvin on the Hiddenness of God," *The Journal of Religion* 53, no. 3 (1973): 263–92.
5   Brian A. Gerrish, *Grace and Gratitude: The Eucharistic Theology of John Calvin* (Philadelphia: Fortress, 1993), 22. Gerrish quotes from William B. Selbie, *The Fatherhood of God* (London: Duckworth, 1936).
6   Selbie, *Fatherhood of God*, 75–76.
7   Selbie, *Fatherhood of God*, 75–76.
8   Charles Hodge, *Systematic Theology*, vol. 1 (Grand Rapids: Eerdmans, 1997), 575.

9   Karl Barth, *The Theology of John Calvin*, trans. Geoffrey W. Bromiley (Grand Rapids: Eerdmans, 1995), 117.

10 John Calvin, *Institutes of the Christian Religion*, ed. John T. McNeill and trans. Ford Lewis Battles (1559 ed.; Philadelphia: Westminster, 1960), 1.2.1 (1:41). References are to book, chapter, and paragraph (and references in parentheses are to the volume and page number) of the Westminster edition.

11 Gerrish, *Grace and Gratitude*, 27–28. For the claim about the distinctness of fatherly love, see Calvin, *Institutes*, 3.20.36 (2:899). To anticipate obvious objections from feminist quarters, Gerrish shows with textual references that Calvin also speaks repeatedly of God's motherly love. Gerrish, *Grace and Gratitude*, 40–41.

12 Gerrish, *Grace and Gratitude*, 24.

13 See ch. 7, p. 147.

14 Terry J. Wright, *Providence Made Flesh: Divine Presence as a Framework for a Theology of Providence* (Eugene, Ore.: Wipf & Stock, 2009), 25.

15 Here, Thomas' work *Calvin's Teaching on Job* is a useful source. I have also used Arthur Golding's translation of Calvin's sermons on Job, *Sermons of Maister John Calvin*.

16 Calvin, *Institutes*, 1.16.1 (1:197).

17 See Charles Partee, *Calvin and Classical Philosophy* (Leiden: Brill, 1977), 47.

18 Partee, *Calvin and Classical Philosophy*, 47. Although Calvin does not mention Aristotle in this connection, the entire section appears to be directed against philosophers who see God only as the first cause of all motion. He only mentions the "Sophists"— *Sophistae*—which in his days was used to refer to the Scholastics. Calvin, *Institutes*, 1.16.3 (1:200).

19 Calvin, *Institutes*, 1.16.3 (1:200).

20 Calvin may have had in mind the thought that providence only regards the order of the universe and the general motion of things at large. The thought is explicit in the second book of Cicero's *De natura deorum*, where he claims that the gods mind great things but neglect the small (*magna di curant, parva neglegunt*). Cicero, *De Natura Deorum*, ed. Arthur S. Pease (Darmstadt: Wissenschaftliche Buchgesellschaft, 1968), II, 167.

21 Calvin, *Institutes*, 1.16.3 (1:200).

22 Calvin, *Institutes*, 1.5.2 (1:53).

23 Wright, *Providence Made Flesh*, 27.

24 This "or else" indicates the skepsis referred to in the introduction to this chapter: people will rest safely in God's protection; if not they will bear their fate in patience, because there might be a purpose, in what they have to bear, that is beyond human understanding.

25 Calvin, *Institutes*, 1.5.3 (1:54).

26 Calvin, *Institutes*, 1.5.5 (1:57–58).

27 Calvin, *Institutes*, 1.5.5 (1:57–58).

28 Calvin, *Institutes*, 1.5.4 (1:56). Calvin may have had Cicero in mind, who quotes from Ennius the phrase of nature as the "father of gods and men." The quote is from Cicero, *De Natura Deorum*, II, 25.

29   Calvin, *Institutes*, 1.5.5 (1:58). Calvin appears to aim directly at the Stoics with this
      phrase. For the Stoics taught that God is not independent from nature; God is nature
      and vice versa. The universe is its own creative force and its own source of activity,
      and change. See Marcia L. Colish, *The Stoic Tradition*, vol. 1 (Leiden: Brill, 1985), 24
      ("God, or the universe, is not only its own cause; it is the one cause and explanation
      of all things"). Hence, there is the famous Stoic dictum *deus sive natura*. Hence, there
      is also the fact that for the Stoics providence is apparently not a power held by God,
      because "god," "nature," and "providence" are names for one and the same being. Jaap
      Mansfeld, "Providence and the Destruction of the Universe in Early Stoic Thought,"
      in *Studies in Hellenistic Religions*, ed. M. J. Vermaseren (Leiden: Brill, 1979), 36.

30   Calvin, *Institutes*, 1.16.3 (1:201). Later in his text, Calvin will argue explicitly against
      the Stoic belief in fate that was grounded in the idea of nature as a necessary chain of
      causality: "We do not, with the Stoics, contrive a necessity out of the perpetual con-
      nection and intimately related series of causes, which is contained in nature; but we
      make God the ruler and governor of all things." Calvin, *Institutes*, 1.16.8 (1:207).

31   Calvin, *Institutes*, 1.5.6 (1:59).

32   Coming back to Martha Beck's experience with providence as taught in the Mormon
      church, one cannot help but think that it entirely lacked this pastoral sense, such
      that Martha came to know God only as an arbitrary and volatile operator of obscure
      retributive formulas, and that in the hour of her deepest despondency, she found the
      Bunraku puppeteers arriving to fill this gap. Despite her complete lack of understand-
      ing of what is going on, she cannot but let herself be rescued and be safe in their hands
      (see ch. 3, pp. 56–58).

33   Calvin, *Institutes*, 1.16.3 (1:201).

34   Calvin, *Institutes*, 1.16.1 (1:197).

35   Calvin, *Institutes*, 1.5.2 (1:53). Calvin has a quite effective array of metaphors for the
      responsibility of proper understanding. Even without "pure and clear knowledge of
      God," human beings cannot pretend ignorance, he argues, because there is no excuse
      "for a man to pretend that he lacks ears to hear the truth when there are mute crea-
      tures with more than melodious voices to declare it"; or "to claim that he cannot see
      with his eyes what eyeless creatures point out to him"; or "to plead feebleness of mind
      when even irrational creatures give instruction." Calvin, *Institutes*, 1.5.14 (1:69).

36   Calvin, *Institutes*, 1.16.4 (1:203).

37   Calvin, *Institutes*, 1.16.1 (1:197); see also 1.5.14 (1:68).

38   Calvin, *Institutes*, 1.16.1 (1:197). Calvin's view on the task of understanding has clear
      moral overtones, e.g., when he reminds his readers that the true knowledge of God is
      not one that pleases the brain with empty speculation, but it is a knowledge that will
      be fruitful "if it takes root in the heart." Calvin, *Institutes*, 1.5.10 (1:62).

39   Calvin, *Institutes*, 1.16.1 (1:197).

40   Calvin, *Institutes*, 1.16.1 (1:197–98).

41   Calvin, *Institutes*, 1.16.2 (1:198).

42   Calvin, *Institutes*, 1.16.2 (1:198–99). Earlier in book 1, Calvin quotes extensively from
      examples found in Psalm 107 to prove the falseness of this view. The Psalmist shows

that what are thought to be chance occurrences are just so many proofs of God's "fatherly kindness." Calvin, *Institutes*, 1.5.8 (1:60).

43   Calvin, *Institutes*, 1.16.2 (1:199).

44   Calvin, *Institutes*, 1.16.3 (1:200). I take "confused motion" here to indicate the coming together of two powers: God's power of channeling the water into rivers, and the rivers' channels to guide the flow of the water through the land. This view is what Calvin rejects.

45   Calvin, *Institutes*, 1.16.4 (1:202).

46   Calvin, *Institutes*, 1.16.4 (1:202). In his treatise *A Defence of the Secret Providence of God*, Calvin seems to work with a threefold distinction between *providentia generalis*, *providentia specialis*, and *providentia specialissima*. John Calvin, *A Defence of the Secret Providence of God*, in *Calvin's Calvinism: Treatises on the Eternal Predestination of God and the Secret Providence of God*, trans. Henry Cole (Grand Rapids: Reformed Free Publishing, 1987). The first regards God's governance of his creatures by the order of nature according to which all creatures follow their own distinct properties; the second regards God's governance by special ordinance through which he directs each and every creature; the third regards the governance of the faithful. See Partee, *Calvin and Classical Philosophy*, 126–27. According to Partee, the main purpose of Calvin's discussion regards the distinction between the first and the second. His point is to argue that God governs all creatures according to his will, and not only according to the natural order once established (129). Quoting from Calvin's commentary on Isaiah, Partee observes, "Calvin says that he does not wholly repudiate the doctrine of universal providence provided it is granted that God rules the universe by watching over the order of nature and exercising special care over each of his works" (131).

47   Calvin, *Institutes*, 1.16.4 (1:202).

48   Calvin, *Institutes*, 1.16.4 (1:202).

49   Taken in this sense, the distinction appears early in the philosophical history of the notion of providence. Plotinus, in his treatise *Peri Pronoias*, also makes the distinction between two kinds of providence. The first is the providence that regards the *kosmos*; it is the *kosmos* as it structured by *nous*, the spirit that precedes all being, and, therefore, is properly named *pronoia*. The second is providence as regards individual things and events. It is the domain of the *logos*. The occurrence of individual things and events is guided by divine deliberation, which is why it is called *logos pro ergou*. In Plotinus' view, there is not only a division of labor, however, because the distinction between the two also reflects a hierarchical order. Augustine combines the pastoral meaning of the two elements of providence—God's foreknowledge and God's care for individual human beings—in exactly this manner when he speaks of *cura dei hominibus* as implication of his *praescientia*. Norbert Scholl, *Providentia: Untersuchungen zur Vorsehungslehre bei Plotin und Augustin* (Freiburg: Dissertation Universität Freiburg, 1960), 65.

50   Calvin, *Institutes*, 1.16.4 (1:202).

51   Calvin, *Institutes*, 1.16.4 (1:202).

52   Calvin, *Institutes*, 1.16.2 (1:199).

53   Calvin, *Institutes*, 1.16.2 (1:199).
54   Calvin, *Institutes*, 1.16.2 (1:199). Emphasis added.
55   See Partee, *Calvin and Classical Philosophy*, 130.
56   Calvin, *Institutes*, 1.16.1 (1:197); see also 1.5.14 (1:68).
57   This reading is further supported by the fact that Calvin regards the philosophical conception of providence—as *providentia generalis*—as a competing religious view. See above, n. 19.
58   Calvin, *Institutes*, 1.16.4 (1:203). See also Wright, *Providence Made Flesh*, 28.
59   Calvin, *Institutes*, 1.16.4 (1:202). For the sake of argument, Calvin considers what it would entail to say that the beginning of motion is with God, but that otherwise all things are moved by the inclination of their natural impulse. The rhythm of the seasons would be set by God, but extreme dryness or unseasonable rains that ruin the crops would be beyond his control. Calvin comments, "In this way no place is left for God's fatherly favor, nor for his judgments." Calvin, *Institutes*, 1.16.5 (1:203–4).
60   Calvin, *Institutes*, 1.16.6 (1:204–5). To prove this point, Calvin quotes from the book of Jeremiah: "I know, O Lord, that the way of man is not his own, nor is it given to man to direct his own steps" (Jer 10:23).
61   See ch. 7, pp. 148ff.
62   Wright, *Providence Made Flesh*, 37–39.
63   See ch. 6, p. 139.
64   Calvin, *Institutes*, 1.16.9 (1:209). One wonders in this connection what Calvin's mind would have made out of the pattern we have been tracing in the stories we have read, for it does seem to convey that even in the midst of people's woundedness, there is a sense of hope that there must be a way out. It seems as if he believed this ineradicable sense of hope to be itself the work of God's providence. That this phenomenon does not necessarily require a religious explanation is shown in Viktor Frankl's notion of "the will to meaning," which signifies the same sense of hope. In Frankl's work this is grounded in his anthropology. Viktor E. Frankl, *Man's Search for Meaning: An Introduction to Logotherapy*, 4th ed., trans. Ilse Lasch (Boston: Beacon, 1992).
65   Bouwsma speaks of Calvin's "intellectualized Christianity" appearing from the fact that "Calvin sometimes gives the impression of believing that human beings can understand much in God's mind." Bouwsma, *John Calvin*, 98, 106. But precisely with regard to Calvin's reflections on the question of how God governs the world, Bouwsma points to the Reformer's conviction that God's plans and purposes are incomprehensible even to believers (168). The reputation of intellectualism is particularly strange in view of the fact that Calvin follows by and large what the Christian tradition always has said on the subject (see Schreiner, *Where Shall Wisdom*).
66   Augustine, *Retractationes*, I, 1, quoted from Calvin, *Institutes*, 1.16.8 (1:207–8).
67   Calvin, *Institutes*, 1.16.9 (1:208). Bouwsma takes this remark to indicate that "as a practical matter, Calvin's providence is not far from Machiavelli's fortune." Bouwsma, *John Calvin*, 168. To show why this comment is incorrect is the burden of the present section.

68 "In fact, with regard to those events which daily take place outside the ordinary course of nature, how many of us do not reckon that men are whirled and twisted about by blindly indiscriminate fortune, rather than governed by God's providence?" Calvin, *Institutes*, 1.5.11 (1:63).

69 In the book of Genesis, Joseph speaks to his brothers about their crime of selling him to merchants on their way to Egypt, but what "really" happened was something very different: "God sent me before you to preserve for you a remnant on earth, and to keep alive for you many survivors. So it was not you who sent me here, but God." (Gen 45:7-8). In this claim the term "really" is tricky, of course, in that it suggests that God's action overrides human action, triggering the question that concerns Wright's book on providence. See, e.g., Wright, *Providence Made Flesh*, 41. We will return to the Joseph story extensively in chapter 8 (pp. 169ff.).

70 Calvin, *Institutes*, 1.16.9 (1:209). In the same section, he writes, "As far as the capacity of our mind is concerned, all things therein seem fortuitous." Calvin, *Institutes*, 1.16.9 (1:209).

71 Calvin, *Institutes*, 1.16.9 (1:210).

72 Calvin, *Institutes*, 1.16.9 (1:210).

73 Apart from the occurrence of lightning, there may be facts about the case explaining why the young man went into the open field—for example, the fact that he planned to meet his girlfriend there.

74 As a coincidence the accident might as well not have happened—for example, when the young man would not have missed the phone call from his girlfriend to cancel their appointment shortly after he left home.

75 Calvin, *Institutes*, 1.16.9 (1:210). Calvin gives the example of David hiding in the fields with his men for King Saul. Saul's army was clamping down on David and his men, when a messenger arrived to inform Saul that he had to return immediately because the Philistine army was raiding the country. Calvin comments that we ought always to reckon with the fact "that whatever changes are discerned in the world are produced from the secret stirring of God's hand." Calvin, *Institutes*, 1.16.9 (1:210).

76 Calvin, *Institutes*, 1.17.1 (1:211).

77 Calvin, *Institutes*, 1.17.1 (1:211).

78 See ch. 5, n. 4.

79 Calvin, *Institutes*, 1.17.1 (1:211).

80 Calvin, *Institutes*, 1.17.1 (1:211).

Chapter 7

1 See ch. 5, n. 18.

2 See ch. 5, nn. 16 and 22.

3 Quoted in the current edition of Calvin's Institutes from James Moffatt, trans., *A New Translation of the Bible* (New York: Harper, 1934).

4 Calvin, *Institutes*, 1.17.2 (1:212).

5   Luther famously made the distinction between the *deus revelatus* (God as revealed in the incarnation) and the *deus absconditus* (God as the author of the eternal decrees, by which God rules over all of existence), indicating that those who are faithful in following the former need not fear the absolute power of the latter. Contrary to his intention, however, the distinction opened the gateway to those strands in Protestantism that were occupied with the darker, and frightening, side of divine omnipotence. On the development of the notion of divine omnipotence, see Gijsbert van den Brink, *Almighty God: A Study of the Doctrine of Divine Omnipotence* (Kampen, The Netherlands: Kok Pharos, 1993).

6   Calvin, *Institutes*, 1.17.2 (1:212).

7   Calvin, *Institutes*, 1.17.2 (1:213–14).

8   Calvin, *Institutes*, 1.17.2 (1:214).

9   On the relation of Calvin to these schools, see David Steinmetz, *Calvin in Context*, 2nd ed. (Oxford: Oxford University Press, 2010).

10   Calvin, *Defence of the Secret*, 248.

11   See Partee, *Calvin and Classical Philosophy*, 41.

12   Calvin, *Institutes*, 1.17.2 (1:214).

13   Calvin, *Institutes*, 1.17.2 (1:212).

14   See ch. 6, n. 67.

15   Calvin, Institutes, 1.17.2 (1:214).

16   Calvin, Institutes, 1.17.2 (1:215); see also 1.17.1 (1:210).

17   Calvin, Institutes, 1.17.4 (1:216).

18   Here we should notice that the difference from Martha Beck's puppeteers—to which I have pointed earlier in connection with the story of God's wager with Satan (see ch. 5, n. 31)—is pertinent again: God does not make human agents move as if they were puppets.

19   Calvin, *Institutes*, 1.17.4 (1:216).

20   We have already seen that Calvin discusses the sun as an instrument of the divine will (*Institutes* 1.16.2 [1:199]), which indicates that he does not reject the notion of providence in its naked form entirely.

21   Calvin, *Institutes*, 1.17.5 (1:217).

22   This was already the case during his lifetime, which is why Calvin wrote *A Defence of the Secret Providence of God*, a polemical treatise against the critics accusing him of determinism.

23   Recall Calvin's earlier quote from the book of Proverbs, "A man's mind plans his way," which seems to indicate just this (see ch. 7, p. 149).

24   Calvin, *Institutes*, 1.18.1 (1:229). Calvin's rejection of the doctrine of permission has led David Bentley Hart to deny that Calvin had an authentic doctrine of divine providence, because without the former the latter cannot be anything other than a doctrine of absolute divine determinism. The reason is, according to Hart, that in Calvin's use the distinction between primary and secondary causation fails to do any work: secondary causality is merely a modality of primary causality. See David B. Hart, "Providence and Causality: On Divine Innocence," in *The Providence of God*, ed. Francesca

A. Murphy and Philip G. Ziegler (Edinburgh, Scotland: T&T Clark, 2009), 36. I will return to Hart's comments below.

25   See, e.g., his comment on Psalm 88:6, where the psalmist accepts that his hardships come from God, which leads Calvin to argue that the victim can only pray to God to take away his affliction because "it is the divine hand that smites him," showing "that nothing happens by chance." John Calvin, *Commentary on the Book of Psalms*, vol. 5 of *Calvin's Commentaries V* (Grand Rapids: Baker, 2003), 411.

26   Calvin, *Institutes*, 1.18.1 (1:230) (referring to Acts 4:48); see also Acts 2:23 and 3:18.

27   In comparison, the Thomist tradition on providence seeks to avoid both determinism *and* indeterminism—and rejects the view that limits providence to "foreknowledge," thereby making God's will for its efficacy dependent upon human decisions to act in accordance with it. It therefore has adopted the doctrine of "physical premotion": God as the primary cause of all causes is the efficient cause of all things, including all actions. David Hart summarizes the Thomist position as follows: "As God is the primary cause of all causing—so the argument goes—he must be the first efficient cause of all actions, even those that are sinful; and yet, as he operates in a mode radically transcendent of the mode of the creature's actions, he can do this without violating the creature's freedom. From eternity, God has infallibly decreed which actions will occur in time, and he brings them to pass either by directly willing them or directly permitting them." Hart, "Providence and Causality," 38.

28   Calvin, *Institutes*, 1.2.1 (1:41).

29   Calvin, *Institutes*, 1.17.9 (1:221–22).

30   Calvin, *Institutes*, 1.17.9 (1:221–22).

31   Calvin, *Institutes*, 1.17.4 (1:216).

32   See ch. 4, pp. 58ff..

33   Calvin, *Institutes*, 1.18.2 (1:231).

34   Calvin, *Institutes*, 1.18.2 (1:231) (referring to Isa 29:10, Exod 9:12, et passim).

35   Wright, *Providence Made Flesh*, 1, 8, 11, 13, 18, et passim.

36   It appears that here Hart's comment on Calvin's use of secondary causation as a modality of primary causation is relevant (see above, n. 27). In Hart's view the question regarding Calvin's position is not whether they are genuine causes, but whether their secondary causality is distinct from primary causality.

37   In Calvin's view, God's will not only causes the actions of human beings, but also determines their will to act. God's will makes human beings *want* to do what they do. This triggers the objection that Wright pursues. If my intentions are caused by the divine will, this seems to go at the heart of my human agency, because what could possibly be more mine than my intentions? If I can no longer claim my intentions as my own, what could it possibly mean to say that I am the one who acts? Persuasive as these questions may appear, however, they do not seem to do much harm to the notion of *simultaneous* causation. How does the fact that someone—or something—determines my intentions eliminate the fact that they are nonetheless mine, and remain so? Intention involves a conception on my part of what I am doing in performing my act. I cannot be said to act willingly without a particular mental state with

regard to what my act is. If so, how could I be said *not* to act upon my own intentions, *even when* God determines them? The fact of God's determination does not cancel my psychological capacity of acting, but rather presupposes it. To return to an earlier example, if someone willfully performs a killing, how could he disclaim responsibility for this act by saying that it was God who caused his willing it? "His willing it" is the decisive clause to show that his own will must be involved. Simultaneous causality is a principle underlying any number of theories on human behavior—in the social and medical sciences, not to mention jurisprudence—that will explain various conditions—biological, neurological, cultural, social, economic, linguistic—that may shape our mental states. These theories imply that I may hold certain beliefs about what I am doing that are shaped by external conditions out of my control. How could this conditionality eliminate the fact that they are still *my* beliefs? Neither psychologists nor therapists would have a profession without the assumption that some of the things we believe about our own beliefs are caused by factors (our past, other people's views, etc.) that we do not know are having an effect upon us.

38   Here it seems to me Calvin deserves more credit than Hart is prepared to give him. Calvin's claim to epistemological abstinence here at least indicates that he was aware of the problem of using the distinction between primary and secondary causality within one and the same framework of causal explanation, which is basically Hart's point that is driving his critique of *both* Calvinist and Thomist positions: "It is one thing, for a theologian simply to assert that God's 'mode of causality' is utterly different from that of the creature, and that therefore God may act within the act of the creature without despoiling the latter of his liberty; but such an assertion is meaningful only if all the conclusions following from it genuinely obey the logic of transcendence. For, as primary cause of all things, God is first and foremost their ontological cause." Hart, "Providence and Causality," 40. God imparts *being* to what in itself has no being. What God creates possesses its own contingent being, and exists therefore as other than God, which is "the effect of a truly transcendent causality" (40). This radical transcendence, however, leaves the language of causality near to being void of any analogical content: "This donation of being is so utterly beyond any species of causality we can conceive that the very word 'cause' has only the remotest analogous value in it" (40). In other words, contrary to where Wright locates the problem of simultaneous causation—the anthropological question of free will and responsibility—Hart locates it in the doctrine of divine transcendence. This logic forecloses the possibility that God's will operates within the realm of natural causes. To ignore this is to violate a basic rule in Christian theology— namely, that an ontological difference needs to be maintained at all times between the Creator and creatures (see Wright, *Providence Made Flesh*, 13). Acknowledging that he does not know how to explain how God's will as primary cause works, Calvin at least indicates that he saw the problem.

39   Calvin, *Institutes*, 1.17.2 (1:212).

40   Wright, *Providence Made Flesh*, 15. It should be added that Wright is following Karl Barth's criticisms very closely in this respect.

41 Wright, *Providence Made Flesh*, 14. Wright quotes Paul Fiddes: "Reflection on the Trinity with regard to the 'causative power' of God seems to be at best an unnecessary complication, and at worst irrelevant." Fiddes, *Participating in God: A Pastoral Doctrine of the Trinity* (London: Darton, Longman & Todd, 2000), 117.

42 Wright, *Providence Made Flesh*, 14.

43 Barth, *Church Dogmatics*, III.3, p. 31.

44 Wright, *Providence Made Flesh*, 15.

45 Calvin, *Institutes*, 1.17.2 (1:212).

46 What follows is based upon Wright's constructive argument, which replaces the notion of a determining divine will with the notion of divine presence, and then defines providence as "God's sovereign action within creation to remain faithful to the promise he made to it." Wright, *Providence Made Flesh*, 222.

47 See Psalm 138:8.

48 God blesses mankind and hands over the earth to become fruitful.

49 Wright, *Providence Made Flesh*, 119.

50 Wright, *Providence Made Flesh*, 214–15 (quoting Gerald F. Hawthorne, *The Presence and the Power: The Significance of the Holy Spirit in Jesus' Life and Ministry* [Eugene, Ore.: Wipf & Stock, 1991], 230).

51 See ch. 6, p. 138.

52 Having read the argument for rethinking providence from a Trinitarian perspective, some readers will have been waiting for an account of the role of the church, particularly in the last section. The reason for refraining from taking this step is partly theological, and partly pragmatic. To begin with the former, the spirit of discernment is the promise that people will be able to see how the gap between the "before" and "after" may be bridged, but this promise is not the exclusive prerogative of Christians. The gap will be bridged by the promise of God's love, in which all things were created and which holds all things together. The promise that God's love has not faded from their lives is therefore a promise to the whole of creation. However, since the ability of "seeing" in this connection requires a transformation of the human heart, the question arises of how this transformation occurs. This question would lead to an account of the role of the church. Providence as the promise of God's presence in Christ, Immanuel, involves the ability to see. But this ability is not a given; it requires "epistemic virtue," which has to be learned and practiced. To develop this into an ecclesiological counterpart of providence is a further step, which to develop would take considerable space of its own. This consideration of space is the pragmatic reason for not taking this step in this inquiry.

53 Calvin, *Institutes*, 1.18.2 (1:231). Emphasis in original.

54 Calvin, *Institutes*, 1.18.1 (1:228).

55 Calvin, *Institutes*, 1.17.6 (1:218). In his biblical references, Calvin again leans heavily toward the book of Psalms as well as the Prophets: Pss 54:23, 55:22, 90:1, 91:1, 91:12; Isa 49:15, 49:25; Jer 1:18, 15:20; Zech 2:8.

56 Barth, *Church Dogmatics*, III.3, p. 31.

57 Calvin, *Institutes*, 1.13.14 (1:138).

58 Wright, *Providence Made Flesh*, 25 (quoting Calvin, *Institutes*, 1.13.18 [1:143]).
59 Wright, *Providence Made Flesh*, 28 (quoting Calvin, *Institutes*, 1.12.1 [2:465]).
60 Calvin, *Institutes*, 1.17.7 (1:220).
61 Calvin, *Institutes*, 1.17.10 (1:223).
62 Calvin, *Institutes*, 1.17.8 (1:220).
63 Calvin, *Institutes*, 1.17.8 (1:221).
64 Calvin, *Institutes*, 1.17.11 (1:224).
65 Berkouwer, in his book on providence, leaves us with the confession of a "mystery" when it comes to all the "deep" questions that this doctrine confronts us with, both with regard to the relation between providence and the reality of evil, and between divine determination and human freedom. Berkouwer's analysis shows that all attempts to square these notions fail because of their desire for a "logical synthesis." They introduce specific distinctions to sustain human responsibility, while leaving God's rule intact—for example, the distinction between his decree and his command (whereby the first determines our will, but the second does not), or between the formal and material aspect of human acts (whereby the former is shaped by God's will, but the latter is not). By introducing such distinctions, the attempt at logical solutions inevitably does one of two things, according to Berkouwer: it either restates the problem without solving it, or it identifies divine and human agency as two mutually limited kinds of agency, thereby defining it away. Berkouwer, *The Providence of God*, 137–72.
66 Calvin, *Institutes*, 1.7.2 (1:214–15).

Chapter 8

1 Becker, *A Good and Perfect Gift*, 95.
2 Becker, *A Good and Perfect Gift*, 95.
3 Becker, *A Good and Perfect Gift*, 96.
4 Becker, *A Good and Perfect Gift*, 96–97.
5 Becker, *A Good and Perfect Gift*, 25. Emphasis in original.
6 Becker, *A Good and Perfect Gift*, 30.
7 Becker, *A Good and Perfect Gift*, 33.
8 Becker, *A Good and Perfect Gift*, 27. Emphasis in original.
9 Becker, *A Good and Perfect Gift*, 35. Emphasis in original.
10 Becker, *A Good and Perfect Gift*, 11. Emphasis in original.
11 Becker, *A Good and Perfect Gift*, 68.
12 Becker, *A Good and Perfect Gift*, 70.
13 Becker, *A Good and Perfect Gift*, 83.
14 Becker, *A Good and Perfect Gift*, 84–85.
15 Becker, *A Good and Perfect Gift*, 85.
16 Becker, *A Good and Perfect Gift*, 86.
17 Becker, *A Good and Perfect Gift*, 88.
18 Becker, *A Good and Perfect Gift*, 88.
19 Becker, *A Good and Perfect Gift*, 89.

20 Becker, *A Good and Perfect Gift*, 97.
21 Becker, *A Good and Perfect Gift*, 99.
22 Becker, *A Good and Perfect Gift*, 111.
23 Becker, *A Good and Perfect Gift*, 112.
24 Becker, *A Good and Perfect Gift*, 121.
25 Becker, *A Good and Perfect Gift*, 122.
26 Becker, *A Good and Perfect Gift*, 122. Notice here again how the leading character of the story is at the receiving end. Finding a new self entails the discovery that one has been changed.
27 Becker, *A Good and Perfect Gift*, 141.
28 Becker, *A Good and Perfect Gift*, 141. The last phrase refers, of course, to Jesus' response to his disciples' question of why a man they met in the street was born blind (John 9:1-3).
29 Becker, *A Good and Perfect Gift*, 141.
30 Becker, *A Good and Perfect Gift*, 165.
31 Becker, *A Good and Perfect Gift*, 166.
32 Becker, *A Good and Perfect Gift*, 166.
33 It may be noticed, in the same connection, that when God has restored Job in his fortune, his brothers and sisters, and all that knew him before, come to visit him at his house, and "they showed him sympathy, and comforted him for all the evil that the Lord had brought upon him" (Job 42:12). The fact that God has changed his future apparently does not eradicate the suffering of evil. Again, there would have been no evil to overcome, unless it was real to begin with.
36 Selbie, *Fatherhood of God*, 75–76.
37 See ch. 7, n. 23.

BIBLIOGRAPHY

Adams, Nicholas. "The Goodness of Job's Bad Arguments." *The Journal of Scriptural Reasoning* 4, no. 1 (2004). Accessed July 21, 2013. http://jsr .lib.virginia.edu/issues/volume4/number1/ssr04-01-e03.html.

Andersen, Francis I. *Job: An Introduction and Commentary*. Tyndale Old Testament Commentaries. Downers Grove, Ill.: InterVarsity, 1980.

Anderson, Robert C., ed. *Graduate Theological Education and the Human Experience of Disability*. Binghamton, N.Y.: Haworth, 2003.

Barnes, Albert. *Notes, Critical, Illustrative, and Practical on the Book of Job with a New Translation*. Vol. 1. New York: Leavitt, 1852.

Barth, Karl. *Church Dogmatics*. Edited by G. W. Bromiley and T. F. Torrance. Edinburgh: T&T Clark, 1957–1975, III.3.

———. *The Theology of John Calvin*. Translated by Geoffrey W. Bromiley. Grand Rapids: Eerdmans, 1995.

Barton, George A. *Commentary on the Book of Job*. New York: Macmillan, 1911.

Bauby, Jean-Dominique. *The Diving Bell and the Butterfly*. Translated by Jeremy Leggatt. New York: Harper Perennial, 2008.

Beck, Martha. *Expecting Adam: A True Story of Birth, Rebirth, and Everyday Magic*. New York: Berkley Books, 1999.

Becker, Amy Julia. *A Good and Perfect Gift: Faith, Expectations, and a Little Girl Named Penny*. Minneapolis: Bethany House, 2011.

————. "Raising Children with Disabilities in an Age of Achievement." Presentation for The Summer Institute on Theology and Disability, Catholic Theological Union, Chicago, July 18, 2012 (unpublished).

Berkouwer, Gerrit C. *The Providence of God.* Grand Rapids: Eerdmans, 1952.

Black, Kathy. *A Healing Homiletic: Preaching and Disability.* Nashville: Abingdon, 1996.

Bouwsma, William J. *John Calvin: A Sixteenth Century Portrait.* Oxford: Oxford University Press, 1988.

Brink, Gijsbert van den. *Almighty God: A Study of the Doctrine of Divine Omnipotence.* Kampen, The Netherlands: Kok Pharos, 1993.

Brock, Brian. *Singing the Ethos of God: On the Place of Christian Ethics in Scripture.* Grand Rapids: Eerdmans, 2007.

Brueggemann, Walter. *The Message of the Psalms: A Theological Commentary.* Minneapolis: Augsburg, 1984.

————. *Theology of the Old Testament: Testimony, Dispute, Advocacy.* Minneapolis: Fortress, 1997.

Buckley, Michael J., S.J. *At the Origins of Modern Atheism.* New Haven, Conn.: Yale University Press, 1987.

Calvin, John. *Commentary on the Book of Psalms.* Vol. 3,, *Calvin's Commentaries V.* Grand Rapids: Baker, 2003.

————. *A Defence of the Secret Providence of God.* In *Calvin's Calvinism: Treatises on the Eternal Predestination of God and the Secret Providence of God.* Translated by Henry Cole. Grand Rapids: Reformed Free Publishing Association, 1987.

————. *Institutes of the Christian Religion.* 1559 ed. Edited by John T. McNeill. Translated by Ford Lewis Battles. 2 vols. Philadelphia: Westminster, 1960.

————. *Sermons from Job.* Introduction by Harold Dekker. Translated by Leroy Nixon. Grand Rapids: Eerdmans, 1979.

————. *Sermons of Maister John Calvin, upon the Booke of Job.* Translated out of French by Arthur Golding. London: Bishop, 1574. Facsimile reprint. Carlisle, Pa.: The Banner of Truth Trust, 1993.

Cicero. *De natura deorum.* Edited by Arthur S. Pease. Darmstadt: WBG, 1968.

Colish, Marcia L. *The Stoic Tradition.* Vol. 1. Leiden: Brill, 1985.

Collins, Francis. Foreword to *Playing God? Genetic Determinism and Human Freedom*, by Ted Peters. London: Routledge, 1997.

Cotton, David. "I Don't Know What to Pray For." In *Brain Injury: When the Call Comes; A Congregational Resource*. New Brunswick, N.J.: The Elizabeth Boggs Center, 2001.

Creamer, Deborah. "Finding God in Our Bodies: Theology from the Perspective of People with Disabilities." *Journal of Religion in Disability & Rehabilitation* 2, no. 1 (1995): 27–42.

Crimmins, Cathy. *Where Is the Mango Princess? A Journey Back from Brain Injury*. New York: Vintage Books, 2001.

Dau, Isaiah. "Facing Human Suffering: A Biblical and Theological Perspective." In *Suffering, Persecution and Martyrdom: Theological Reflections*, edited by Christof Sauer and Richard Howell, 107–35. Johannesburg: AcadSA, 1995.

Dell, Katharine J. *The Book of Job as Skeptical Literature*. Beihefte Zur Zeitschrift Fur Die Alttestamentliche Wissenschaft 197. Berlin: de Gruyter, 1991.

———. "Job: Sceptics, Philosophers, and Tragedians." In *Das Buch Hiob und seine Interpretationen*, edited by Thomas Krueger, 1–20. Zürich: Theologischer Verlag, 2007.

Dollar, Ellen Painter. *No Easy Choice: A Story of Disability, Parenthood and Faith in an Age of Advanced Reproduction*. Louisville, Ky.: Westminster John Knox, 2012.

Dorris, Michael. *The Broken Cord*. New York: Harper & Row, 1989.

Dumelow, J. R., ed. *Commentary on the Holy Bible by Various Authors Complete in One Volume*. New York: Macmillan, 1909.

Eiesland, Nancy L. *The Disabled God: Toward a Liberatory Theology of Disability*. Nashville: Abingdon, 1994.

———. "Liberation, Inclusion, and Justice: A Faith Response to Persons with Disabilities." In *Impact: Feature Issue on Faith Communities and Persons with Developmental Disabilities* 14, no. 3 (2001/2): 2–3. Published in Minneapolis by the University of Minnesota's Institute on Community Integration and edited by A. N. Amado, B. Gaventa, V. Gaylord, R. Norman-McNaney, and S. R. Simon.

Fiddes, Paul. *Participating in God: A Pastoral Doctrine of the Trinity*. London: Darton, Longman & Todd, 2000.

Frankl, Viktor E. *Man's Search for Meaning: An Introduction to Logotherapy.* 4th ed. Translated by Ilse Lasch. Boston: Beacon, 1992.

Fraser, Gregory. *Strange Pièta.* Lubbock, Tex.: Texas Tech University Press, 2003.

Fritzson, Arne. "Disability and Meaning." In *Interpreting Disability: A Church for All,* edited by Arne Fritzson and Samuel Kabue, 1–23. Geneva: World Council of Churches, 2003.

Frye, DeAnna, and JoAnn M. Ovnic. "Memory Problems after Brain Injury." *Blog on Brain Injury,* November 9, 2009. www.lapublishing. com/blog/2009/-memory-brain-injury.

Gaventa, William C., Jr., and David L. Coulter, eds. *Spirituality and Intellectual Disability: International Perspectives on the Effect of Culture and Religion on Healing Body, Mind, and Soul.* New York: Haworth, 2001.

Gerrish, Brian A. *Grace and Gratitude: The Eucharistic Theology of John Calvin.* Philadelphia: Fortress, 1993.

———. "'To the Unknown God': Luther and Calvin on the Hiddenness of God." *The Journal of Religion* 53, no. 3 (1973): 263–92. Reprinted in *The Old Protestantism and the New: Essays on the Reformation Heritage,* 131–49. Chicago: University of Chicago Press, 1982.

Gilson, Etienne. *The Spirit of Medieval Philosophy.* Notre Dame, Ind.: The University of Notre Dame Press, 1934.

Goodey, Chris F. *A History of Intelligence and of Intellectual Disability: The Shaping of Psychology in Early Modern Europe.* Burlington, Vt.: Ashgate, 2011.

Govig, Stewart D. *Strong at the Broken Places: Persons with Disabilities and the Church.* Louisville, Ky.: Westminster John Knox, 1989.

Hailer, Martin. *Die Unbegreiflichkeit des Reiches Gottes.* Neukirchen-Vluyn: Neukrichner Verlag, 2004.

Hall, Douglas J. *God and Human Suffering: An Exercise in the Theology of the Cross.* Minneapolis: Augsburg, 1986.

Hart, David B. "Providence and Causality: On Divine Innocence." In *The Providence of God,* edited by Francesca A. Murphy and Philip G. Ziegler, 34–56. Edinburgh: T&T Clark, 2009.

Hauerwas, Stanley M. *Naming the Silences: God, Medicine, and the Problem of Suffering.* Grand Rapids: Eerdmans, 1990.

Hawthorne, Gerald F. *The Presence and the Power: The Significance of the Holy Spirit in Jesus' Life and Ministry.* Eugene, Ore.: Wipf & Stock, 1991.

Henry, Matthew. "Matthew Henry's Complete Commentary on the Whole Bible:Job6." StudyLight.org.AccessedJuly25,2012.http://www.study light.org/com/mhc-com/view.cgi?book=job&chapter=006.

Heschel, Abraham J. *Man Is Not Alone: A Philosophy of Religion*. New York: Farrar, Straus & Giroux, 1951.

Hodge, Charles. *Systematic Theology*. Vol. 1. Grand Rapids: Eerdmans, 1997.

Hubach, Stephanie O. *Same Lake, Different Boat: Coming alongside People Touched by Disability*. Phillipsburg, N.J.: P&R Publications, 2006.

Hume, David. "Enquiry Concerning Human Understanding." In *Dialogues Concerning Natural Religion*, edited by Norman Kemp Smith. London: Thomas Nelson, 1947.

Isarin, Jet. *De Eigen Ander: Moeders, deskundigen en gehandicapte kinderen*. Amsterdam: Damon, 2002.

Kabue, Samuel, Esther Momba, Joseph Galgalo, and C. B. Peter, eds. *Disability, Society, and Theology: Voices from Africa*. Limuru, Kenya: Zapf Chancery, 2011.

Kooi, Cornelius van der. *Als in een spiegel: God kennen volgens Calvijn en Barth*. Kampen, The Netherlands: Kok, 2002.

Kushner, Harold S. *When Bad Things Happen to Good People*. New York: Avon, 1981.

Leathes, Stanley. "Job." In *An Old Testament Commentary for English Readers by Various Authors*, edited by Charles John Ellicot. Vol. 4. London: Cassell, 1884.

Levering, Matthew. "Aquinas on the Book of Job: Providence and Presumption." In *The Providence of God*, edited by Francesca A. Murphy and Philip G. Ziegler, 7–33. Edinburgh: T&T Clark, 2009.

Lyotard, Jean F. *The Inhuman: Reflections on Time*. Translated by Geoffrey Bennington and Rachel Bowlby. Cambridge: Polity, 1991.

Mairs, Nancy. *On Being a Cripple*. http://thelamedame.tumblr.com/post/30938417648/on-being-a-cripple.

Mansfeld, Jaap. "Providence and the Destruction of the Universe in Early Stoic Thought." In *Studies in Hellenistic Religions*, edited by M. J. Vermaseren. Leiden: Brill, 1979.

Martone, Marilyn. *Over the Waterfall*. CreateSpace Community, 2011.

Mintz, Susannah B. "Ordinary Vessels: Disability Narrative and Representations of Faith." *Disability Studies Quarterly* 26, no. 3 (2006). Accessed July 29, 2011. http://www.dsq-sds.org/issue/view/34.

Moffatt, James, trans. *A New Translation of the Bible.* New York: Harper, 1934.

Morris, Henry. "Study Notes on Job." In his *The Defender's Study Bible: King James Version.* Emeryville, Calif.: World Publishing, 1996.

Nouwen, Henry. *Adam: God's Beloved.* Maryknoll, N.Y.: Orbis, 1997.

Oddy, Michael, and Ian Fussey. "Why Me?" Brain Injury Rehabilitation Trust. Accessed August 10, 2011. http://www.birt.co.uk.

Partee, Charles. *Calvin and Classical Philosophy.* Leiden: Brill, 1977.

Peters, Ted. *Playing God? Genetic Determinism and Human Freedom.* London: Routledge, 1997.

Potgieter, Pieter C. "Perspectives on the Doctrine of Providence in Some of Calvin's Sermons on Job." *HTS Theological Studies* 54, no. 1–2 (1998): 36–49.

Reinders, Hans S. *The Future of the Disabled in Liberal Society: An Ethical Analysis.* Notre Dame, Ind.: The University of Notre Dame Press, 2000.

———. "Is There Meaning in Disability? Or Is It the Wrong Question?" *Journal of Religion, Disability & Health* 15, no. 1 (2011): 57–71.

———. *Receiving the Gift of Friendship: Profound Disability, Theological Anthropology and Ethics.* Grand Rapids: Eerdmans, 2008.

———. "Theology and Disability: What Is the Question?" In forthcoming volume by Julie M. Claassens and Leslie Schwartz.

Reynolds, Thomas E. *Vulnerable Communion: A Theology of Disability and Hospitality.* Grand Rapids: Brazos, 2008.

Ricoeur, Paul. "Evil, a Challenge to Philosophy and Theology." *Journal of the American Academy of Religion* 53, no. 4 (1985): 635–50.

Sadler, Gregory. "Saint Anselm's *Fides Quaerens Intellectum* as a Model for Christian Philosophy." *The Saint Anselm Journal* 4 (2006): 32–58.

Schenkhuizen-Lok, Hilly *Een kind als Clary.* Kampen, The Netherlands: Kok, 1983.

Scholl, N. *Providentia: Untersuchungen zur Vorsehungslehre bei Plotin und Augustin.* Diss., University of Freiburg-i.-B., 1960.

Schreiner, Susan E. "Exegesis and Double Justice in Calvin's Sermons on Job." *Church History* 58 (1989): 322–38.

———. "'Through a Mirror Dimly': Calvin's Sermons on Job." In *Calvinism and Hermeneutics,* edited by Richard C. Gamble, 231–49. New York: Garland, 1992.

————. *Where Shall Wisdom Be Found? Calvin's Exegesis of Job from Medieval and Modern Perspectives.* Chicago: University of Chicago Press, 1994.

Selbie, William B. *The Fatherhood of God.* London: Duckworth, 1936.

Sonderegger, Katherine. "The Doctrine of Providence." In *The Providence of God,* edited by Francesca A. Murphy and Philip G. Ziegler, 114–57. Edinburgh: T&T Clark, 2009.

Steinmetz, David. *Calvin in Context.* 2nd ed. Oxford: Oxford University Press, 2010.

Surin, Kenneth. *Theology and the Problem of Evil.* Oxford: Blackwell, 1986.

Swinton, John. *Raging with Compassion: Pastoral Responses to the Problem of Evil.* Grand Rapids: Eerdmans, 2007.

Synapse. "Why Me? Possible Answers to Tricky Questions." *Bridge* 2 (2011): 27–28. Magazine of Synapse, Brain Injury Association of Queensland.

Taylor, Charles. *A Secular Age.* Cambridge, Mass.: The Belknap Press of Harvard University Press, 2007.

Teasdale, Graham and Bryan Jennett. "Assessment of Coma and Impaired Consciousness: A Practical Scale." *Lancet* 2 (1974): 81–84.

Thomas, Derek. *Calvin's Teaching on Job: Proclaiming the Incomprehensible God.* Geanies House, Scotland: Christian Focus, 2004.

————. "When Counseling Doesn't Help: Job 4–7." First Presbyterian Church of Jackson, Mississippi website. Accessed July 24, 2012. www .fpcjackson.org/resources/sermons/Derek's_SERMONS/job.

Wagt, Gabri de. *Mijn zoon en ik: Leven met een gehandicapt kind.* Bloemendaal, The Netherlands: Nelissen, 1994.

Waters, Larry J. "Elihu's Theology and His View of Suffering." *Bibliotheca Sacra* 156 (1999): 143–59.

————. "Reflections on Suffering from the Book of Job." *Bibliotheca Sacra* 154 (1997): 436–51.

Webb-Mitchell, Brett. *God Plays Piano Too: The Spiritual Lives of Disabled Children.* New York: Crossroad, 1993.

Wilke, Harold H. *Creating the Caring Congregation: Guidelines for Ministering with the Handicapped.* Nashville: Abingdon, 1980.

Williams, Thomas. "Saint Anselm." In *The Stanford Encyclopedia of Philosophy* (Spring 2011 edition), edited by Edward N. Zalta. Stanford

University, 1995–. Article first published May 18, 2000 and substantially revised September 25, 2007. http://plato.stanford.edu/archives/spr2011/entries/anselm/.

Windheim, Dan. "Living with Traumatic Brain Injury." *The ARC Light Magazine* 10, no. 3 (1995).

———. *Out of My Mind*. 1997–2000, http://www.tbi-life.org.

Wolterstorff, Nicholas. *Lament for a Son*. Grand Rapids: Eerdmans, 1987.

World Council of Churches. "A Church of All and for All: An Interim Statement." Geneva: WCC, 2003.

Wright, Terry J. *Providence Made Flesh: Divine Presence as a Framework for a Theology of Providence*. Eugene, Ore.: Wipf & Stock, 2009.

Ziglar, Zig, and Julie Ziglar Norman. *Embrace the Struggle: Living Life on Life's Terms*. New York: Howard Books, 2009.

Yong, Amos. *Theology and Disability: Reimagining Disability in Late Modernity*. Waco, Tex.: Baylor University Press, 2007.

INDEX

ableist, ableism, 8, 9, 11, 13,
Adams, Nicholas, 203, 205, 207, 221
Andersen, Francis, 203, 221
Anselm, 195, 226, 227, 228
Augustine, 48, 138–39, 151, 187, 198,
   211, 212

Barnes, Albert, 202, 206, 221
Barth, Karl, 129, 157, 164, 188, 191,
   209, 217, 221, 225
Barton, George, 202, 203, 206, 221
Bauby, Jean-Dominique, 27, **77–83,**
   93, 95, 142, 163, 170, 207, 221
Beck, Martha, 26, 27, 37, 38, 43,
   53–72, 73, 92, 94, 124, 154, 163,
   170, 171, 174, 177, 182, 185, 197,
   198, 199, 207, 208, 210, 214, 221
Becker, Amy Julia, 29, 37, **171–86,**
   189, 192, 196, 197, 218–19, 221
Berkouwer, Gerrit, 19, 193, 194, 195,
   196, 199, 218, 222

Bouwsma, William, 127, 204, 208,
   212, 222
bridging the gap, 26, 29, 74, 80, 82, 86,
   93, 94, 97, 98, 99, 110, 118, 124, 157,
   158, 167, 168, 183, 189, 210, 217
Brink, Gijsbert van den, 214, 222
Brock, Brain, 193, 222
Brueggemann, Walter, 194, 203, 222

Calvin, John, 16, 28, 99, **125–44,**
   145–66, 181, 186, 187, 188, 193,
   204, 208–18; on divine ("double")
   justice, 28, 108, 127, 141, 143,
   146–48, 151, 152, 187, 204, 205,
   206, 226; on divine will, 131, 132,
   133, 135, 137, 139, 140–41, 145,
   147–50, 152–56, 157, 187, 188, 211;
   on Job, 106, 108, 187, 202, 205, 207;
   on (primary and secondary) causation, 28, 149, 150, **153–56, 187,**
   188, 214, 215, 216; on ("special" and

"general") providence, 62, **125–44, 145–66**, 211
cause (natural and supernatural), 2, 9, 13, 34, 37, 39, 44, 63, 64, 133, 138, 139, 147, 149, 150, 151, **153–55**, 156, 165, 188, 208, 209, 210, 215, 216
Colish, Marcia, 210, 222
Collins, Francis, 25, 196, 223
contingency, 15, 26, 139, 140, 141, 163.
Crimmins, Cathy, 27, 75, 76, 77, **83–92**, 93, 94, 117, 163, 170, 174, 183, 184, 185, 201–2, 223

Dekker, Harold, 205, 222
Dell, Katherine, 202, 203, 223
disability: as a blessing, 12, 13, 72, 190; as "defect," 9, 11, 24, 57, 87–88, 95, 117, 118, 170, 173, 178; as injustice, 10, 14, 38, **43–47**, 50; "making sense" of, 3, 4, **5–11**; as punishment, 2, 12, 14, 16, 38, 44, 45, 106; religious explanations of, 2–3, **11–13**, 14, 16; as "tragedy," 5, 29, 49, 57, 159, 177, 179, 190
Dollar, Ellen Painter, 196, 223
Dorris, Michael, 197, 198, 223
Down syndrome: the experience of, 26, 37, 38, 47, **53–72**, 73, 92, 124, 170, **171–80**, 181, 183, 185, 200

Eiesland, Nancy, 6, 8–11, 12, 192, 193, 200, 223

fortune and chance, 3, 9, 14, 24, 39, 46, 50, 119, 125, 138, 142, 156, 159, 181
Frankl, Viktor, 212, 224
Fraser, Gregory, 2, 3, 4, 191, 224
Fritzson, Arne, 6, 192, 224

Gaventa, William, 191, 192, 223, 224
Gerrish, Brian, 127, 128–30, 205, 208, 209, 224
Gilson, Etienne, 195, 224
Glasgow Coma Scale (GCS), 40, 197
God: as Creator, 4, 24, 28, 50, 104–5, 106, 110, 119, 120, 123, 131–33, 134, 136, 148, 155, 165, 187, 196, 204, 206, 208; and incomprehensibility, 16, 37, 110, 119, 122, 124, 126, 127, 143, 146, 166, 187, 193, 205; and inscrutability, 28, 107, 109, 110, 145, 146, 205; and justice, 106, 107, 122, 145; as the Spirit, 25, 26, 29, 157, 160–65, 167, 180, 183–85, 188, 189, 190; the will of, 3, 13, 14–16, 194, 215, 218
Goodey, Chris, 192, 224

Hailer, Martin, 193, 224
Hart, David Bentley, 214, 215, 216, 224
Hauerwas, Stanley, 48, 195, 198, 224
Henry, Matthew, 205, 225
Hodge, Charles, 128, 208, 225
Hubach, Stephanie, 197, 200, 225
Human freedom, 25, 138, 143, **151–53**, 164, 184, 186, 215, 218
Hume, David, 19, 194, 225

Job, **97–124**; on divine (retributive) justice, 104–6, 109, 110, 115–16, 118, 119, 120, 122, 126, 145, 205; on divine majesty, 28, 118, **103–7**, 111, 112, 119, 120, 121, 122, 145, 204; on punishment for sins, 46, 113, 116, 118, 122

Kabue, Samuel, 6, 191, 192, 224, 225
Kooi, Cornelius van der, 205, 225
lament, 17, 18, 19, 35, 36, 47, 48, 49,

50, 75, 93, 98, **101–3**, 124, 159, 186, 188, 189, 195, 198, 228
Leathes, Stanley, 204, 225
Levering, Matthew, 207, 208, 225
locked-in syndrome: the experience of, 27, **77–83**, 93, 95, 142, 163, 170, 207
Lyotard, Jean-François, 50, 198, 225

Mairs, Nancy, 46, 198, 225
Manfeld, Jaap, 210, 225
Martone, Marilyn, 197, 225
Mintz, Susannah, 191, 225
Morris, Henry, 204, 226

Oddy, Michael, 34, 35, 36, 196, 198, 225

Partee, Charles, 209, 211, 212, 214, 226
Peters, Ted, 24, 196, 223, 226
playing God, 24–25, 196, 223, 226
Plotinus, 211
Potgieter, Pieter, 205, 207, 226
providence, 1, 4, **13–17**, 21–24, 25, 26, 27, 29, 51, 53, 56, 59, 64, 65, 71, 92, 93, 94, 99, 119, 157, 167, 169, 171, 173, 181, 183, **186–90**, 194, 199, 217, 218; deism's understanding of, **21–25**, 62, 195; as divine control, 13, 14, 16, 22, 25–26, 27, 28, 126, 149, 154, 188, 212; a (Trinitarian) theology of, 15, 16, 17, 26, 28, 72, 124, **156–59**, 167, 188, 217
Psalms, 15, 59, 72, 131, 152, 194, 215, 218, 222

Reinders, Hans, 191, 192, 193, 226
retribution, 10, 13, 15–16, 98, 118, 122, 207

Reynolds, Tom, 2, 191, 192, 193, 226
Ricoeur, Paul, 48, 198, 226

Selbie, William, 128, 208, 227
Schreiner, Susan, 127, 202, 205, 208, 212, 226
Silence, 38, 39, **47–51**, 102, 124, 159, 186, 188, 198, 224
Sonderegger, Katherine, 195, 227
story (stories), 10, 26, 48, **64–65**, 74, 80, **92–95**, 97, 118, 125, 170, 178, 179, 185, 186, 188, 190, 207
suffering, 6, 14, 17, 18, 19, 39, 48, 57, 74–77, 81, 98, 102, 109, 117, 119, 122, 158, 162, 194, 198, 206, 219, 223
Surin, Kenneth, 20, 195, 196, 227
Swinton, John, 17–21, 47, 48, 49, 78, 93, 159, 167, 194, 198, 227

Taylor, Charles, 21, 22, 23, 195, 196, 227
theodicy, **17–21**, 26, 193, 194, 196
Thomas, Derek, 127, 202, 204, 208, 209, 227
transformation, 23, 26, 29, 65, 67, 72, 73, 162, 168, 170, 173, 177, 180, 182, 185, 190, 217
Traumatic Brain Injury (TBI): the experience of, 7, 27, 33, 34, 35, 36, **39–41**, 42, 43, **73–95**, 118, 184

Waters, Larry, 193, 206, 227
Webb-Mitchell, Brett, 31, 196, 227
"why" question, the, 3, 5, 9, 15, 18, 26, **32–36**, 37, 39, 43–47, 48, 49, 50, 72, 74, 93, 97, 98, 117, 123, 125, 157, 159, 164, 167, 172, 180, 181, 186, 188, 194, 198
Williams, Thomas, 195, 227

Windheim, Dam, 41, 43, 197, 228
Wolterstorff, Nicholas, 50, 195, 198,
    228
Wright, Terry, 155, 156, 157, 159, 160,
    165, 167, 209, 212, 213, 215, 216,
    217, 218, 228

Yong, Amos, 194, 228

Ziglar, Zig, 196, 200, 228